THE TREND
FOLLOWING BIBLE

Founded in 1807, John Wiley & Sons is the oldest independent publishing company in the United States. With offices in North America, Europe, Australia, and Asia, Wiley is globally committed to developing and marketing print and electronic products and services for our customers' professional and personal knowledge and understanding.

The Wiley Trading series features books by traders who have survived the market's ever-changing temperament and have prospered—some by reinventing systems, others by getting back to basics. Whether you are a novice trader, a professional, or somewhere in between, these books will provide the advice and strategies needed to prosper today and well into the future.

For a list of available titles, visit our Web site at www.WileyFinance.com.

THE TREND FOLLOWING BIBLE

How Professional Traders Compound Wealth and Manage Risk

Andrew Abraham

WILEY

John Wiley & Sons, Inc.

Library of Congress Cataloging-in-Publication Data

Abraham, Andrew.
  The trend following bible : how professional traders compound wealth and manage risk / Andrew Abraham.
      pages cm. — (Wiley trading series)
  Includes index.
  ISBN 978-1-118-40774-5 (cloth); ISBN 978-1-118-42186-4 (ebk),
  ISBN 978-1-118-43439-0 (ebk), ISBN 978-1-118-41763-8 (ebk)
 1. Investment analysis. 2. Portfolio management. 3. Investments. 4. Risk management. I. Title.
  HG4529.A27 2013
  332.64'5—dc230

                                                        2012043888

10 9 8 7 6 5 4 3 2 1

To my Family, Ruthie, Gabrielle, Ariel, Micael, my mother, and all those who supported me along my journey of trend following, thank you.

CONTENTS

Foreword   ix

Preface   xiii

Introduction   My Journey as a Trend Follower   1

CHAPTER 1   Get a Savvy Start   9

             Can You Really Make a Living as a
             Trend Follower?

CHAPTER 2   Getting the Most Out of This Method   25

CHAPTER 3   Why Trend Following?   35

CHAPTER 4   How Successful Trend Followers Trade   49

CHAPTER 5   Managing the Risks when Trend Following   81

CHAPTER 6   Your Complete Robust Trading Plan   95

CHAPTER 7   Trend Breakouts   107

CHAPTER 8   Trend Retracements   121

CHAPTER 9   The Trend Follower Mindset   137

CHAPTER 10   My Trading Journal   161

             Conclusion   193

             Disclosure   195

             Index   197

I've been trading for investors for over 30 years. My first fund, Tactical Commodity Fund, started in mid-1981. Tactical's current program began in 1993 as an offshoot of that first fund but with lower leverage and some evolutionary changes. I've learned a lot over the years. I've seen a lot of markets, a lot of bull moves, a lot of bear moves. And I can tell you I wish I had read this book 30 years ago. I would have made more money, especially near the beginning. Do yourself a favor. Read it. Now.

My trading-for-investors career began not long after gold peaked around 870 and a bit over a year before the S&P bottomed near 100. I subsequently watched gold drop more than 70 percent over 19 years and then rally over 700 percent in the next 12. I watched the stock market rally for over 17 years with just one big, brief pullback along the way only to witness two retracements greater than 50 percent in the next 10 years.

I've seen almost too numerous to remember booms and busts in the commodity, currency, and interest rate markets. I've seen things happen that everyone said never would and watched as things didn't happen that everyone said were inevitable. I've traded and held positions in these markets nearly every single day since mid-1981.

Tactical was one of the first systematic, computerized fund managers. We started out on a Radio Shack TRS 80, before the first Apple. Historical data that costs pennies now took months to type in by hand. We ran Fourier transforms and proved there were in fact no repeatable hidden cycles in the markets while everyone else was still talking about them. We tested all the market lore to see what was true and what wasn't. We tested the early mechanical systems that were touted and found most of them didn't hold up. Indicators that people still use today we learned years ago don't really give you a statistical advantage.

I wrote my own back-testing software and tested everything I could think of. When personal computers advanced we bought the latest. For a number of years we had two Sun workstations running 24/7 doing systems testing when those were state of the art. Of course, now you can do the same things much faster on a laptop. But that was then and this is now. We kept testing. We kept learning.

I read every book I could get my hands on about trading. I listened to the old traders. When I worked during summer breaks in college at a brokerage firm at the Chicago Board of Trade I kept my ears open as the old-timers related their adventures, their successes, their failures. I tried to understand the psychology of the winners and how it differed from that of the losers. I got the idea that the psychology of the trader was as important if not more important than anything in success or failure.

I spent a lot of time learning things the hard way, a lot of trial and error, a lot of hard knocks. Trading is still a lot of hard knocks. Drawdowns can go on seemingly forever. You can have days, weeks, even months on end without much in the way of profits. It can feel as if you are a punching bag or a movie double who takes all the hits. But that's the nature of the game, of the business.

Even after you've learned how to do it, you still take your hits. To succeed, you just need to stand up every time you get knocked down. You need to have the confidence that standing up is the right thing to do. You need to know when to stand back up and how. And just by standing up again and again and staying standing as long as you can before you get hit again, well, you can actually make more money than you lose over the long run in trend trading. It's quite an amazing process.

Very few people succeed in this process. The learning curve is too steep and the correct psychology is too hard to implement. If you have any attachment to making money, and who doesn't, it is very tough to trade correctly.

This brings me to the book you hold in your hands. To reiterate: I surely wish I had had it 30 years ago. It would have saved me a lot of work. And I would have made more money, especially in the early years. More specifically, I would have lost less money and that would have put me farther ahead today. Andy Abraham has written a gem. His writing style is enjoyable, clear and entertaining. He covers all the main ingredients needed for successful trend trading. He tells the truth.

What impresses me most about Andy's writing is his honesty. He doesn't sugarcoat things. He doesn't tell you it's easy to make money. He tells you that you need patience and discipline. (By the way, "Patience and Discipline" has been Tactical's slogan since its inception.) Andy tells you drawdowns and losses are part of the business. He presents a track record of one of his own programs that he started just a few years ago that has not made new highs in 17 months. That's exactly how it works sometimes. What is so refreshing is Andy's honesty about it. The man has integrity.

A characteristic of those traders who have been successful over many years is honesty with respect to their trading. You need to understand your own psychology, where you are mentally strong and weak, how you deal with baser emotions, particularly fear and greed. If you lack honesty with yourself, you will almost certainly fail. Andy's honesty, more than anything, tells me he understands trading psychology and gives me confidence he is qualified to teach others what he knows. I have yet to run across a trading book that emphasizes the psychological aspect of trading better than this one.

This book is not a cookbook. It does not outline a mechanical system. It explains the psychology needed to succeed in trend trading, gives some examples of traders who have applied it, and sets out the underlying principles that should be followed for success—trade the best markets, trade with the trend, bet small, use stop-losses, cut losses, ride winners, don't overtrade, be patient, be disciplined.

As a bonus, Andy gives you the scaffolding for a particular methodology that works for him as an example of everything he sets out in the basic rules. Just as you would never think of moving into a new house that has been framed but before the roof, walls, and interior are finished, you cannot and should not attempt to trade Andy's "system" without doing all the finishing carpentry. You need to do your own back-testing—doable these days with off-the-shelf software he describes—to fill in the parameter values and to learn how his trade-the-best market portfolio ranker shuffles which market signals you take. For those who don't have a clue where to begin, Andy gives you his exact pattern to follow. Your own back-testing fills in the parameter blanks.

✔Andy advises everyone that they must trade a style that fits their personality. I believe very strongly that he is absolutely correct. You will not follow a system that does not suit you. In his wisdom Andy thus does not give you all the parameter values for the formulas in his personal trading scaffold. He wants you to do your own back-testing, to find a methodology that you are comfortable with yourself and have confidence in. When all is said and done, your approach may be identical to his with your own parameter values. It may be significantly different. Regardless, you cannot develop the confidence to pull the trigger after multiple losses in a row without having done the work yourself. Guaranteed.

It's a fair bet to say that any trend following methodology likely to succeed over time will employ the general psychological and fundamental trading rules Andy outlines. The specifics of everyone's approach will vary, but the broad principles outlined here will be present in one form or another in virtually all robustly successful trend following approaches. People say that markets have changed and new rules are needed for the new game. I've heard that for over 30 years. The markets do change but the underlying fundamental rules for success don't seem to. They are all outlined here. How great.

You are lucky to have picked up this book. If you are a seasoned trader, reviewing the basic elements of winning psychology makes this book worth perusing cover to cover. We can all use reminders, yours truly always. If you are new to trading, this book can save you years of trial and error and monetary losses. This book is now on my short list of recommended reading material for traders. I sincerely thank Andy for having written it. Have fun reading it. I wish you all the best in your trading.

Dave Druz
Tactical Investment Management
CTA / CPO since 1981
Haleiwa, Hawaii
November 2012

I wanted to write a book that I wished I could have read when I first began to trade. This book is unique and I hope it will give you all the tools needed to help you become a successful trader over time. I have had help along the way of my journey of trend following. Writing a book that encompasses all aspects of trading is my way of giving back and helping new and aspiring traders. By teaching and enlightening others I know I will make a difference in many aspiring traders.

Hopefully you will learn from my mistakes and avoid the 18-year learning curve I have been on so far. The lessons I have presented in this book will help you achieve the goals that you are seeking.

I wanted to share my insight—from the perspective of a professional who trades for a living—what one goes through on a daily basis and what a trader needs to know and internalize to become a consistent and successful trader over time. The majority of books I have read over the years seemed to try to boost my confidence by demonstrating how easy trading success can be. Trading for a living is not easy by a long shot.

My goal is to illustrate the major issues and challenges that traders face. I would assume there are those readers who would prefer to seek the "easy." It really does not exist! My purpose and goal was to dispute all the snake oil, hope, hype, unrealistic get rich quick falsehoods. There is no easy money in the markets. You will have to work hard to achieve success. You will make plenty of mistakes; however, look out the front window and learn from your mistakes.

I would assume that many of you have picked up this book because you are hoping to improve your trading. My goal is to give specific methods instead of vague generalities that can be used in your everyday trading and improve it. My goal is that you instill in yourself that ultimately you are the only one responsible for your success or failure. It is never the market, never the broker, or me, with my advice. I want you to realize that the markets can be cooperative at times and giving, as well as also ruthless and unforgiving. No matter what stage of trading you go through, there will be times of severe aggravation (if you let it). How you react to the realities of trading will determine if you will be part of the 90 percent who lose money or the small group of 10 percent who are consistent winning traders over time. My goal is to have you be part of the 10 percent club of winners; however, it is up to you to truly internalize what I am trying to instill in you.

Introspectively there were other reasons why I wrote this book. Writing about trading actually helps me overcome the inherent difficulties of trading. No one is immune to the difficulties of trading. Even money managers who have assets in the hundreds of millions of dollars must face the mental challenges. I have had a blog, TrendFollowingmentor.com, in which I speak and try to educate about trading. Nothing is sugarcoated. I have been told by many colleagues that I focus almost too much on telling readers how trading is difficult. The reality is that trading is hard. I learned this fact the hard way. This is probably the complete opposite of what you would have thought when you purchased this book. You probably thought you could buy this book and be immediately on your way to making money. Trend following, however, is like a marathon, and I hope it becomes a lifetime strategy for you.

On October 31, 2011, MF Global went bankrupt and shocked the futures markets. It is not just the fact that MF Global went bankrupt but that over $1.6 bbillion of client segregated funds supposedly "vaporized." I was a client of MF Global and their predecessor EDF Mann since 1994. Along with many others, I was in shock about what was allowed to transpire. This had never happened in the futures markets. Another firm, Refco, blew up due to fraud and the next day clients were made 100 percent whole. Not so in the case of MF Global. What helps me overcome this frustration was to write. Over the Christmas holidays in 2011 I decided to write a book on trend following and trading for a living that would be different from all of the existing books on the market.

It was partly due to a catharsis and in conjunction with the request by my oldest daughter who has been trading with me since she was 13. She had asked me to teach some of her friends how to trade. I had time on my hands and started to write.

My bookshelves are full of trading books. I have read books regarding Warren Buffett, Value Investing, and all the books you can ever imagine on technical trading, but none of them got me to the point that 18 years of struggle did. I thought the more books, the more successful my trading would be. This is why I really believe my book will stand out among the many other trading books. I continued on this holy grail search with trading systems and formulas. I was so overwhelmed with courses and gurus. I could not figure out why everyone wasn't rich. I could not understand why more than 90 percent of traders fail. Many of these 90 percenters are engineers, pilots, and successful people in all types of fields. I read the various success stories of traders in *Market Wizards* by Jack Schwager whom I called the 10 percenters and was encouraged. There are other great books in recent years that focus on successful traders such as Michael Covel's books *Trend Commandments: Trading for Exceptional Returns*, *Trend Following: How Great Traders Make Millions in Up or Down Markets*, and *The Little Book of Trading.* There is a great deal of fantastic information to be gleaned from these books and I strongly recommend them.

A driving force for me was to succeed in trading. I did not assume the lure of so-called "easy money"; I did not assume it would be easy. I read about Larry Williams who in a trading contest took $10,000 to approximately $1 million. I read in *Market Wizards* about Michael Marcus who started with $30,000 and took that sum to $80 million. Richard Dennis was also featured; he started with $400 and ran it up to over $200 million. These numbers were amazing but also dangerous to novice traders like myself at the time. Everyone who trades wants to achieve these results. Just because someone else succeeded, this might really help you. You do not hear of all those who failed and how long it took the ones to survive to become successful.

Most traders have no concept of what is needed in order to achieve these lofty goals. I assume that all too many traders think this is easy and instead of focusing on what needs to be learned, they focus their time and energy on all the ways they could spend their new-found riches. Then there are those who invest all their time in search of holy grail indicators and systems that aren't.

In every business venture before one starts the norm is to make a business plan. To the contrary, too many new traders are more focused and anxious to get rich rather than to make a business plan. They think they do not have time for the plan. The lure of easy money is a Pandora's box of problems. The dangers of unrealistic expectations are more than prevalent. Instead of focusing on all the dangers of trading, too many are focusing optimistically on their new-found easy wealth. I can humbly say I made countless mistakes and I paid for these mistakes, but introspectively I was of the camp seeking holy grail systems and indicators, which was a waste of time. These mistakes were required learning lessons for me in order to become a consistent trader even though I had people trying to help me. It is not just me. Behind all the glory of the *Market Wizards* was the reality. Richard Dennis, the teacher of the Turtles, lost 50 percent of his and his investors' accounts and has stopped trading. Michael Marcus borrowed money from his mother and lost it before he internalized his mistakes! Larry Williams, whose claim to fame was in a trading contest and book, *How I Made One Million Dollars Last Year Trading Commodities,* lost a million dollars the following year.

There are countless stories of unknown traders who have blown up. They focused too much attention on the easy profits they thought they would make. They had no concept of risk management. They had no concept of hard work. Too many believed they could buy a trading system or trading robot and find their proverbial retirement in a box.

The reality of successful trading comes down to several basic tenets and the realization that you have to work hard:

1. Robust trading plan applicable to all time frames and markets.

2. Complete risk and money management.

3. The patience and discipline to follow the trading plan and follow the risk and money management guidelines.

On my business card I have written on the back the tenets of successful trend following:

1. Trade with the trend.

2. Cut your losses.

3. Let your profits run.

4. Don't let the big profits get away.

One who follows these simple rules is light years ahead of so many traders. These four rules are similar to the Ten Commandments. If one follows them, one will be "blessed" over time with the trading results. When combining these tenants one puts one's self in the position to potentially create extreme wealth.

A vast majority of traders spend all of their time and energy trying to predict or guess what will occur in the markets. The right activity for traders is look at what is happening right now. Be in the moment and just follow the plan (hopefully they have a plan). The question needs to be asked, has the market taken out the X period high? Has the market retraced and is offering me a low-risk retracement trade? Bloomberg and CNBC are based on predictions. Everyone wants to be smart and show they know the future. Successful trend followers have internalized that it is nothing about being right or predicting. The point that these successful trend followers have internalized is to identify where they are located currently in relation to the trend and just take the trade if they have one.

As I believe any trade is 50/50, you never know which trade will work. Too many traders are looking for certainty. Certainty does not exist in the markets. Traders want to know when trends start and stop. The reality is you never know. The flipside of the 50/50 is that you do not know how bad a trade can go against you. The concept of cutting losses is a paramount issue if one wants to stay in this business. If losses get out of control, one can easily be overwhelmed financially and emotionally.

Letting profits run is very hard for some traders. They have that urge to ring the cash register. They do this primarily out of fear. In trend following one needs these rare big winners to offset all of the inherent small losses. Your trading plan must have the contingent for following trades that are working. This is the key to making money in the long run and building your positively sloping equity curve. With a trading plan there is no "Should I", "Could I", "Would I", "Shoot, why didn't I take that trade," or worse, "Why did I let this happen to me?" When we trade, we should trade for the primary reason to make money and build a positive equity curve. This primary reason is so powerful we are all trying (should be) to better our trading. This is why we try to perfect our trading. This leads us at times to second guess ourselves. We second guess because we don't have a plan and do not have discipline. If you are in this state I believe my book will truly help you develop "the plan" based on risk management, a robust trading methodology, and the proper mindset in which you do not second guess yourself.

One must plan in trading. The extent of planning determines success or failure in trading. The more developed and stringent a trading plan with all potential outcomes preplanned, the greater the potential for success over time. There will be times you will think to violate your trading plan. You know that you should not; however, rationalization is a powerful tonic. You try to justify your decision to violate your plan. No one is standing over you and asking you why are you breaking your own rules? You just do it, wrongly though. Ironically, Mr. Market might even reward you for breaking your own rules. This is even worse for your psyche! Breaking your own rules becomes a slippery slope. It becomes easier and easier, and by the way you made some money last time.

The big issue is you just bought yourself a one-way ticket to the 90 percent club of failed traders who lose money. The only way you can even hope to join the 10 percent club of consistently successful traders over time is being consistent in your trading plan. Consistent means seeing the same type of trade, recognizing it, and taking action. This is repetitive in nature. Actually I was recently told that this was boring. My answer was, I am not trading for excitement. I like boring.

Without a trading plan how would you know where you are going?

Clearly you would not!

Even with your trading plan there will always be problems and surprises. Thousands of traders were caught in the MF Global debacle. A situation in which client segregated accounts were violated was an industry first. On Halloween 2011 MF Global went bankrupt. Client accounts were frozen. Not just cash was frozen; positions could not be offset for days. Frantic traders were calling 24 hours for days trying to exit their positions. I know traders that flew to Chicago to try to exit their positions. Another colleague of mine had three people on speed dialer trying to get through to the trade desk, to no avail. This was a nightmare for traders as well as the futures industry. The fortunate traders who had multiple accounts were able to offset their positions. Other traders who fortunately had the majority of their funds at Treasury Direct (the U.S. Federal Reserve bank) or at a cash management firm such as Horizon survived. Planning saved traders. Those that did not plan are not in business. Thank God I planned for the unthinkable and had a vast percentage of assets at Treasury Direct (the U.S. Fed). Luckily due to my paranoia and the advice of a colleague I transferred out some funds from MF Global before they collapsed. I still got burned, however, but not destroyed. The MF Global issue was extreme; anything can and anything will happen in trading. The only certainty is uncertainty. Who would have thought the Nasdaq would still be down 10 years from the highs? Who would have really believed the Japanese stock market would be down from 39,000 to approximately 9,000? What is shocking is that for 22 years Japan has been in a bear market. If someone told you this could happen in the U.S. stock markets you would think they were crazy. Who would have ever thought gold could go from a couple hundred dollars to almost $2,000 over approximately 10 years? Once you truly internalize that anything can happen, you realize the absolute need for a complete plan. The markets will always throw you a curveball. Investing your time and energy in your trading plan will reward you more than the futile search for predictions, indicators, and mechanical systems. In my book I am giving you my trading plan. What a great bargain.

A solid trading plan is the holy grail if there really is one!

ANDREW ABRAHAM

My Journey as a Trend Follower

Things that happen many times are not a coincidence. Probably today and even more so in 1994 very few people had ever heard of the phrases "trend follower" or "trend following." I stumbled on the phrase "trend following" by sheer luck. I sold a business that I started in college in 1994. I had saved the majority of the money over the years and even acquired more money upon the sale of the business. I had no idea how to invest it. I was not comfortable with the stock market after witnessing the 1987 stock market crash as well as the stock volatility in the early 1990s. As I have always done, I tried to surround myself with the smartest people I could. I asked my accountant what he suggested. He told me that he had a client who owned a commodity brokerage firm who was very successful and suggested I meet him. My accountant was in his mid-60s with a rather large practice, therefore he had seen a very large pool of clients, and I trusted his unbiased opinion.

I wanted to learn how my money could work for me and compound over time. I was overwhelmed with all the books and courses that offered so-called magical success and millionaire traders who really weren't.

I started my journey of learning. *Market Wizards* by Jack Schwager mesmerized me and has encouraged me. My journey of trend following began. This journey was more like a marathon and still is.

I probably made every mistake possible. Working past mistakes and a bad memory is very tough due to the emotional baggage we carry. I personally overtraded; I did not follow my trading plan, or better said, hardly had one; I did not follow my money management plan, as well as did not follow a correlation plan. After the many losses I encountered I felt frustrated, angry, and just plain lousy. Besides these emotional issues, there were the financial issues. I felt beaten up and poorer. I knew there had to be a better way. I wanted to dig myself out of this negative sand trap and join the rare group of 10 percent consistently successful traders that I read about in *Market Wizards* by Jack Schwager.

Even though I had those who guided me, the fact is that you can be told exactly what to do but unless you internalize it, it is worthless! It was only from mistakes and losses that I learned. I had the extreme desire to learn and grow!

I believe most traders really make mistakes due to fear, greed, or ego. There is this illusion or lure of supposed easiness or easy money out there. Why waste any time planning or working? I have heard, "I can buy a Forex robot and grind out the profits." I chuckle to myself and think: How can it be so easy? Why isn't everyone rich if all they needed to do was to buy a Forex robot? The fact is everyone wants success and wealth, but are we really ready to work so hard for it? Not many!

My journey has been two-pronged with the goal to compound money over time. I started my own trend following in 1994 as well as invested with hedge fund managers and commodity trading advisors who were trend followers. Investing with other commodity trading advisors has offered me diversity and helped me build my equity curve over the years. I allocate between 2–5 percent of my family's net worth in any one particular money manager. I have a group of managers. Year in and year out they have different returns. In some years I have outperformed them, in others not, but my goal was to diversify. It helped me very much during the MF Global debacle that I was diversified. Two of my commodity trading managers had some exposure to MF Global. The rest had no exposure whatsoever. In trading, as Salem Abraham from Abraham Trading Group has so aptly stated, you never know what can kill you. This underscores the need for a well-thought-out plan. My way of staying in the marathon is to spread it out. I look for managers as aware of risk as myself. My wife tells me I am compulsive obsessive paranoid. Before the MF Global debacle I would thank her and took it as a compliment. We sold our private home at the top of the housing bubble in January 2006. I did not feel comfortable with how prices were skyrocketing, and we were contemplating moving overseas. Fate occurred and we luckily sold at the top. This is probably the only time in my career I can claim such luck. After the MF Global debacle I wish I had been more paranoid. However, as in my trading, it was a good learning lesson, and I am not focusing on the past but on the future. I have opened up with numerous futures commodity merchants, and at the slightest smell of smoke I will wire the cash out of the futures commodity merchant and offset my positions.

When I allocate to other commodity trading advisors, I have positive advantages. I have a diversification to clearinghouses, trading styles, and markets in addition to how I trade. That is the good news. The bad news is that to some degree this diversification costs me and eats into my compounding of my money over time. Most commodity trading advisors and hedge fund managers charge a 2 percent management fee and 20 percent incentive fee. I even have one manager who charges a 25 percent incentive fee. He gets 25 percent of my profits. However, he has done very well for me over the years, albeit there are periods in which he goes through severe drawdowns. I am willing to pay the fees as I have been able to compound money over the years in this process, and this should be your goal as it is mine.

My personal trend following has been a work in progress. The commodity broker I started with in 1994 learned under Ed Seykota, Van Tharp, and was an avid student of Mark Douglas. He taught me to focus on how to think as a trend follower. He taught me to think in terms of probabilities and to accept the risks when trading. I learned the only certainty in trading is uncertainty. No one provided the holy grail of a magical indicator or system, rather how to think, how to be disciplined and patient.

■ A Great Learning Lesson

 Discipline and patience are the foundations of the holy grail.

Discipline means knowing exactly what you need to do at every moment and actually doing it. The easiest thing to do is to put off taking a trade that causes emotional distress. However, this is exactly what you need to do with discipline. A lack of discipline can be expressed as failing to do what you should be doing in every given event. A lack of discipline will destroy even professional money managers. In this book I have highlighted numerous examples. Simply telling someone to build his discipline is a lot easier said than done and trite. No one is perfect and discipline is not like a light switch you can just turn on. Every trader including myself has failed in some degree of discipline. However, I learned and internalized the absolute need for complete discipline. The discipline became enhanced over time, and when I completely internalized my trading plan, I became rigid in my plan, which built my discipline, and at the same time I became more accepting of my returns and the expectations of my trading returns. I was willing to learn from all of my mistakes. I strived to get to the point at which I did not make the same mistakes again. I learned to follow my plan and not be deluded by the fact I made a mistake when I did not follow my plan and even profited. Breaking my own plan or rules and profiting is what makes discipline so hard. Been there and done it. However, I learned this would not get me to my goals of compounding money and I was negatively rewarded.

In order to make money on my money, I started to invest with (who I thought were very successful) hedge fund managers and trend followers. I invested "luckily" with Monroe Trout as well as Julian Robertson. I did not know the questions to ask; rather, I basically chased their prior returns.

In retrospect this was a mistake and yet also a great lesson.

Going back to my first two hedge fund managers that I allocated to in 1994, a valuable lesson was to be learned. Julian Robertson from the 1980s had a compounded annual return in the 20 percent-plus range. All I thought about was the rule of 72. Yes,

I was blinded by greed and thinking it would be easy. I had no concept of how he was managing the risk nor even worried about it. How could a guru lose money, I thought?

The rule of 72 is how many years until your money compounds. You divide the percent returns by 72 and this determines how many years for your money to double. I was honestly blinded by greed. The interesting fact is twofold and I learned a fantastic lesson in investing. First of all, there are no gurus, and second, never allocate more than 5 percent of your net worth to any idea or money manager, including me.

I invested $200,000 with Julian Robertson through a feeder fund in 1994. All I could think about was I am going to be rich. I was doing the math of 20 percent returns and thinking all the way of compounding my way to wealth. Well, not everything ends as you planned it. Things were proceeding nicely in 1995, 1996, and thereafter until 1998. In 1998 there was the Asian contagion as well as the Russian debt crisis.

Unfortunately Julian Robertson made a big bet on borrowing Japanese yen and buying U.S. Treasuries. For years this trade was a no brainer until Mr. Murphy entered the reality. The Japanese yen took off in value and the borrowing rate changed dramatically, and quickly this trade was a disaster. All of the years of compounding money were shot and big losses shot up. In shock (thank God), I closed out my investment with Julian Robertson.

What did I learn? Very simply that there are no gurus and that anything can happen. I still made money but did give back a lot of my profits.

On the other hand, Monroe Trout was still grinding out profits irrespective of the stock market. I also invested $200,000 with him in 1994. The account just kept on growing. In 2005 or 2006, after years in the market, Trout decided to retire. My $200,000 had compounded over the years after taking some money out to approximately a valuation of $1,400,000. This taught me the lesson of compounding money. As Jesse Livermore stated, patience is what can make money. In all truthfulness it was rather easy with Monroe Trout. There was not a lot of volatility or aggravation. In retrospect it grew to a big percent of my net worth and should have taken profits off as it was compounding. Once Trout decided to retire, I thought to myself, thank you and time to move on.

To highlight the dangers of simply chasing returns, in 2011 there was a manager called Dighton who had a great record. On a simplistic level it would have been easy to invest with him. Over the last six years or so he compounded money at around a 30 percent rate. Many naïve investors threw him money and were blinded by his returns. Dighton was managing upwards of $200 million dollars. In July 2011, however, Dighton blew up and lost 80 percent of his fund. Dighton was a countertrend trader who blew up over one trade with the Swiss franc. Think about it, six years of hard work to be blown up by one trade.

This is not unique. I remember in 1998 that Niederhoffer, a so-called "guru," was compounding money for years. Many had no idea what he was doing other than printing money. Until one day in late 1997 he made one bad trade after another and later blew up. Niederhoffer believed he was right and the market was wrong (even though he was eventually right). In the meantime he blew up and left a debt of approximately a $20 million margin call. Institutional investors are no better than most when allocating to commodity trading advisors and hedge fund managers. The same greed is evidenced in institutional investors. I learned over the years not to be like them. As it is easier to buy when a commodity trader or hedge fund manager is doing well, too many do this. There is a herd mentality with institutional investors. The bigger the fund, the more confident they are in not just generating returns but the safety of their investments. This axiom was proven wrong in 2011 with John Paulson's funds. Paulson had a fantastic run when he called the housing crisis. He is the founder and president of Paulson & Co. Paulson became a billionaire by short-selling subprime mortgages during the housing crisis in 2007. He personally made $3.5 billion that year. Institutional investors flooded him with their money to manage. However, in 2011, he made various bad trades in banking stocks such as Bank of America and Citigroup. I conjecture he got caught up in the fraud of the Chinese company Sino-Forest Corporation, which further tarnished his record. His flagship fund, Paulson Advantage Fund, was down over 40 percent as of September 2011. Using this as an example, bigger is neither always safer nor better. Many institutional investors buy the equity highs and sell the equity lows. So many of these investors lose money even with profitable hedge funds and commodity trading advisors. They do not have the patience to permit compounding money over time to occur. They want their profits now!

What I do is the opposite of most investors and institutional investors. I buy the drawdowns of commodity trading advisors who have done well for years, who understand and prepare for risk, yet in the current environment have a drawdown. To me it is pretty much common sense and somewhat of a way to mitigate the inherent risks when investing. This is counterintuitive to how most investors think. However, nothing is perfect. As in trend following, you never buy the bottom. Because a commodity trading advisor is experiencing a 25 percent drawdown, for example, there is absolutely nothing promising you or guaranteeing you it will not get worse or even that the commodity trading advisor could blow up. This is the reason that in trading I risk a small percentage on any investment or allocation. I try to take a low-risk bet when investing in a hedge fund or a commodity trading advisor. I accept the risks and the uncertainty. I do not sit month in and month out praying or hoping. I set the trade and say to myself, let's see how this will look in 10 years. Don't get me wrong, I do my extensive due diligence before I invest. I speak to the managers on a current basis and monitor them daily when I have the luxury of having a managed account with them. I am not chasing quantitative numbers solely. The qualitative is much more important. The qualitative are many matrixes based on integrity and honesty. When I speak to a commodity trading manager, I want to understand the risk measures they utilize. These risk and money management parameters dictate to what degree the manager "tries" to prevent losing my family's money. It is not pertinent to me what exactly gets them into a trade or their exact system. The most important issues are the risk and money management aspects. After the MF Global debacle a major source of interest is where the money sits if I invest in a fund, as well as how many futures commodity merchants they have accounts with. These have become major issues and aspects of risk management that prior to MF Global I truly did not consider. As trading is my passion, besides researching and building models for me to utilize for my own trading, a good part of my day is speaking to other traders and brokers. I am not seeking any trading tips. I am seeking new trading talent that I am not familiar with. I am always exchanging thoughts and ideas with others who invest in commodity traders like me. There are two individuals who I feel fortunate to have come in contact with, Harry from Texas and Alan from Chicago. These two individuals get it more than any institutional investor I have ever spoken to. In addition, I always try to surround myself with people that have considerably more experience and knowledge than me. There is a broker in Chicago that has a small group of very experienced clients, and his specialty is to allocate to commodity trading advisors. Todd Fulton from Pioneer futures has his ear to the pavement and seems to know everyone in the industry. I have had numerous conversations with him and have learned a great deal.

I have been to numerous conferences at different times such as the MFA conferences, Alphametrix, and the CTA Expos. I have had coffee and drinks with Sovereign Wealth fund managers as well as large fund of funds managers. Comparatively, the individuals from Texas and Chicago as well as Todd have so much more vast experience and knowledge. Harry from Texas has been investing since 1987. He told me one of his first managers was Paul Tudor Jones. All one has to think of is the compounding over the years Harry has accomplished. One manager whom I know went through a terrible drawdown in one of his programs from February 2009 till May 2010. He told me about a client of his who bought this drawdown and without mentioning names I understood who it was. Buying drawdowns and diversifying are some of the tools of investing with commodity trading advisors I have used over the years.

At the last Alphametrix conference in Miami Beach, I had the luck to sit at a presentation of a commodity trading advisor, and Alan from Chicago sat down with us. I had never met Alan before and was honored he sat in on the meeting. He was giving me and the commodity trading advisor great insight into many trading issues and ways he has profited over the years. It was a great lesson.

It is not easy to find the upcoming new managers. It has to be your passion. It is not just about going to conferences, as many family offices or fund of funds try to do. Nor is it quantitatively looking at databases. As much as I strongly recommend Iasg. com, Autumn gold, Altegris, Alphametrix, and Barclays, however, the best is to meet managers face to face. Both the CTA Expo and Alphametrix conferences offer that possibility. Meeting someone face to face is personal and much can be gleaned.

Contrary to the institutional investors who think they are "safer" to invest in the huge funds such as Winton or Transtrend with their billions of dollars under management, I feel it is more prudent to invest with a manager who is a PHD—Passionate, Hungry, and Dedicated—who is not managing a ton of money. When a money manager is trading less money, he is more nimble and can trade markets the aircraft carrier funds cannot trade due to liquidity issues. It would be impossible for a large fund to try to trade cocoa or orange juice. It would be like an elephant in a china store. Many investors were deluded in 2011 because many of these big funds did well because of the Treasury markets. The big funds can only trade the biggest markets such as stock indexes, currencies, interest rates, and so on. In 2010 one of the big winners was cotton. This was a market that the big funds could possibly get into but exiting would have been difficult and full of slippage. Investing with other commodity trading advisors is an essential aspect of my way of compounding wealth over time.

As in your own trading as well as investing with money managers you need an exact plan.

■ Have a Plan and Follow it

It is surprising to me that such a large number of traders who enter the markets have no plan whatsoever or no plan based on risk. Too many traders do not have the vaguest concept of how they plan to succeed in the long run. They are so anxious to actually get started that they have not thought of any of the preparations that are necessary. In the futures markets they are cannon fodder for the 10 percenters who take money out of the market over time. This lack of preparation explains the reason for the extremely high rate of failure of traders. The next great danger in trying to trade for a living is the danger of high expectations. To highlight this example, I had a conversation with a new trader who told me he expected to make at least 25 percent a year on his money. I asked him if he had ever heard of the rule of 72 (how many years it takes to double your money). Clearly he never heard of it. I enlightened him and expressed to him that some of the best traders who manage the risks, who have a plan, ONLY make, over time, on average 15 percent. These money managers are managing in excess of hundreds of millions of dollars. Traders that focus too much on the money end up losing their money. New traders need to focus on their learning and perfecting their plan to be consistent. I cannot say that enough!

As far as my personal trend following journey, I wanted to learn from my broker who was succeeding at his firm and what they were doing right. The most successful client of the brokerage was a dentist. He was not a Harvard graduate nor a partner in Morgan Stanley or Goldman Sachs.

■ A Lesson in Compounding: The Dentist

The dentist invested $200,000 in a robust trend in 1979. He let that money compound over time. Today the dentist has pulled out over $12,000,000 over the years and has a $5,000,000 trading account as well as accounts for his children and grandchildren.

The dentist did not have any magical holy grail formula!

He is a trend follower who had a simple robust methodology and, more importantly, knew how to properly condition his thought processes to get through all the tough drawdowns and long periods when he did not make money (even though he complained about it).

The dentist was the exception, though. Most clients of the brokerage were not successful. The vast majority of them lost money and ended up quitting. I did not want to be one of those unsuccessful clients that lost money and quit. My goal in this book is to help you to not become the typical trader who loses money and quits.

My goal is to help traders like you to achieve your trading goals, so that you, too, can live the lifestyle you want, afford to buy the things you want to have, be more relaxed, and have more time for the things you enjoy doing and that are important to you. Do not expect overnight success. There will be losses and drawdowns. You will need to work on your patience and discipline. The dentist's goal was, and still is, compound money over long periods of time.

I want to teach you to think like a successful trend follower. I am giving you exactly the methodologies I have used on a daily basis for the last 18 years. They are not any magical holy grail; rather, they are robust ideas that give you the ability to make low-risk trades and try to catch trends when they are present.

You can take my ideas and apply them to your own personality and risk tolerance. Your trading must match your personality. An example of this is Dave Druz, who learned under Ed Seykota. Dave took ideas from Ed and matched them to his own trading. Both of them are trend followers, yet they trade different styles matching their personality.

Hopefully this will be the same with you as well. I will share with you and instill in you all of my knowledge gained over the last 18 years. However, we are dealing in the unknown, and there are also risks when trend following. You need to apply your own risk tolerances.

If you are interested, I will teach you how to invest with other trend followers via my courses or webinars. The reality is that some years I outperform the money managers I invest with, and then there are years I underperform them. I am not on any ego trip as my ultimate goal is to compound money over long periods of time and diversify. I do not care if I do better than the group of money managers or if some do better than me. The bottom line is that I am compounding my way to wealth, and this is the key to success.

I do a combination of things in order to try to smooth out my returns and compound money over time. As I have previously stated, I invest with groups of trend followers as well as do my own trend following. There are many who believe that all trend followers are the same. I know for a fact that this is not the case as I have money invested in various money managers via managed accounts. Sometimes we can be in the same trades. However, we get in or out at different points or have different position sizing, thus we generate different returns. My goal is to compound money over time.

I do not allocate more than 5 percent of my family's net worth to any trading idea and look to let the odds work over time. In many cases I allocate even less with the goal to diversify.

The fact that I can compound money over these years means you might be able to as well if you have the mental fortitude! The dentist compounded money over all of these years and you might be able to as well!

CHAPTER 1

Get a Savvy Start

Can You Really Make a Living as a Trend Follower?

W hat I have said to countless people is: If I can do this, you can do this. I did not go to Harvard nor is it even needed to succeed as a trend follower. However, it will be a journey! Many first-time traders want to start too quickly without a well-thought-out plan. This can be very dangerous to one's financial health. Very few of these new traders are successful right off, and if they get lucky on a trade, this can even be worse for them. They learn not to have a strong appreciation of the inherent risks in the markets. What does that help, though, if you have learned via a mentor or had a pedigree education at another trading firm? Many of the traders I have invested with over the years have come out of other successful organizations and have learned there. I had people help me along my journey. Not with the elusive holy grail; rather, how to think, how to accept the inherent risks in the market, and how to implement additional risk filters in my trading models.

Understand, trend following is full of risks, and you need to risk your money to trade. I assume you heard this warning several times: "Don't trade with money that you can't afford to lose." You might think that this is just the typical disclaimer that every professional in the trading industry has to use, but it's not. It's much more. You need to be realistic and start slow. I would not suggest you quit your day job to start trend following. Even the most successful trend followers who have been trading for decades on average over time return approximately 15 percent. What makes you think you will outperform them?

In one of the further sections I detail some examples of some of these trend followers. Do not think their returns are representative of those of all trend followers or that you can easily generate these numbers. The reality is probably that you can't, and the databases are full of trend followers who blow up or do not achieve these returns.

As I stated in one of the earlier sections, I do my own trend following and I am sharing with you my exact methodology. I also invest with groups of other trend followers who I feel understand risk as I do. However, anything can and will happen when we are trading.

Successful trading requires knowledge, skill, and experience.

Trend following can be simple, but don't make the mistake of thinking it is easy! There are countless websites and late-night infomercials that try to tell you differently. They make you think that you just have to read a few pages or attend an online class, and then, magically, you'll become a successful trader.

■ Trading as a Profession

If you have a regular job or run your own business, the probability is that you're working at least 40 hours per week.

Comparing trend following to any business is an eye opener. Consider the following differences:

- No employees to hire.

- No set, exact hours to keep.

- No inventory.

- No rent.

- No overhead.

- No customers who complain.

- No accounts receivable.

- Very little equipment needed.

- No bank loans needed.

You are truly dependent on yourself! In order to start you need to take the following seven steps:

1. Determine how much you want to start trading and risking.

2. Open a brokerage account.

3. Decide on which trading platform you want to use.

4. Decide on which group of markets you want to trade. Do you want to trade stocks, forex, or futures?

5. Have a well-thought-out plan and trading methodology with exact rules for entries, exits with a loss, exits with a profit, what markets to trade, and have built-in risk controls such as stop-loss orders to "try" to minimize or mitigate your drawdowns.

6. Back-test and truly believe in the viability of your strategy.

7. Be mentally prepared for the inevitable drawdowns.

Simply, trend following is not like any other business venture. The only three fixed costs you have are:

1. A computer or laptop.

2. An Internet connection for your data.

3. A trading platform.

Trading is like every other profession: You learn the basics, you apply them, you gain experience, and then you take the attributes and make them part of your personality.

◼ Trend Following Is a Journey

I am glad you realize this is a journey or rather a marathon. It is full of ups and downs. Actually more times there are drawdowns and nothing happening than up and profitable periods. Drawdowns are the bane of trading. When you are profitable, you do not think of these inevitable losses. When the losses mount, however, the doubts increase. This is why I am presenting the reality to diminish your disappointment when reality sets in and there are the eventual drawdowns. There are times the drawdowns extend for periods of times that it actually becomes painful. Doubts about returning to prior equity peaks are brought up. In my personal experience, at the darkest moments were the upcoming light and the end of the drawdown. Drawdowns are not easy to digest. However, when you experience a drawdown and have been conditioned ahead of time what to expect, it becomes less painful. If you never anticipated that you would go through a 20 percent-plus drawdown and you are in the thick of it, it is much harder than if you had been educated that drawdowns can even be worse than this and that your worst drawdown is ahead of you. If you really never accepted the fact that you will encounter a drawdown like so many other traders, it will be very difficult to maintain your trading posture and confidence. This leads me to enlighten you on what you can realistically expect from your trading, both the good and bad, in terms of potential profitability and potential losses.

I'm glad you're different from the masses that want a stock tip or insider information.

You decided on my book of trend following because you're serious about becoming a successful and consistent trader over time. My goal is to help you in your quest to achieve this. However, please be aware and be realistic. Just reading this book will not automatically make you an instant millionaire. There is nothing instant with trend following. You will hear the word *marathon* quite often.

Lifetime Strategy

Trend following is a lifetime strategy for me, full of challenges and obstacles.

You'll learn the basic ideas and concepts about trend following, but in order to make the most out of this book and become the trader you want to be, you'll have to internalize and believe in them. I will present you with example after example and most importantly help you in order to achieve the proper trend following mindset. You don't have to go to college for years to learn trend following. Unlike most other professions, years of experience are not necessary either. You have to have the desire and passion. I firmly believe that everybody can learn how to become a successful trader. (Later in this book you will learn about the turtles who did exactly this.)

I am resolute that this manual will save you both money and time when it comes to your trading goals. I'm convinced that it will help you become the trader you want to be. You made the right choice. You could have done as I did for almost a decade, looking to pick up ideas and concepts regarding trading, but now you have me as your mentor. You will learn from all of my costly mistakes throughout the years. The irony I want to point out is that I had people who had helped me along the way, and I can even call them mentors, however, only when I truly internalized what they were trying to teach me did I succeed.

Yes, You Need a Broker

You may wonder if you really need a broker. The answer is yes. If you intend to trend follow, then you must have a broker. And it doesn't matter whether you are trading stocks, futures, forex, or options: Unless you are a member of the exchange, you won't be able to place your orders without a broker. Stock, futures, and options brokers are required to pass different tests in order to obtain their licenses. These tests ensure that the broker knows his or her business and will be able to support you if needed. I personally go directly to a futures commodity merchant (FCM). Trading in this fashion, I get the best price for my trades and I trade through the commodity trading advisor desk.

What you will not need is a full-service broker. After you finish the book you will be able to make your own decisions based on the trend following methodology. If you want, I will share with you the name of one of the brokers I use personally. Just shoot me an email.

Don't Be Misled!

There are no shortcuts in trend following. My own experience has been a journey of almost a decade of learning and finally internalizing what was needed in order to succeed over time when trend following.

As in all professions, you need a solid education before you get started. Many go to college for years in order to learn and earn a degree. Even with going to college there is no guarantee of success, especially these days. My goal of trend following has been to compound money over time and achieve financial freedom. My goal was never to work by the hour, but to create a lifestyle that many think is unachievable.

What is shocking is that many aspiring traders think they don't have to learn a single thing. Some believe that they can buy a "magic system" or "trading robot" that will be retirement in a box. Some beginning traders think that they can learn everything they need to know from a "free" e-book that they downloaded from the Internet. Then there are those who read the *Wall Street Journal*, *Barron's*, *Smart Money,* and countless other magazines looking for tips in which to invest. If it were only that easy, we would all be rich!

■ Make Sure You Are Properly Funded before You Start

If you don't have sufficient funds to trade, then you need to start doing something about it now. Either save more money or do not even begin. Trading without being amply funded will only lead to disaster. With a small account one can trade stocks or mini commodity contracts.

The question is asked, "How much do I really need to start trading?"

That is a personal question. It depends on your time frame and the markets you want to trade. The lower the time frame, the less funds are needed. If you decided to trend follow stocks, you need less than if you trend follow futures. If one were to day trade via trend following, one would not need much money due to margin requirements. This is regardless of stocks, forex, or futures.

I personally prefer a daily time frame as it gives me greater freedom and no pressure. If looking at dailies, I suggest for stocks a minimum could be $10,000. For futures traded on a daily time frame the minimum is at least $50,000 and quite possibly more, up to $100,000. Regardless of these estimations, it is a personal decision, and you do not want to risk more than 1 percent of your account on any one trade. This would be the best formula for you to decide how much you should start trading with. Start slowly and build confidence over time. Rome was not built overnight nor will your trading career. Focus on learning before trying to make money.

Many beginning traders think they should trade all of their savings. This is financially reckless and increases trading pressure. To determine how much money you should trade, you must first determine how much you can actually afford to lose and what your financial goals are. There is a traders' joke among futures traders. The question is, what is the easiest way to make a million dollars trading futures? The answer is to start with two million. In all seriousness this is the reality. You do not want to impact your or your family's lifestyle. This only puts more pressure on you.

The more capital you can afford to lose without negatively affecting your lifestyle, the greater the possibility that you will be successful. The more money you start with gives you greater longevity and cushion in the event of a drawdown. There will always be drawdowns and losses. There will always be ugly periods. These bad periods can extend not just for months but personally I have lived through periods of durations that were greater than two years. The more capital accompanied with proper risk management such as a risk per trade of 1 percent reduces the emotional drag on your psyche.

You do not want to be emotionally attached to the aspect of money. Successful traders look at percentages, not money. Thinking of money in terms of itself is a terrible thing for a trader to do. They think of the things they could have purchased or done with the money. I think of money as chips. I am betting and I have a small edge. I have heard traders say, after a winning trade, I am going to buy this car or that car. I know at this point they are destined to fail. I think what happens when they have a losing streak; they clearly will not be buying that car. Trading must be thought of a game. You need to play the game without emotions such as fear and greed.

Let's begin by determining how much of your savings should remain in your savings account. It's important to keep at least six months of living expenses in a readily accessible savings account, so set that money aside, and don't trade it! You should never trade money that you may need immediately or for daily living expenses. Do not borrow money from your parents or in-laws (even though David Einhorn did and now is managing billions of dollars).

Take a good look at how much money you can currently afford to trade.

I would not suggest you even think about trading if you have less than $10,000. The reason I say this is that I am a strong believer that you should not risk more than 1 percent of your account on any trade. One percent of $10,000 is $100. That is really tough to do in the real world. It is the lower limit if you plan on day trading stocks. The above concept accentuates why it is better to have a larger trading account. Better means a greater chance to succeed over time.

If you have the fear of losing this money, it will almost become a self-professing reality. As well, if you cannot afford to lose this money, my opinion is that you will lose this money either by fear or through mistakes. If you do not have enough money, wait!

You don't want other parts of your life to suffer when you tie your money up in a trade or lose money on a trade. I promise you, you will have many losing trades, so make sure to consider what these savings were originally for. Never borrow money to trade, and never use money that you can't afford to lose!

If you do not have enough money to trade, some traders rationalize that they can just specialize in one market. They are deluding themselves. I know there will be those that will disagree with me, however, there will be periods or time frames when nothing seems to happen in any particular stock or market. As well, there will be times in which the volatility will be too great in which they cannot put on a low-risk trade (1 percent of their account size). These traders think to lower the time frame and go to tick charts. They end up being cannon fodder for floor traders or the 10 percenters (consistently successful traders over time). At first thought it would seem that it would be easier to focus all of their energy on a single market and supposedly become an expert in that market. However, in reality I believe that it is extremely hard to always make money in any single market. As I am an open person, I would assume some traders have succeeded focusing on just one market; however, I believe this is the realm of floor traders or market makers in stocks.

I am a proponent of utilizing a robust trading methodology that trades all markets and time frames the same (more on this in Chapter 2). I want to make myself available for potential opportunities. The way I do this is to trade a basket of diversified markets. I never know which market is going to move. I know that markets go from periods of quiet orderly trading to volatile periods. It is very difficult to trade volatile markets.

■ Establish Your Trading Goals

Before you start, you need to determine what your goals are. What do you hope to achieve with your trading activities? How much time do you have to trade? Another great question is why do you want to trade? Before you trade a single penny, really think about what you hope to achieve with trading. Knowing what your goal is will help you stay motivated when you're facing an inevitable drawdown, and it'll help you all along the way.

What *Really* Are Your Goals?

Maybe this is a very obvious question, and the answer is probably simple: You want to make money. There has to be a trade-off, however, between simply making money and the drawdowns one has to endure to get to one's goals.

No matter how profitable one's trading is, the volatility of returns must be taken into account. If the volatility is too great, there will be a period when one cannot continue to trade. This cessation in trading could be due to an emotional breakdown or lack of risk trading capital. Consider this example. One trader makes 60 percent returns; however, he goes through periods in which he experiences 40 percent-plus drawdowns. Quantifying these numbers over a 10-year period with an initial amount of $50,000 compounds to $5,497,558.14.

FIGURE 1.1 DUNN Capital Management: DUNN Combined Fund (DCF)
Source: Chart Courtesy of IASG.Com

That is the great news; however, at one point in year 10 you lose 40 percent of that much. Does losing $2,199,023 leave you feeling comfortable? The answer is obvious: probably not! Do you really think he can stomach that year in and year out? Would you invest with him? I would personally find it very hard. In the real world there are trend followers like Bill Dunn of DUNN Capital Management who have had some wild swings. You mostly hear of the fantastic periods, not the drawdowns. There were points at which Bill Dunn managed funds in excess of $2 billion. In his program, the Combined Fund DCF, he is currently managing $22 million.

Bill Dunn has been managing money since the 1970s. He is considered a legend in the trend following world. Dunn has experienced extreme volatility throughout the years. When times are good, people throw him money, and when he goes through drawdowns, his investors panic. As much as DCF has returned 100 percent one year he has had drawdowns in the 70 percent range. Dunn had five years in a row in which he sustained losses and the following year he returned 100 percent.

I have heard from many investors that they can withstand a 20 percent drawdown; however, when it actually occurs, that is a different story. They quickly translate 20 percent into what that is in a dollar basis. The fear of the 20 percent drawdown increasing to 30 percent or greater sets in very quickly. In my proprietary trading account I consider how much risk I need to take on in order to generate reasonable returns. This keeps me in the race.

I believe the lower the volatility in a trading account, the more apt one is to stay in the game. Going through any drawdown is not fun or easy. However, there are many investors that are not satisfied with this either. They want the big returns without the big drawdowns. They seem to want their cake and eat it too, as that phrase goes.

Traders need to be realistic and mature when weighing between these two options. Reducing the magnitude of a drawdown enhances the probability that the trader will stay in the game by two accounts. This reduces the risk of ruin and makes it much less emotionally challenging to go through big swings not just in percentages but also in real dollar terms.

Some of the biggest mistakes I have seen are when traders are in drawdowns. They stop to think logically and fear kicks in with irrational behavior. These traders forget their trading plan and try to trade their way out of this bottomless pit of a drawdown. They double up, they tighten stops when they shouldn't, or they will do the exact opposite by widening stops. Basically they are out of control and trading in a rage. You do not want to get to this point. This is why it is a paramount issue to "try" to keep losses and drawdowns to a tolerable level. I want to emphasize the word *try*. We are dealing with uncertainty, and the only certainty is uncertainty.

We can put stops in the market, but this is no guarantee that we cannot get caught in a limit move against us. Limit moves are set by the exchanges of a maximum permissible move allowed in a particular market. There are times when, as much as we want to exit, we cannot. The other reason I stress the word "try" is that there will be overnight gaps and moves, which as much as they can benefit us, are more apt to hurt us.

Stick to Your Plan

Another hard mistake for traders to overcome is that they do not follow their plan (if they have one) and exit a trade that is working due to the proverbial fear of losing money, greed of taking the money, or ego of being right or smart. Initially they might feel good and then Mr. Murphy shows up and the trade in which they exited prematurely ends up being a runaway trade. The trader has left a substantial amount of money on the table. The emotional roller-coaster starts with a great deal of disappointment and anxiety. I wish I had stayed in that trade. Why was I so stupid? The list can go and on. My solution is first, look out the front window. What has happened is over. All you can do is go forward and learn from it. What one needs to learn is the necessity of a plan and following it exactly.

A Look on the Bright Side

Going back to being slightly more positive, there is more to the idea than you want to make money. Do you want to be rich or wealthy? In my neighborhood I have both types of neighbors. I have wealthy ones and rich ones. What is the difference?

"Being rich" means that you have a lot of money. "Being wealthy" means that you actually have **time** to enjoy your money, time to do what you want to do when you want to do it.

I live five minutes from the beach and see many people early in the morning walking. I walk pretty much every morning, most of the time with my wife. What stuck out to both of us was that a very famous businessman would walk on the beach whenever it seemed he would have financial issues as reported in the newspapers. In 2008 we saw him for the first time. He walked with his head down in deep thought and concern. Again this year we would see him. What I gleaned from this was that he was rich but he was not wealthy. He owned one company after the other and was leveraged to the hilt. On the surface of it he seems unable to enjoy his money.

Contrarily, I am wealthy. I can do whatever and whenever I please. I take my trading with me. I have time for my family as well as charity work. I can only attribute this to trend following over the years. I compounded money over time. It has not been easy as I have gone through countless drawdowns, but I was patient and disciplined to keep in the marathon and not give up.

In retrospect I was fortunate that I struggled when I first started trading. This struggle planted the seeds in my psyche that trading is not easy and that I had to work. I am happy I did not encounter immediate short-term success that would have deluded me. I believe if I had had some amazing trades right from the get-go, I would have underestimated what is truly entailed for trading success. I might not have realized how quickly the market can take away my hard-earned profits. I probably would not have developed the risk profile in which I trade today.

You decide which you prefer!

■ Trading Pitfalls

With great excitement and probably nervousness you put on your first trade. Do not expect it to work (make money). It will be much better for you if your first couple of trades do not work. This will serve as a wakeup call on how hard trading really is. I would strongly suggest that you start small with money you can afford to lose, as you will make mistakes. Remember, 90 percent-plus of traders lose money and quit. I wish that you will become one of the 10 percenters who are consistently successful over time. I truly believe my book is unique and gives you all the tools.

On my blog, TrendFollowingMentor.com, there are many free educational pieces to help you and guide you. Reading my book and my material on my Web page, TrendFollowingmentor.com, should help you with one of the most important aspects of trading, patience and discipline.

Traders lack discipline for several emotional reasons. There is the fear element, greed element, and the ego element. These are all based on human nature. We all should trade for one paramount issue, to build an ever-increasing equity curve—greed. Who would ever want to put on a trade if they stood the distinct possibility of losing money? That is human nature. We want to be right; this is ego. Who really likes to lose money? This is where the fear comes into play. We are hard-wired for these human emotions. This is why discipline is hard to achieve. When we cut a loss, several interesting things happen. We are wrong and our ego could be damaged and our pocketbooks are damaged with a loss. Not too many people like being wrong and losing money at the same time. What a head trip! It is not human nature! Wouldn't it be so much easier just not taking the loss and hoping the trade will come back? Yes, it would be emotionally easier; however, this is one of the quickest ways to stop trading. Small losses morph into large losses.

Successful trend followers know that if they do not take small losses, these small losses can morph into big losses and cause both financial and emotional damage. This is why successful traders have built the discipline. They have let small losses turn into these big losses, and they do not want to have it happen again.

Lack of discipline can be evident in various other aspects of trading. Exiting a profitable trade contrary to your rules is due to lack of discipline and fear. Ego comes into the picture when people want to be considered right or smart on a trade. If they lock in the profit, all of a sudden they are right. These types of traders are lacking discipline. Taking their profit prematurely, they face the distinct possibility of missing the big trade of the year. They need that trade to offset all the numerous losses they will encounter.

Another example of lack of discipline are the traders who violate their trading plan (if they really have one), and once a trade goes against them, they average down and double down. They believe they are right and the market is wrong. It is almost funny to say this, but even professional traders have made this mistake of discipline and have blown up.

Conversely there are the type of traders who, when/if a trade starts to work, immediately add to that position. They want to make a killing. They want to get rich. This is ego. This enhanced leverage works both ways and is a double-edged sword. When a trade works and leverage is used, that is great. However, the more probable instance is when these trades do not work, leverage is used, and both financial and emotional pain is generated. I am not a psychologist; however, I have seen these types of instances in the market.

Discipline is really a hard attribute to build. It is almost like a muscle that needs to be built. You need to build a discipline muscle as well as a patience muscle. Discipline is one of the most difficult aspects of trading to overcome. You can have your exact trading plan and the "best" system, but it is for naught if you either do not take the next upcoming trade or fail to exit when you are supposed to.

You do not want to fail to pull the trigger on a trade. You do not want to miss a trade you should have taken. You do not want to let a small loss grow into a nightmare. If you miss one trade, you might miss an entire year of profits. The lack of discipline comes at the most critical time for a trader. Discipline is needed when you are in the thick of it or in a difficult situation. There are those that think simulated trades teach one discipline. I disagree wholeheartedly. There is a new feeling when you have real money and real risks on the line. All the supposed planning and preparation can go out the window. It is trite to tell a trader that he or she needs to control fear and greed. These are very strong emotions. When one is consistent (over time) the ability to overcome fear and greed are slightly easier to handle. Consistent means seeing a familiar situation that you have seen before and acted upon in exactly the same manner. You repeat the same action and are open and accepting of the consequences. You completely accept that the trade is 50/50, and if the trade does not work, you move on and take the next trade without any fear. Mechanical trading systems can assist in discipline, but it is still up to you to take the trade and be responsible for the outcome.

Interpreting charts is somewhat difficult. At times, if you do not have an exact plan with patterns that are recognizable, you might interpret the charts differently. Differently means you are not consistent. Consistency builds discipline and controls the inherent fear, greed, and ego.

The learning never stops. Do you really expect to make millions of dollars after only investing a few hours of time in your education? You wouldn't trust a lawyer or doctor whose only education was from a course or webinar!

If you're not willing to spend the time learning the techniques of trend following, not working on yourself as far as discipline and patience are concerned, then trend following might not be for you.

■ It's Your Choice

Trend following is all about making decisions, but before you actually begin trading, there are a few important things you'll need to consider. The basic decisions you should make deal with your chosen software platform, your trading time frame, and what markets you want to trade.

My trend following methodology is very simple and robust, and it will work on all platforms, time frames, and markets.

Your Charting Software and Computer System

You don't need the latest computer, and you don't need the most expensive or so-called fastest system. Basically, any computer or laptop that you've purchased in the past couple of years is fine. I trade with an ASUS laptop from a year ago. I have everything backed up on a desktop, an external hard drive, and a cloud. You do not need anything fancy, just solid, reliable, and durable. Forget about all the speed stuff that is touted.

Choosing the *right* charting software is a very personal decision. What another trader chooses may be different from what you choose, and vice versa. That's why it's important for you to carefully evaluate a list of features, considering both advantages and disadvantages before you make a decision on a data feed and charting package.

You can use *Stocks & Commodities* magazine's Reader's Choice as a starting point and try out various software platforms. I have been using Metastock, probably since around the time it came out in the marketplace, and I use Tradingblox, as well. There are pros and cons to both platforms.

Metastock Metastock was probably the first trading platform in the world that gave you the ability to create, test, and fully automate your own rule-based trading strategies on a daily basis. When you're ready for your first trade, Metastock can watch your trading rules and even carry out your trades 100 percent automatically. It is similar to autopilot, but I suggest you still try flying the plane yourself, at least initially.

Metastock is designed to help you discover some potential market opportunities and then perform your trades more professionally than you could ever do on your own. Metastock essentially monitors the markets for you tick by tick, in real time on the Internet, and seeks out all of the opportunities based on your trading plans.

The instant an opportunity arises based on your custom buy or sell rules, it's designed to automatically generate your entry and exit orders and send them to the marketplace within fractions of a second of the market move.

You can automate practically all of the trading strategies you could ever think of, including multiple orders, entries and exits, profit targets, protective stops, trailing stops, and more. It allows you to back-test, program custom indicators, and modify indicators to your needs. Then, with just a single click of your mouse, it will back-test your strategy on up to 20 years of authentic, intraday market data, giving you the simulated results. Metastock will provide you with information on all of the trades you would have positioned, your simulated net profit or losses, and much more, before you even risk one dollar from your real trading funds.

When you first set up Metastock, it may be a little overwhelming because of all the features and functions. However, for $1,395 (plus data charges) you can utilize Metastock's award-winning features and be off to a good start.

Tradingblox As I stated, there are reviews in *Stocks & Commodities* magazine to help you figure out what works best for you. On a portfolio level, I use Tradingblox. It lets me test out how my ideas test on a portfolio level. I would suggest walking before running. Walk forward means testing different periods of time in order to confirm that you have similar results both in percent profits and percent drawdowns. Try Metastock and if you are satisfied, purchase it for your trend following strategies. I teach with Metastock in my mentoring courses due to its robustness and simplicity.

You need to be comfortable with the platform and it is entirely your choice.

Time Frames for Trend Following

The term *time frame* refers to the length of time you plan to hold your trade. This is totally a personal decision based on your personality, risk profile, and account size. Day traders exit all of their positions at the close of the market. Position traders can hold trades for weeks or even years. You have to decide on your time frame. Do you want to trade short-term, long-term, or somewhere in between? This is a paramount decision regarding your trading career. Each time frame has its own prerequisite of both time and emotional energy.

Whatever time frame you chose, it must fit your personality as well as time constraints. Some traders simply do not have the patience to wait for an outcome of a trade. They are not emotionally built to hold a trade for month or longer. Traders like this should not even consider longer-term time frames. Conversely, if you have a full-time job, do not delude yourself that you can bop in and out of a position while you are juggling your real job. Can you imagine if you went to an attorney for a pressing issue? Suppose he comes in late for the meeting because he was watching his trading screen of five-minute S&P 500 bars. In the course of the meeting, he gets an alert on his BlackBerry to buy the S&P 500 futures and bolts out the door to place the order. I doubt that the lawyer will be successful nor that you would have confidence in the lawyer representing you. The lawyer thinks he can make easy money. He is lured into the money trap and cannon fodder for professional traders. I have heard stories like this, as ridiculous as they sound. You must trade your time constraints and there is no free lunch out there.

Day traders swear by their time frame and why it is optimal. Position traders will swear by their time frame and state their reasons. In both cases these traders are trading their personality. There is no *best* time frame. The best time frame is one that matches your time constraints and personality. There are traders who change time frames like some change their hairstyles. These traders are seeking the holy grail and have not accepted the inherent risks while trading. There is no way to avoid losses other than not trading. If I can put my two cents in, there is the inherent advantage to trade less to avoid slippage and commissions. This is just my opinion. I have found that more position traders over time are more successful than day traders. There is less emotional demand and stress on position trading than day trading.

Trade your personality as far as time frame; determine for yourself what time frame works the best for you.

You can sit in front of a computer and day trade or you can do as I do with daily bars. Personally, when I am trading daily bars from start to finish, I am usually finished in less than one hour. With the methods of trend following I will teach you, it is all the same. I download my data early in the morning and within less than one hour I am finished for the day. **I know what I need to do exactly.** I have exact entries, exits, and exact amounts of contracts or shares to buy. I am prepared and my orders are in the markets. It really does not matter what your exact entries are. A mechanical systematic trader might look for a breakout trade or a retracement trade (as I do). A fundamental trader might look for a favorable earnings report. Then there are those who rely on astrology or cycles. Don't laugh, I am serious, people even seek out astrology. The key is to have some type of realistic entry method that is replicative and identifiable so that once you see it on another trade you can repeat the action.

Regardless of the entries, they are one of the smallest pieces of the puzzle. Any trade is 50/50. The more important issues are the risk considerations such as how much to buy or sell and when to exit with either a profit or a loss.

Aspects of the Exit   Exiting a trade is much more important than the entries. One of the hardest things for traders to do is actually take the appropriate exit as per their trading plan (if they have one). Trend followers need to ride major trends to make up for all of the small losses they encounter and maximize their profitability. Day traders, on the other hand, are happy to make a few ticks on the majority of their profitable trades. Both of these issues are personal issues that need to be addressed before trading commences. What I have found is that one of the hardest issues for a beginning trader is to have the patience to let the trade work. Once the trade starts working or trending fear or greed kicks in, there is the urge to lock in the short profit as opposed to letting it run. This will have devastating effects on a trader's account. Most trades do not work when one trend follows and cutting profits short is the direct route to failure in trading. One must have these rare big winners to offset the multitudes of trades that do not work and incur (hopefully) small losses. The reality of trend following is doing the uncomfortable. Trend following requires work. This work is developing your patience and discipline to let these trades run their course and not cut them short due to fear or greed. It is very easy to ring the cash register, and then this leads to another major issue of disappointment. Can you imagine if you had a trade that was working and out of fear or greed you took your quick profit only to watch it afterwards hitting multiyear highs or lows? This is the reality. Trends go to extremes. Do not feel bad. This is human nature. I once heard a lecture by Leo Melamed from CME who spoke about a silver trade he was in. Leo Melamed, the chairman of CME, exited a silver trade during the Hunt brothers' escapade thinking that it had gone far enough.

The Hunt brothers tried to corner the silver market in the late 1970s. Silver went from $11 to $50 during the Hunt brothers' manipulation. Fortunes were made and lost. Beginning in the early 1970s, the Hunt brothers started accumulating large amounts of silver. By mid-1979, the Hunt brothers virtually cornered the total global silver market. The brothers made a tremendous profit estimated at between $2 billion to $4 billion due to their enormous silver bet. In today's terms, this amount I would assume would be in the tens of billions or possibly more. Silver prices ultimately returned from the stratosphere and collapsed to below $11 eventually. The largest single-day drop in the price of silver occurred on so-called Silver Thursday. The Hunt brothers ended up filing for bankruptcy in September 1988, largely due to lawsuits incurred as a result of their silver speculation. However, during this period trend followers who had a plan and the tenacity to follow their plan created fortunes for themselves and their grandchildren. Trends will go to extremes. You need to have the patience and fortitude to let them run without interfering.

As much as cutting losses is important to long-term success while trend following, the aspect of exits and when to exit may have more of an impact in your long-term success as exemplified in the preceding paragraphs.

You have to have the drive, dedication, discipline, patience, and passion to give yourself the potential for success in trading.

CHAPTER 2

Getting the Most Out of This Method

Do not delude yourself. You will not instantly become successful the minute you finish reading this manual. You run the possibility of making your money over a long series of trades. You need to have realistic expectations of yourself and my trend following methodology. Once you internalize the fact that you will make your money *over a series of trades,* it makes it a lot easier to handle the inherent losses when trading. You will come to grips with the fact that any trade in any month or any year does not really matter as long as you have kept your losses small.

Too often, people start trading with dreams of becoming rich overnight. I am of the belief of trying to compound your money over time. I do not like taking big risks when I trade. It's much safer to maintain a trading strategy that will allow your account to grow at a slower pace over time, which can ultimately be used for retirement or a child's education.

Compounding your way to wealth is not a get rich quick endeavor.

There will be no surprises when you trend follow as I outline in the book. You will have losses. You will have long periods when you might not make money, but if you stick with the strategy and stay in the marathon, you stand the potential to compound money over time.

My goal is to give you the realistic picture that I have personally encountered over the last 18 years of my trend following career. Trend following is not retirement in a box! You will have to do the work. You will have to work on yourself. You will have to build your discipline and patience muscles. There will be times when it will be very hard. In order to succeed over time you need to believe in the concepts. You'll learn key concepts that you can apply to your trading right away.

I am giving you my exact *plan*. There is nothing held back.

There Are No Secrets!

My plan is not perfect but it is robust and can be traded on any time frame and any market. Without a well-thought-out plan, trend following is very risky. However, with the right risk measures and the knowledge to use these in an efficient and effective manner, you put the odds of success on your side. Your trading plan requires a great deal of work. You need to develop the plan to match your personality, and it is even harder to follow the plan. You will have to follow through on difficult decisions and choices. Your plan must cover all the key elements of trading with risk, money management, and having the proper discipline and patience.

Developing a trading plan with all the time, energy, and effort devoted toward your future success still does not guarantee you your trading success. The markets need to move. With this movement the best you can try to do is not lose too much money. The market has a way of throwing you curveballs and unexpected twists. You need your strategy or your plan to get you through all of the unexpected outcomes prevalent in the market. Too many traders only consider the context of a plan after they have lost money. The plan consists of all potential precarious events before they happen. The plan should answer all the potential outcomes.

An example of this, as you will learn further on, I trail my stops with a trailing average true range stop indicator version that I wrote about in *Stocks & Commodities* magazine in 1998. The question as part of my trading plan is, if I touch my average true range stop, do I exit or do I have to close below it? The trading plan must answer this because in the heat of trading you do not want to be surprised. There is no free lunch when we trade. There will be times that the stop is touched and reverses. Frustration can easily be had.

Conversely, if one were to wait for a close below the average true range stop, the loss can be greatly enhanced. The only solution is to accept the risk and accept the outcome as part of your plan. You must not change your plan or rules in midstream. You strive for consistency. This consistency lowers the pressure as well as gives you the ability to repeat the trade process over and over again. Trading patterns repeat themselves over and over again. There are always an endless stream of potential trades on all time frames and all markets. You just have to be available.

Do You Want to Be Right or Make Money?

I have this question posed to me all throughout my journey. I prefer to make money and compound it over long periods of time. The funny thing is that many traders and investors don't like trend following. It is not intuitive, too long term at times, or simply not exciting enough. I am not in need of excitement.

Clearly there is nothing perfect in life or trading. You will have losses but these losses, as long as they are kept small, will be manageable. You will have ups and downs in your trading account. You will go through drawdowns. Losses are as natural as breathing.

Many cannot take losses. That is why they flocked to Madoff. They did not want to take small losses only to take total losses.

You decide; **nothing is perfect! There is no free lunch.**

In my opinion there is no other strategy out there that offers **liquidity, transparency, and profit potential** as much as trend following. Trend following strategies work on all markets, forex, stocks, and commodities. Trend following works on all time frames. If you want to day trade, the same rules apply as they do to trading daily charts. Trend following is not something new; it goes back decades!

Even with the success of trend following there are periods when profits are elusive. Many people consider trend following dead during these periods. In all honesty, my wife has asked me over and over again during my drawdowns if maybe trend following is over.

People, including my wife, ignore the tremendous track record that trend followers have built over the decades. They argue it is outdated; it has too many participants; or it simply just does not work anymore. Again and again they are proven wrong. At the darkest point comes the light.

Actually these are the best times to invest in trend following.

Trend following entails having a defined plan and strategy to put money into trades to achieve one and only one goal: **profit.**

Trend followers do not care what they own or what they sell or buy as long as they end up with more money than they started with. Trend followers will go short as often as they will go long, thus giving them the potential to make money in both up and down markets.

The fears associated with a potential market crash do not exist; the greed associated with a runaway bull market does not exist.

Trend followers do not worry about what the markets are going to do tomorrow. They have an exact plan with all contingencies thought out ahead of time. Trend followers are like surfers and look to ride the waves.

Trend followers have an exact plan. This plan is based on an objective and automated set of rules.

Trend followers follow their plan without second guessing it. They believe in it! A trading plan makes life easier by eliminating emotions from the trading decisions. A trading plan forces discipline. If you do not follow the trading plan, you will not succeed. Do not even start if you cannot follow the plan.

■ Basic Tenets of Trend Following

The single biggest mistake traders make is thinking that investing and trading is easy.

They allow themselves to fall for advertisements promising, "You can get rich by trading" or "Earn all the income you've ever dreamed of" or "Leave your day job forever and live off your day-trading profits." Trend following is not retirement in a box.

You Have to Work

The actual tenets of successful trend following are basically simple and intuitive in nature. However, in practicality trend following is very difficult due to our greed and fears.

In order to succeed over time with trend following you will need to internalize these tenets and make them part of your trading.

It is imperative for your long-term success to always **cut losses short and take low-risk trades**. You will realize when you start trend following, if you haven't already, that many trades simply do not work. Taking low-risk bets and keeping losses manageable are the cornerstone of successful trend following.

Don't trade to get rich quick. At best it takes a long time to compound money and there are no guarantees for the future. **The only certainty is uncertainty!**

Have realistic expectations. Losses are part of our business. There will be many. A trading system that doesn't have losses is "too good to be true." The only truth about that trading system is that it will not make money in the real world.

Start Small

Remember to start small—walk before you run. When you are trend following successfully you trade **only in the direction of the trend**. There is no second-guessing or debating. You do not let your opinions get in the way. You have an **exact plan** to follow trades that are working as well as an **exact plan** to exit quickly trades that are not working.

I use only a few rules and they are very easy to understand. Do not confuse easy-to-understand with easy-to-do. The more rules you have, the more likely that you've "curve-fitted" your trading strategy to past data, and such an overoptimized system is very unlikely to produce profits in real markets.

At the same time, it takes time to develop a successful strategy. This is why you should start small. Test potential rules before deciding to include them in your trading. It's important that your rules are easy to understand and execute. This ensures that your strategy is robust, adaptable, and easy to manage.

Compound Your Money over Time

Patience is also important when it comes to finding trading success. Every trader—no matter how experienced—has losing trades. I recommend keeping a long-term view.

This can help you keep your emotions in check so you can quickly recover from losses, behave rationally, and follow your trading *plan* instead of getting distracted.

■ Compounding Your Way to Wealth

Repeatedly I have stressed that trend following is not easy nor the only way to compound your way to wealth.

There is a drawdown out there that can make one stop trend following. As they have not followed their plan, even had a plan, or took on too much risk.

Regardless of the strictest risk and money management filters, there will be numerous losses. In order to compound money we must try to keep them small and manageable, otherwise we will not be compounding money. You will experience gaps that go against you as well days that are limit up or down. You cannot avoid or control these.

There will always be drawdowns and extended periods of elusive profits. In all honesty, trend following is the easiest yet the hardest thing to do. You will have deep and extended drawdowns that seem never to end. However, eventually there is light at the end of the tunnel. Out of nowhere trends appear, and accounts regain their lost values and hit new equity peaks.

Everyone has his or her belief system of how to try to compound money or simply invest. There are those who do real estate, invest in hedge funds, as well those that invest in their own personal business. As I stated, trend following is not the only solution to compound money over time, but it is the strategy I adhere to and I have personally been able to compound money over time.

There are no guarantees, however, that trend following will be right for you. Trend following is liquid and transparent where other strategies are not.

As much as nothing is for sure except uncertainty, I am confident that trend following will continue to work over time regardless of bull markets, bear markets, inflation, and deflation.

We all have heard of the Rule of 72 and the magic of compounding at some point in our education. However, for me, compounding money was elusive for a period of time. The reality is that for most traders it is also elusive. It took me many years until I was able to take money out of the markets.

Compounding Money Is the Key to Building Our Net Worth

Albert Einstein called compound interest "the greatest mathematical discovery of all time."

Richard Russell, known from his work, *The Dow Letters*, has stated, "Compounding is the royal road to riches." He also said, "Compounding is the safe road, the sure road, and fortunately anybody can do it.

This means possibly you.

Table 2.1 details what would happen to a $100,000 investment if one were able to compound that initial investment at an annual rate of between 10 percent and 20 percent.

TABLE 2.1 **Compound Interest on $100,000 over Time**

Initial Investment	Annual Interest Rate	Time	Total
$100,000.00	10%	5 yrs	$ 161,051.00
$100,000.00	10%	10 yrs	$ 259,374.25
$100,000.00	10%	15 yrs	$ 417,724.82
$100,000.00	10%	20 yrs	$ 672,749.99
$100,000.00	15%	5 yrs	$ 201,135.72
$100,000.00	*15%*	*10 yrs*	*$ 404,555.77*
$100,000.00	*15%*	*15 yrs*	*$ 813,706.16*
$100,000.00	15%	20 yrs	$1,636,653.74
$100,000.00	20%	5 yrs	$ 248,832.00
$100,000.00	20%	10 yrs	$ 619,173.64
$100,000.00	20%	15 yrs	$1,540,702.16
$100,000.00	20%	20 yrs	$6,814,608.25

The chart tells us that a $100,000 investment compounding at 15 percent would grow in excess of $400,000 over a 10-year period. If that investment continued to compound at 15 percent per year, it would grow to over $800,000 five years later. Simple terms: in 10 years @ 15 percent you have 4 times your money and in 15 years you have 8 times.

In the manual I present real-time and real-money audited returns of some money managers. Now that you see Table 2.1 you can understand how these money managers were able to compound money to such extremes.

One of the key points that I will keep on reminding you is about keeping losses small. If losses grow to extremes, it negatively impacts our compounding or even may lead you to quit trend following.

Table 2.2 reflects the mathematics of recovering from losses.

TABLE 2.2 **Recovering from Losses**

Starting Portfolio Value	If Your Portfolio Drops	New Value of Portfolio	% Gain Needed to Recover
$100,000	10%	$90,000	11%
$100,000	20%	$80,000	25%
$100,000	30%	$70,000	43%
$100,000	40%	$60,000	67%
$100,000	50%	$50,000	100%

This table actually shows us the importance of trying to mitigate losses. The bottom line is that it is very difficult to recover from large losses.

Figure 2.1 is a chart from American Century Investment that shows an equity curve of a portfolio that suffered a 50 percent decline. This chart indicates just how difficult it is to recover from large losses. A positive 8 percent compounded return for eight years will only bring your account back to even after initially suffering such a large loss. It is simply not easy to recover from large losses, and yet all markets will likely suffer 50 percent declines at some point. The power of compounding can work for you only if you do not suffer large losses.

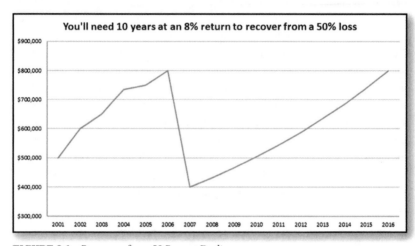

FIGURE 2.1   Recovery after a 50 Percent Decline

All we can control is our risk. This is why it is so important to adhere to strict risk and money management rules. There always exists a draw down that can stop you from trend following. If you want to make trend following a lifetime strategy you must include strict risk & money management.

Keep It Simple and Stupid

Many people (including myself when I first began) think that the fancy Ivy schools or reams of research reports will bring trading profits. **My proprietary robust ideas are more successful than complicated analysis.** When I first began my journey of learning I sought out the holy grail. I thought there was some secret method, Fibonacci, Elliott wave, or Gann idea that would enable to me to make money. I personally have not been able to figure out or predict when a market will move. I reached the point where I realized that I could not nor can anyone else accurately predict over time when a market will move.

I started to doubt that gurus really existed. Prechter was still a perma bear years after his great call of the stock market in 1987. Once I really internalized this, my anxiety level fell and I was okay not even thinking about or trying to predict or know why a market moved. **I learned that anything can happen and will happen**. I realized all information was in the price. I did not need to predict anything to be successful.

More so, I realized that no one knows anything more than me. I have invested with many commodity-trading advisors over the years. In the beginning I thought they were smarter or simply just better than my own trend following. I realized this is not the case. Some years I have had better returns in my trend following than some of the managers I invest with and some years I have worse. It does not matter, though, as I am looking to compound my money over long periods of time and want to try to smooth it out as best I can.

Eventually I learned that trying to predict anything was a waste of time and not possible. That is I why I decided to follow trends. That is why I have been successful over the years since 1994 even though it has been some journey. I never know when a trend starts or stops. I just take small bets, ask myself how much it is going to cost me to see if the trade will work, and try to follow trends. A small position is like a tugboat. Sometimes these small positions can pull a great deal of weight and show tremendous returns. As an example, I was lucky to have a cotton trade in 2010 and just on one contract $20,000 of profit was attributed. This is a rare case; most trades actually do not work.

I cannot guess how far a trend will go. It is impossible! No one knows how high or how low a market can go. No one knows when a market will move or a trend will begin.

■ Requirements for Successful Trend Following

Successful trend followers strive for the goal of consistency. In order to achieve consistency you need a solid, robust plan that gives the potential to produce consistent trading profits over time. As I stated earlier, if you want to succeed in trend following you must do your work. You MUST invest both time and money to acquire the knowledge that you need as well as the discipline to follow the plan and the patience to let the plan work over time.

You are **accountable** for your trading decisions and actions, and you must take **responsibility** for your trading.

You are responsible for your trading results, nobody else.

Perseverance and Commitment

With these attributes, over time, success can possibly be achieved.

Trend following is not for everyone. Yes, there are many advantages, but there are also realities that many do not want to face. One of these realities is that you will encounter many losing trades. If you do not want to lose on a trade, do not start trend following.

Successful trend followers, regardless of whether they are managing money for others or simply for themselves, have robust trend following strategies and the discipline to stick to their trading plan even through the inevitable drawdowns.

Unfortunately, even with a tested, proven trading strategy, you are not guaranteed trading success. It takes something else. It takes discipline and patience. A proven strategy is useless without discipline. Successful trend followers must have the discipline to follow their system rigorously. Simply purchasing a trend following book (even mine) does not guarantee your success as a trader.

A Positive Attitude and Realistic Expectations

As I have already stated and want to reiterate, trading can be simple, but it is not easy. Along the line, you will face losses, but you need to get up every single morning believing in yourself, the robust methodology, and the potential of compounding money over time.

Give Yourself a Time for Introspection

Evaluate yourself. Be honest with yourself. Maintain a trade journal and evaluate yourself. I strongly suggest using it for every trade and then reviewing it. Here are some sample questions and reminders to address in your journal.

Did you follow the exact plan?

Did you overtrade this week?

Did you put on too large a position because you thought the trade would work?

Did you put on too small a position due to fear?

Did you let your emotions get the better of you?

Did you let fear or greed overcome you?

What about ego? Did you have to be right on a trade?

If you made mistakes—do not beat yourself up.

Look out the front window, not the back window!

I have yet to meet a perfect person!

Take responsibility for your actions and your decisions.

Admit a mistake, learn from it, and move on.

Be Committed!

Trading success will not happen overnight. It requires commitment, time, and effort on your part.

There are already too many "traders" in the market who think they know every-thing they need to, who think they don't have to learn anything; they believe there are trading robots out there that will place their trades for them and make them rich. You and I know that this is a sure path to failure.

Keep Your Cool

The markets can behave very wildly and move very fast, and you won't have time to calculate complicated formulas in order to make trading decisions. Think about suc-cessful floor traders: The only tools they use are a calculator and pivot points, and some make thousands of dollars every day.

You follow the trend! Let profits run without any fear or greed. Simply detach yourself, see what is happening, and *follow the exact plan.*

You will have an exact plan in which at every point you know exactly what you should be doing. When you are letting your profits run you will be exposed to profit-able opportunities due to trending markets. You will not be in areas that are illiquid such as the housing bubble or on the wrong side of major trends such as the dot.com bubble or the October 2008 stock market meltdown.

I will teach you how successful trend followers both approach the markets and how they think.

You will have an exact plan. You will need to follow it exactly in order to succeed.

You will not overtrade.

You will take low-risk bets with the understanding that these trades do not have to work.

You will immediately take losses when trades do not work out without a second thought.

You will allow profits to run when trades do work and not cut them short.

You will have the proper mindset to overcome all the challenges, drawdowns, and durations of drawdowns.

You will learn the proper mindset of patience and discipline.

You will not blame your broker, the market, or even yourself.

You know there is no perfect methodology or trading system.

You will not jump into a trade prematurely.

You do not need to be right. Trading has nothing to do with being right.

The right mindset is one of the keys to investment success, and most traders fail to understand this.

CHAPTER 3

Why Trend Following?

You have all kinds of ways to make money as well as lose it. Many have tried the buy-and-hold (or buy-and-pray) method of stock market investing or real estate and realized it is not the way.

Trend following is natural and not that complicated. However, *complicated and easy* is a misnomer. Trend following probably has to be one of the hardest and easiest things to do because of our emotional baggage.

Markets can only do several things.

Markets only go up, down, or sideways.

Trend following entails following the markets when they go up as well as following them when markets go down!

When you trade with a well-thought-out plan, you will not take out a large percentage of your business day if you decide to trade daily bars. You might only spend between 30–60 minutes a day as I do when I put on my trades. It is your choice to sit in front of a screen and day trade (which is a definite possibility) or to download daily data and determine what action you need to take, if at all. You can trade stocks, forex, or commodities. The same principles apply to all.

It is that simple! But it is not simple due to our mental baggage such as fear, greed, and ego.

Too many times we try to make simple things more complicated! There are those who think simple means unsophisticated or impossible to generate money. They are very wrong and track records going back decades from many trend followers prove them wrong.

The key to success or compounding money over time is the ability to stay focused, stay disciplined, follow the plan, and have patience. **This is the holy grail!**

Trend following in itself is basically simple. You do not have to overanalyze it. You just have to just do it, as Nike says.

■ Why Not Fundamental or Even Technical Analysis?

Fundamental analysis is defined by an examination of the financial statements of the company to determine its current financial strength, future growth, profitability prospects, and current management skills in order to estimate whether the stock's price is undervalued or overvalued. **One must almost be an accountant!**

A great deal of reliance is placed on annual and quarterly earnings reports; the economic, political, and competitive environment facing the company; as well as any current news items or rumors relating to the company's operations.

And then with all the analysis the stock or commodity can do the unexpected. That is why I hold very little faith in fundamental analysis.

Technical Analysis

Technical analysis is defined by the fact that the stock's current price or commodity price discounts all information available in the market: that price movements are not random, and that patterns in price movements, in many cases, tend to repeat themselves or trend in some direction.

It's easier (and therefore faster) to learn technical analysis than to even attempt fundamental analysis.

You can learn the basics by reading a couple of books, but you might be deluded or confused with all the countless indicators and still might not have a plan. Technical analysts look at charts the same way a doctor would look at X-rays. Technical analysts examine the charts for information on the future direction of the markets. Again, once they think they have it figured out, then the market does something unexpected. There are many ideas about support and resistance. Too many traders believe those are lines in the sand, not to be broken. However, they are broken all the time. So again you need a plan.

Mechanical Trading Systems

With the upgrades in computers, trading system development has become the rage. Too many make mechanical trading system development a hobby, as a way to compound money over time. Too many traders focus all their time and energy searching for new and elusive indicators and better mechanical trading systems. To some degree, this is an admirable quest. However, having the patience and discipline to follow a simple robust trading methodology is preferable to a complicated "supposedly" mechanical trading system. I had a conversation with an engineer who works on helicopters regarding trading. His astute opinion was that the fewer moving parts in a trading system, the better. He made the comparison to a helicopter. The more parts, the more potential defects or impediments. I thought this was a great analogy. Consider that with enough optimization snake oil mechanical system sellers can make their system look like the holy grail. It is perfect. It sells at the highs and buys at the lows. However, in the real world when money is really on the line, these systems do not hold up and simply blow up. Even if you do not purchase a mechanical system, do not make the mistake of optimization of variables and markets.

I want to put everything in balance. There are many advantages to a mechanical system. I believe you can increase your chances of success over time because a mechanical system removes ego and the emotional dilemmas from a lot of the decision-making processes. The advantage of a mechanical system is that it does not care if Bernanke is speaking or if the crop report is coming out in the next couple of hours. It is completely removed from the emotional issues that can cloud our judgment. The mechanical system simply spits out buy and sell orders based on preprogrammed criteria. Do not confuse this with trading success over time or negating losing trades. The mechanical system makes our trading plan somewhat easier compared to a trader who has no plan and trades based on his gut. The tough decisions have been made and tested with a mechanical system. Before one starts trading a mechanical system, the trader has done some sort of back-testing as to the validity of the concept. Back-testing is not the holy grail either, though. There are traders who overoptimize or pick markets based on past returns. This is another recipe for losses and disaster. Traders also might doubt the validity of their mechanical system once they experience the inevitable drawdown. The danger is if the trader gives up on the program and tries another one during a drawdown.

There is no free lunch or anything perfect in trading. Too many traders think they can buy certainty with a robot that trades for them. Contrarily there are traders that think they know the future and trade from their gut. The only problem is that they are following the news or some guru. First they go short, and then out of panic they think they must buy or cover. The trader hesitates because all of a sudden he is unsure what to do or he simply freezes. The market is unforgiving and gladly takes his hard-earned money, as if he were standing on top of a building and throwing up dollar bills. Examples like this exemplify the benefits of mechanical systems. First, a nonoptimized robust mechanical trading plan eliminates the myriad of emotional and psychological issues of trading. Traders are relieved of having to make consistent and pressing decisions. The mechanical system has the rules implanted; they have been tested and hopefully accepted by the trader. The testing gives confidence to the viability of the trading concept as well as monies needed for trading the account.

In both cases I have attempted to show the reasons we need a well-thought-out plan and need to follow it through thick or thin. Set parameters for entries that are robust, clear, and repetitive; follow the signal with the proper risk and money; and let the possibilities work over time. This gives you the potential for success over time. In conjunction with the entry signals you have to have realistic expectations. Too often traders overexaggerate what they expect. They set themselves up for severe disappointment.

■ My Answer: Trend Following

Let's keep it simple: Money is made if you buy when the market is going up and sell when the market is going down. An uptrend is present when prices make a series of higher highs and higher lows. A downtrend is present when prices make a series of lower highs and lower lows.

Trading can be simple: You buy when the market is going up and you sell when the market is going down. That's how money is made.

Trend followers do the hard thing!

Trend followers buy the highs and sell the lows.

This is clearly counterintuitive as virtually all market participants want to be smart and buy the low and sell the highs, right? In the real world this is impossible. Only liars and people at parties with a lot of drinks in them can call tops and bottoms consistently.

Trend following is the antithesis of what we are taught in school. We are taught to rely on intelligence. We want to prove we are smart. Trend followers take responsibility for their trades and do not need to prove anything. Trend followers are committed to compounding money over long periods of time. Trend followers are committed to the plan. Commitment to trend following through the bad periods as well as the good periods is similar to the commitment of an Olympic athlete.

It is not easy to be an Olympic athlete. Olympic athletes go through rigorous training and have constant coaching. Trend following is no different. Athletes do not become Olympic athletes overnight. They train and go through much pain until they reach their goal. In today's society people want instant gratification. Trend following is not instant gratification. Compounding money is not easy to do in our society that is solely focused on instant gratification. The trend follower's ability to delay gratification and inevitable losses gives him or her the potential to succeed over time.

Have the deep desire to be long-term consistent and successful via trend following if you want to succeed!

Liquidity

One can liquidate one's whole portfolio in minutes. Can you do that with real estate or a hedge fund that has a lockup?

Transparency

With managed accounts you will see every position. Hedge funds are secretive and you have no idea what they are doing with your money.

Profit Potential

The father of trend following, Richard Donchian, traded for 50 years with this strategy. The fact that Donchian traded this strategy profitably for 50 years proves the viability of the concept.

Further on I will show you numerous trend followers who have been compounding money for decades. These are real and audited numbers. Richard Donchian traded up until his 90s.

Trend following challenges the traditional thinking about successful trading and traders. The vast majority of traders want to buy low and sell high. Trend followers do exactly the opposite; they buy high with the anticipation of prices going higher or sell lows with the anticipation that prices will fall further.

Many of you are exploring trend following due to your recent experiences in the stock market. Maybe you are tired of the buy and hold mantras that have been ingrained in our psyche since the start of the great bull market in the 1980s and you have lost a considerable amount of your net worth in the stock market.

People are drawn to manias like moths to a light. From the Great Depression to the dot-com bubble, people have lost their life's fortune. I remember being told to buy tech stocks before they run out!

■ You've Got to Love That Saying!

People have been destroyed from the recent real estate bubble. Everyone was buying second or third homes and flipping them.

The house flipping mania was not that different from the tulip bubble hundreds of years ago. There is very little difference between Enron and WorldCom and today's Netflix.

It was like musical chairs until the music stopped. We are overwhelmed and think we need to have all the information to make prudent financial decisions. Take a look at Figure 3.1 to see the equity curve of the stock market over the past 10 years.

Greed, fear, hope, denial, follow-the-neighbor mentality, and impatience are always the same generation to generation. Faster computers, phones with stock quotes, 24-hour Bloomberg, and more!

All of this is not needed in order to grind profits out of the markets.

My goal is to take you off the rat race and start to try to create income via your trading.

FIGURE 3.1 Equity Curve of the Stock Market with a Compound Annual Rate of Return of 0.39% over 10 Years

Even worse than 10 years of not making any money in the stock market is the chart of the Japanese equity market. The Japanese stock market in 1989 was at a high of approximately 39,000; today the Japanese stock market is fluctuating around 8,500 (Figure 3.2). Can you imagine still being a long-term buyer-and-holder? In Japan it has been buy and lose all of your net worth.

FIGURE 3.2 Japanese Equity Market

Buy and Hold for the Long Term!

Stay the Course!

Buy the Dips!

Has this message been touted by an industry with a conflict of interest?

This is the reality of what happened in the U.S. stock market from 2000 to 2010. What is ironic is that it is not unique. Buy and hold did not do anything for investors from December 1972 until March 1980. This also was a flat period of no profits. Worse are the durations and depths of the bear markets in this century, as shown in Table 3.1.

Do not be deluded. There are losses and drawdowns with trend following.

There is no free lunch out there, and the greatest drawdown is always ahead of you, not behind you.

Once you really internalize the realities of trend following you will be free to decide for yourself. You cannot trust anyone but yourself.

Countless people lost their life's savings due to various market crashes. Many times the politicians and even market legends come out with all types of reasons to delude

TABLE 3.1 Bear Markets since the Great Depression

Bear Market Beginning	Bear Market Ending	Max DD
Sept 1929	June 1932	−86.25 %
July 1933	March 1935	−33.9%
March 1937	March 1938	−54.5%
Nov 1938	April 1942	−45.8%
May 1946	June 1949	−29.6%
July 1957	Oct 1957	−20.6%
Dec 1961	June 1962	−28%
Feb 1966	Oct 1966	−22.2%
Oct 1968	May 1970	−34%
Jan 1973	Oct 1974	−48.2%
Sept 1976	March 1978	−19.4%
Nov 1980	Aug 1982	−27.1%
Aug 1987	Dec 1987	−40.4%
July 1990	Oct 1990	−21.2%
Mar 2000	Oct 2002	−49.1%
June 2008	Mar 2009	−54%

Average Bear Market: −37.3%

Buy and Hold since 1942

Compounded Annual Rate of Return: 8.03%

Maximum Drawdown: 54%

you. There were statements that were made during the Great Depression of 1929 that in retrospect will make your hair stand out.

Below is a sampling of some of that I found through Internet searches.

Bottom Line

Have a plan and have the patience and discipline to let it work over time! Here is some Great Depression advice from a few influential leaders in finance, economics, and politics during that time.

Great Depression 1929 Quotes & Statements

Have no opinion . . . let the markets tell you what to do . . . and manage the risks.

"We will not have any more crashes in our time."
—John Maynard Keynes, 1927

"I cannot help but raise a dissenting voice to statements that we are living in a fool's paradise, and that prosperity in this country must necessarily diminish and recede in the near future."
—E. H. H. Simmons, president, New York Stock Exchange, January 12, 1928

"There will be no interruption of our permanent prosperity."
—Myron E. Forbes, president, Pierce Arrow Motor Car Co., January 12, 1928

"No Congress of the United States ever assembled, on surveying the state of the Union, has met with a more pleasing prospect than that which appears at the present time. In the domestic field there is tranquility and contentment … and the highest record of years of prosperity. In the foreign field there is peace, the goodwill which comes from mutual understanding."
—Calvin Coolidge, December 4, 1928

"There may be a recession in stock prices, but not anything in the nature of a crash."
—Irving Fisher, leading U.S. economist, Ph.D. in economics, quoted in the New York Times, September 5, 1929

"Stock prices have reached what looks like a permanently high plateau. I do not feel there will be soon if ever a 50 or 60 point break from present levels, such as [bears] have predicted. I expect to see the stock market a good deal higher within a few months."
—Irving Fisher, leading U.S. economist, Ph.D. in economics, October 17, 1929

"This crash is not going to have much effect on business."
—Arthur Reynolds, chairman, Continental Illinois Bank of Chicago, October 24, 1929

"There will be no repetition of the break of yesterday . . . . I have no fear of another comparable decline."

—Arthur W. Loasby, president, Equitable Trust Company, quoted in the
New York Times, Friday, October 25, 1929

"We feel that fundamentally Wall Street is sound, and that for people who can afford to pay for them outright, good stocks are cheap at these prices."

—Goodbody and Company market letter quoted in the *New York Times*, Friday,
October 25, 1929

"This is the time to buy stocks. This is the time to recall the words of the late J. P. Morgan . . . that any man who is bearish on America will go broke. Within a few days there is likely to be a bear panic rather than a bull panic. Many of the low prices as a result of this hysterical selling are not likely to be reached again in many years."

—R. W. McNeel, market analyst, quoted in the *New York Herald Tribune*,
October 30, 1929

"Buying of sound, seasoned issues now will not be regretted."

—E. A. Pearce, market letter, quoted in the *New York Herald Tribune*,
October 30, 1929

"Some pretty intelligent people are now buying stocks. ... Unless we are to have a panic—which no one seriously believes, stocks have hit bottom."

—R. W. McNeal, financial analyst, October 1929

"The decline is in paper values, not in tangible goods and services. ... America is now in the eighth year of prosperity as commercially defined. The former great periods of prosperity in America averaged eleven years. On this basis we now have three more years to go before the tailspin."

—Stuart Chase, American economist and author, quoted in the
New York Herald Tribune, November 1, 1929

"Hysteria has now disappeared from Wall Street."

—*The Times* of London, November 2, 1929

"The Wall Street crash doesn't mean that there will be any general or serious business depression . . . . For six years American business has been divert-ing a substantial part of its attention, its energies and its resources on the speculative game . . . . Now that irrelevant, alien and hazardous adventure is over. Business has come home again, back to its job, providentially unscathed, sound in wind and limb, financially stronger than ever before."

—*Business Week*, November 2, 1929

"[D]espite its severity, we believe that the slump in stock prices will prove an intermediate movement and not the precursor of a business depression such as would entail prolonged further liquidation."

—Harvard Economic Society, November 2, 1929

(continued)

"[A] serious depression seems improbable; [we expect] recovery of business next spring, with further improvement in the fall."
—Harvard Economic Society, November 10, 1929

"The end of the decline of the Stock Market will probably not be long, only a few more days at most."
—Irving Fisher, professor of economics, Yale University, November 14, 1929

"In most of the cities and towns of this country, this Wall Street panic will have no effect."
—Paul Block, president, Block newspaper chain, editorial, November 15, 1929

"Financial storm definitely passed."
—Bernard Baruch, cablegram to Winston Churchill, November 15, 1929

"I see nothing in the present situation that is either menacing or warrants pessimism . . . . I have every confidence that there will be a revival of activity in the spring, and that during this coming year the country will make steady progress."
—Andrew W. Mellon, U.S. Secretary of the Treasury, December 31, 1929

"I am convinced that through these measures we have reestablished confidence."
—Herbert Hoover, December 1929

"[1930 will be] a splendid employment year."
—U.S. Dept. of Labor, New Year's Forecast, December 1929

"For the immediate future, at least, the outlook (stocks) is bright."
—Irving Fisher, Ph.D. in economics, early 1930

"There are indications that the severest phase of the recession is over."
—Harvard Economic Society, January 18, 1930

"There is nothing in the situation to be disturbed about."
—Secretary of the Treasury Andrew Mellon, February 1930

"The spring of 1930 marks the end of a period of grave concern . . . . American business is steadily coming back to a normal level of prosperity."
—Julius Barnes, head of Hoover's National Business Survey Conference, March 16, 1930

"The outlook continues favorable."
—Harvard Economic Society, March 29, 1930

"While the crash only took place six months ago, I am convinced we have now passed through the worst—and with continued unity of effort we shall rapidly recover. There has been no significant bank or industrial failure. That danger, too, is safely behind us."
—Herbert Hoover, president of the United States, May 1, 1930

"By May or June the spring recovery forecast in our letters of last December and November should clearly be apparent."

        —Harvard Economic Society, May 17, 1930

"Gentleman, you have come sixty days too late. The depression is over."

        —Herbert Hoover, responding to a delegation requesting a public works program to help speed the recovery, June 1930

"Irregular and conflicting movements of business should soon give way to a sustained recovery."

        —Harvard Economic Society, June 28, 1930

"The present depression has about spent its force."

        —Harvard Economic Society, August 30, 1930

"We are now near the end of the declining phase of the depression."

        —Harvard Economic Society, November 15, 1930

"Stabilization at [present] levels is clearly possible."

        —Harvard Economic Society, October 31, 1931

"All safe deposit boxes in banks or financial institutions have been sealed . . . . and may only be opened in the presence of an agent of the I.R.S."
—President F. D. Roosevelt, 1933

Do not feel bad about what happened in the past in the stock market or if you were deluded by geniuses or legends! Think for yourself with the carefully laid-out plan we will develop in Chapter 6.

Do not look out the back window; look out the front window. Even the father of trend following, Richard Donchian, virtually lost all of his money in the Great Depression. Richard Donchian's trading account basically went to zero. Donchian was above intelligent. During World War II he was one of the Pentagon whiz kids. He was a cryptanalyst who worked with Robert McNamara, secretary of defense under Kennedy and Johnson.

Richard Donchian started the first publicly managed futures fund, Futures, Inc., in 1949. He developed the trend timing method of futures investing and introduced the mutual fund concept to the field of money management.

Richard Donchian is considered to be the creator or father of the managed futures industry and is credited with developing a systematic approach to futures money management. His professional trading career was dedicated to advancing a more conservative approach to futures trading. Donchian traded until his death in his 90s. One of Richard Donchian's famous quotes is, "Nobody has ever been able to demonstrate that a complex mathematical equation can answer the question: Is the market moving in an uptrend, downtrend, or simply just sideways?" He took the complicated and simplified it.

Confirming this is Marty Schwartz, author of *Market Wizards*. He is somewhat of a trend follower and uses very simple techniques. Schwartz looks at moving averages prior to taking a position. Is the price above or below the moving average? Simple question with a simple answer! Schwartz believes this works better than any other tool or indicator. He does not to go against the moving averages; he knows that it is self-destructive. Going with the moving averages is simple trend following in the basic and simplistic approach. Trend following does not need to be complicated.

■ Ed Seykota and *Market Wizards*

Systems don't need to be changed. The trick is for a trader to develop a system with which he is compatible.

—Ed Seykota

Richard Donchian has been an inspiration to all trend followers, including Ed Seykota, a leader in trend following and pioneer of computerized trading. Ed Seykota turned $5,000 into $15,000,000 over a 12-year time period in his model account, which was an actual client account.

Seykota's trading system used exponential moving averages. He improved this system over time, adapting the system to fit his trading style and preferences. With the initial version of the system being rigid, he later introduced more rules into the system in addition to pattern triggers and money management algorithms.

Another aspect of his success was his genuine love for trading and his optimistic attitude. This factor sustained his efforts to continuously improve on his system, although he never changed the response indicators of the system and instead fine-tuned market stimuli.

One of the key aspects of trading systems is the testing for the maximum drawdown and duration of drawdowns. The maximum drawdown is the difference from the highest level of the equity curve to the lowest. Bear in mind that there is no actual floor for a drawdown. Your greatest drawdown is always ahead of you. Previous drawdowns will be exceeded. Hypothetical results also can lead to distortion. When testing systems, since the future is unknown, all we are basing our work on is the past, and the past has extreme limitations. We have read repeatedly that past performance is not necessarily indicative of future performance. It is so true. All we are trying to do is give us a possible impression on what to expect.

Worse than the drawdown is the duration or time period in which you have not made any new money. This is probably what causes traders to either stop trading or start their quest for a new approach. One needs the mental fortitude to continue trading when one has not made money for more than two years. This is reality. Many successful trend followers have durations of drawdowns even exceeding 24 months.

I have seen some in the 30-month range. What sets these traders apart from others is their tenacity to keep on going. These traders know they are in a marathon. They believe in their methodologies and systems; however, even with that said, the demons pop up and questions are asked.

The trading system should have multiple markets and be diversified. As well, the trading system can contain various models that could offset each other. There are traders that encompass multiple time periods even for the same type of system.

The obvious issues to be aware of when testing a mechanical system are curve fitting and optimizing. Through the wonders of computers today one could find the best performing markets in the past, plug in various indicators, and present a holy grail mechanical trading system. The issue is that in the real world at best this system will underperform and in the most likely case not work and lose money. This same optimization can attempt to reduce the hypothetical drawdowns.

In today's world it is very easy to test different type of strategies and mechanical systems. The problem is that traders can so easily jump to another time or mechanical system with a couple of clicks of a mouse. Every system, every trader will encounter rough periods of drawdowns and losses. Traders can get nervous after experiencing a group of trades that do not work. The problem with some of these traders is that this sets them off on their quest for a better mechanical system. They think that all of a sudden they can add an idea that could have prevented the prior losses. What is worse is when a trader is in the midst of a trade and he has tested another mechanical system and it is showing a contrary signal. Confusion and pressure set in. Once you are in a trade, you need to follow your original plan and implement any changes after you exit. You must adhere to your plan. Additions or filters are fine to add to your mechanical system, but not in the midst of a trade. The market does not know your position nor does it care. You need to stay focused and let the odds work out over time. You can never avoid a loss. Do not even try to frustrate yourself. You cannot control the markets. All you can do is control your emotions. After the trade is over, analyze it. Set time aside to invest in your future. The best way to do is this is via a trade journal. Do not let fear, greed, or ego become your personal enemy.

Over the years after trades I have analyzed what I perceived as mistakes and added filters to my model. I believed in the model as it worked for decades for others; however, my goal was to try to mitigate some very evident mistakes. I was an observer of my actions. I was not a participant in my emotions. I added several risk filters after losses such as sector maximum risk and total open trade risk only after analyzing my errors. This is a world apart from tinkering as in a hobby and trying to build the holy grail. Improvement of my model was a well-timed pursuit. Searching and thinking there was something better than what I had would have been a waste of time. I have spoken to traders that have spent years building a system and never trading it. They always think they can make it better. They think they can improve the performance. My reality is that they have not accepted the risks of trading and that they can lose money.

I am a proponent of robust simple trading ideas. In order to test these I have used a rolling testing time frame. I test the system over different data periods. I test two-year periods, five-year periods, staggering them from the 1980s to the present. In order to have confidence, the system should present similar results in returns, in drawdowns, and in the number of trades. Even with this, it is only an estimate or guess of what we will encounter in the real world of trading.

Determining the amount of capital actually demanded by a trading portfolio is not exact. There are proponents who speak about optimal f, but I really believe not just that this is an overlooked issue but that it is a very difficult issue. Failing to plan and allocate enough capital is a disaster waiting to happen. To some degree diversifying your portfolio can reduce the possibility of ruin. As much as markets are correlated, some markets are not correlated or only correlated to a lesser extent. Trading noncorrelated markets will enable us to benefit due to the differences in time when and if markets trend. There are times markets and sectors get quiet. When markets are quiet, trends are absent. Without movement either up or down, generating profits is very difficult.

I was lucky that one of my mentors learned under Ed Seykota. Years ago I invested with David Druz from Tactical who also learned under Ed Seykota. I learned a lot of ways to think from both my mentor and David Druz. There is no magical system or indicator; it is all in how you think. Ed has been a mentor to many via his Trading Tribe. The Trading Tribe is a group of trend followers who are committed to personal growth and receive support from other traders all over the world.

These trend followers know there is no holy grail.

CHAPTER 4

How Successful Trend Followers Trade

It is imperative to remember that the returns of professional trend followers are not representative of those of all trend followers. More so, do not expect your results to be on par with theirs as you begin your journey.

I am not recommending these managers, rather using their history to show what trend following can generate when one trades with a well-thought-out plan and risk management in place. I am giving a short historical background of each of the managers as well. I present here a hypothetical compounding if you had invested with these various managers.

■ The Trend Followers

Before we start, remember: Past performance is not indicative of future performance. The risk of loss in trading commodity futures, options, and foreign exchange (forex) is substantial.

Salem Abraham

Abraham Trading Company
Began January 1988
CAROR 19.18 percent

Salem Abraham does not trade from Wall Street, rather from Canadian, Texas.

The population of Canadian is is approximately 2,000. However, Abraham Trading has been called "The Best Little Hedge Fund in Texas" by *Absolute Return and Alpha* magazine. In 2003 the *New York Times* wrote about Salem. The article was called "A Homespun Hedge Fund, Tucked Away in Texas." I was surprised that Salem made it mainstream and was featured in the business section of the *New York Times*. Salem had been in the trading arena since 1988 and had built an impressive real-time audited hedge fund. He started with money his grandfather gave him. I believe the sum was $800,000, which in 1988 was a large sum of money. The deal was that if he lost the money, he would throw his data provider out the window and work in the family business of cattle and real estate. Salem did not lose his initial stake and has been compounding money over the decades ever since. Salem has a strong awareness of risk as per his statement, "You want your seatbelt to work in a wreck, not when you're not in a wreck." He was quoted in a *Pensions and Investments* article.

His office is not what you would expect for a successful hedge fund. His initial office was 1,000 square feet above a steakhouse. Salem is proof that one does not need to be in Chicago or on Wall Street to succeed in the financial world. He attended the University of Notre Dame starting in August 1984. As I have stated many times, one does not need to go to Harvard or Yale to be successful over time trend following. No one at the company has an Ivy League degree. The members of Salem's Abraham Trading team do not have the financial background you would expect. Salem's coworkers were originally employed at the area's feedlots or natural gas drilling and pipeline companies. "This beats shoveling manure at 6 in the morning," said Geoff Dockray, who was hired as a clerk for Mr. Abraham after working at a feedlot near Canadian. "The financial markets are complicated, but they're not as relentless as dealing with livestock all the time."

None of this has impeded the success of Abraham Trading. Salem has a burning passion to succeed. He did extensive research in the technical and methodological aspects of futures trading, as have most successful trend followers. It is imperative to truly believe in your methodology. He combined information he gathered with ideas that he developed during his research, and he back-tested the profitability and drawdowns of numerous robust trading theories. Salem graduated cum laude with a B.B.A. in finance in December 1987 and moved back to Canadian, where in January 1988, he began to manage customer accounts using his systematic approach. He became registered as a Commodity Trading Advisor in October 1988 and organized Abraham Trading in 1990 to act as a CTA for all customer accounts. The website of Abraham Trading states that 21 years of trading and research make Abraham Trading one of the most experienced traders in the business.

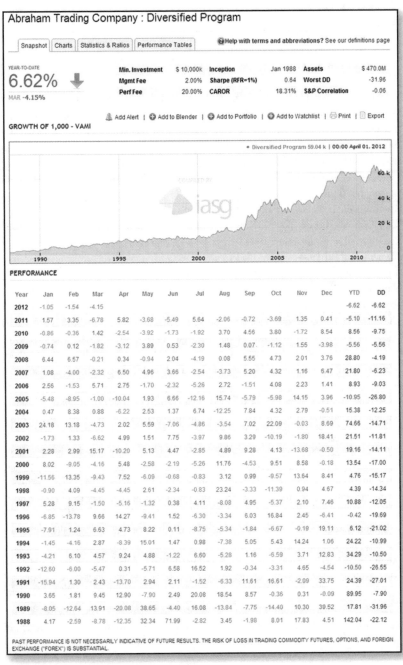

FIGURE 4.1 Hypothetically, if you invested $100,000 in January 1988, today it would be worth $6,743,434.54.

Source: Chart with permission from Iasg.com.

Elizabeth Chavel

EMC Capital Management
Began January 1985
CAROR 21.81 percent

Elizabeth Cheval is the chairman and founder of EMC Capital Management, Inc. It is well known in the trading community that women make better traders. This is not because women are smarter, but because of how women control their emotions in trading. Elizabeth has a B.S. in mathematics from Lawrence University. Not to put down Lawrence University, but it is not an Ivy League school, yet the notion of needing a proper university education such as Wharton is not a prerequisite for trading success. Elizabeth started her trading career at the Chicago Board of Trade. Luckily she landed a job with Richard Dennis. Before working with Mr. Dennis, Ms. Cheval worked with A. G. Becker, a Chicago-based brokerage firm, on the floor of the Chicago Board of Trade. Ms. Cheval has invested in futures since 1983, when she began investing in financial futures for her own account. In 1984, she was lucky enough to be chosen for the investment management training program offered by C&D Commodities. This was the famed Turtle Trader experiment. Richard Dennis and his partner, William Eckhardt, made a bet that traders could be taught how to trade. Some traders did much better than others. Elizabeth did fantastic, however, with volatility. For three years in a row, 1986, 1987, and 1988, Elizabeth returned 134 percent, 178 percent, and 124 percent. In 1990, probably due to the volatilities in the markets, she returned an astonishing 187 percent. However, there is never any free lunch, and there was a period when she experienced a drawdown of 45 percent. She has had periods of one year and longer in which she has had drawdowns exceeding 25 percent up to that dreaded 45 percent. The results of the Turtle Traders varied tremendously even though they all went through the same two-week course. After the Turtle program was disbanded in 1988, Elizabeth formed EMC. EMC, which stands for her initials, was incorporated in May 1988. The EMC trading models invest in over 80 futures markets including stock indexes, currencies, financial instruments, metals, agricultural, meats, energies, and soft commodities. The concept of being diversified is evident in EMC. Elizabeth is available to trade any of the opportunities that become present in these markets. Her proprietary systems include ideas of using multi time frames and multi systems. She uses strong risk management. Her proprietary risk algorithms are based on account equity (core equity), open trade equity, trailing return, and drawdown. Additionally, EMC utilizes proprietary trade-specific risk controls that are independent of the overall portfolio leverage. Market weight factors, system weight factors, and market volatility factors are applied individually to each signal taken at the time of buy or sell. The goal of most managers is to try to mitigate some of the volatilities of returns. After her big drawdown of 45 percent she added filters and enhancement to their Classic Program in July 1996. The goal of these enhancements was to maintain returns consistent with long-term average returns while at the same time trying to reduce the expected drawdown levels and volatility by approximately one half. This is what smart traders do. After a negative run successful CTAs evaluate what happen and try to add filters to mitigate some of these drawdown issues. Her worst drawdown after 1996 was approximately 25 percent. This was a substantial improvement. As per the website of IASG.com, EMC has $110 million under assets. EMC's minimum managed account size is $5,000,000.

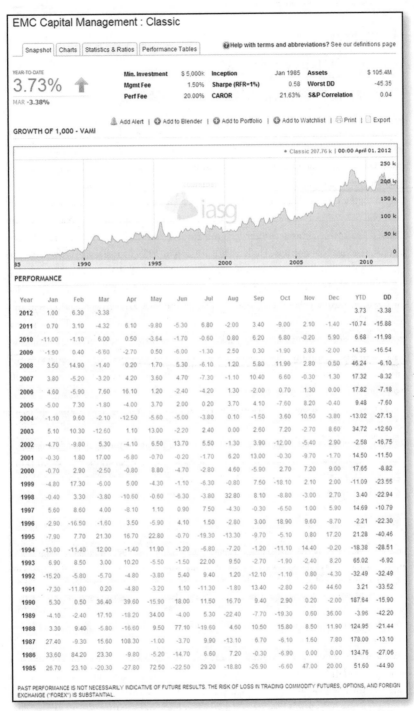

EMC Capital Management : Classic

Snapshot | Charts | Statistics & Ratios | Performance Tables

ⓘ Help with terms and abbreviations? See our definitions page

YEAR-TO-DATE
3.73% ⬆
MAR -3.38%

Min. Investment	$ 5,000k	Inception	Jan 1985	Assets		$ 105.4M
Mgmt Fee	1.50%	Sharpe (RFR=1%)	0.58	Worst DD		-45.35
Perf Fee	20.00%	CAROR	21.63%	S&P Correlation		0.04

🔔 Add Alert | ⊕ Add to Blender | ⊕ Add to Portfolio | ⊕ Add to Watchlist | 🖨 Print | ⬇ Export

GROWTH OF 1,000 - VAMI

● Classic 207.76 k | 00:00 April 01, 2012

PERFORMANCE

Year	Jan	Feb	Mar	Apr	May	Jun	Jul	Aug	Sep	Oct	Nov	Dec	YTD	DD
2012	1.00	6.30	-3.38										3.73	-3.38
2011	0.70	3.10	-4.32	6.10	-9.80	-5.30	6.80	-2.00	3.40	-9.00	2.10	-1.40	-10.74	-15.88
2010	-11.00	-1.10	6.00	0.50	-3.64	-1.70	-0.60	0.80	6.20	6.80	-0.20	5.90	6.68	-11.98
2009	-1.90	0.40	-6.60	-2.70	0.50	-6.00	-1.30	2.50	0.30	-1.90	3.83	-2.00	-14.35	-16.54
2008	3.50	14.90	-1.40	0.20	1.70	5.30	-6.10	1.20	5.80	11.90	2.80	0.50	46.24	-6.10
2007	3.80	-5.20	-3.20	4.20	3.60	4.70	-7.30	-1.10	10.40	6.60	-0.30	1.30	17.32	-8.32
2006	4.60	-5.90	7.60	16.10	1.20	-2.40	-4.20	1.30	-2.00	0.70	1.30	0.00	17.82	-7.18
2005	-5.00	7.30	-1.80	-4.00	3.70	2.00	0.20	3.70	4.10	-7.60	8.20	-0.40	9.48	-7.60
2004	-1.10	9.60	-2.10	-12.50	-5.60	-5.00	-3.80	0.10	-1.50	3.60	10.50	-3.80	-13.02	-27.13
2003	5.10	10.30	-12.60	1.10	13.00	-2.20	2.40	0.00	2.60	7.20	-2.70	8.60	34.72	-12.60
2002	-4.70	-9.80	5.30	-4.10	6.50	13.70	5.50	-1.30	3.90	-12.00	-5.40	2.90	-2.58	-16.75
2001	-0.30	1.80	17.00	-6.80	-0.70	-0.20	-1.70	6.20	13.00	-0.30	-9.70	-1.70	14.50	-11.50
2000	-0.70	2.90	-2.50	-0.80	8.80	-4.70	-2.80	4.60	-5.90	2.70	7.20	9.00	17.65	-8.82
1999	-4.80	17.30	-6.00	5.00	-4.30	-1.10	-6.30	-0.80	7.50	-18.10	2.10	2.00	-11.09	-23.55
1998	-0.40	3.30	-3.80	-10.60	-0.60	-6.30	-3.80	32.80	8.10	-8.80	-3.00	2.70	3.40	-22.94
1997	5.60	8.60	4.00	-8.10	1.10	0.90	7.50	-4.30	-0.30	-6.50	1.00	5.90	14.69	-10.79
1996	-2.90	-16.50	-1.60	3.50	-5.90	4.10	1.50	-2.80	3.00	18.90	9.60	-8.70	-2.21	-22.30
1995	-7.90	7.70	21.30	16.70	22.80	-0.70	-19.30	-13.30	-9.70	-5.10	0.80	17.20	21.28	-40.46
1994	-13.00	-11.40	12.00	-1.40	11.90	-1.20	-6.80	-7.20	-1.20	-11.10	14.40	-0.20	-18.38	-28.51
1993	6.90	8.50	3.00	10.20	-5.50	-1.50	22.00	9.50	-2.70	-1.90	-2.40	8.20	65.02	-6.92
1992	-15.20	-5.80	-5.70	-4.80	-3.80	5.40	9.40	1.20	-12.10	-1.10	0.80	-4.30	-32.49	-32.49
1991	-7.30	-11.80	0.20	-4.80	-3.20	1.10	-11.30	-1.80	13.40	-2.80	-2.60	44.60	3.21	-33.52
1990	5.30	0.50	36.40	39.60	-15.90	18.00	11.50	16.70	9.40	2.90	0.20	-2.00	187.64	-15.90
1989	-4.10	-2.40	17.10	-18.20	34.00	-4.00	5.30	-22.40	-7.70	-19.30	0.60	36.00	-3.96	-42.20
1988	3.30	9.40	-5.80	-16.60	9.50	-19.60	77.10	-19.60	4.60	10.50	15.80	8.50	124.95	-21.44
1987	27.40	-9.30	15.60	108.30	-1.00	-3.70	9.90	-13.10	6.70	-6.10	1.60	7.80	178.00	-13.10
1986	33.60	84.20	23.30	-9.80	-5.20	-14.70	6.60	7.20	-0.30	-6.90	0.00	0.00	134.76	-27.06
1985	26.70	23.10	-20.30	-27.80	72.50	-22.50	29.20	-18.80	-26.90	-6.60	47.00	20.00	51.60	-44.90

FIGURE 4.2 Hypothetically, if you invested $100,000 in January 1995, today it would be worth $20,579,720.22.

Source: Chart with permission from Iasg.com.

Tom Shanks

Hawksbill Capital Management
Began November 1988
CAROR 22.70 percent

Tom was a professional blackjack player in the 1970s. Through playing blackjack he met Blair Hull. Blair Hull is personally credited with buffering the crash of Black Monday in 1987 when he bought the bottom of the market and restored liquidity and confidence to the panicked financial markets. *Trader Monthly* recognized him for having executed one of "The 40 Greatest Trades of All Time," and *Worth* magazine named him one of "Wall Street's 25 Smartest Players." Tom and Blair were a great team. Tom started as a research programmer for Hull Trading and later became operations manager for research of options. He left Hull Trading in 1985 to work with Richard Dennis and Bill Eckhardt. Tom Shanks was an original Turtle Trader like Elizabeth Chavel. He started his Hawksbill program once the Turtle mentor program was disbanded in 1988. Tom, like others, had a better pedigree than a Harvard education. He surrounded himself with legendary traders and honed his skills with them. This is a common occurrence with traders. They all had their mentors. I have invested with what I call a third-generation Turtle Trader, Alex Spies. His knowledge of the markets was not learned out of textbooks or college. He learned over the years by trading and surrounding himself with great traders.

Hawksbill's methodology involves active, aggressive trading. The trading approach emphasizes risk control through proprietary money management rules and diversification of systems and markets within each portfolio. What is unique about Hawksbill is that as much as he is a trend follower he allows for some discretion. Hawksbill is different from most trend followers who are systematic by his use of discretion.

Underpinning the reality of aggressive trading, Hawksbill has returned some outstanding numbers. Hawksbill's returns have historically shown low to no correlation to bond and stock markets, thus offering the potential to diversify a traditional investment portfolio, as well as a portfolio of alternative investments. In 1990 Hawksbill returned 252 percent; in 1993 114 percent; and for those that think the markets changed and outstanding results are not possible, in 2008 he returned 96 percent. However, as I always say, there is no free lunch with trading, and I would only suggest buying drawdowns of traders like Hawksbill. He has had some extremely deep drawdowns. Hawksbill's worst drawdown was after his huge run up in 1990 when he was down 60 percent. In 1994–1996 he was down 50 percent for almost 24 months. In 2004–2007 he was down 31 percent for 37 months. No one ever promised you trend following is easy. However, putting the whole picture into context, he has been able to compound money at a great rate.

Clearly, money managers and investors diversify across the entire universe of ideas from low volatility to high volatility. It could be considered prudent depending on one's risk tolerance to place a small portion of one's portfolio with an aggressive trader such as Hawksbill. There are also individuals and institutional investors who seek high returns and are willing to accept the risk entailed in achieving them.

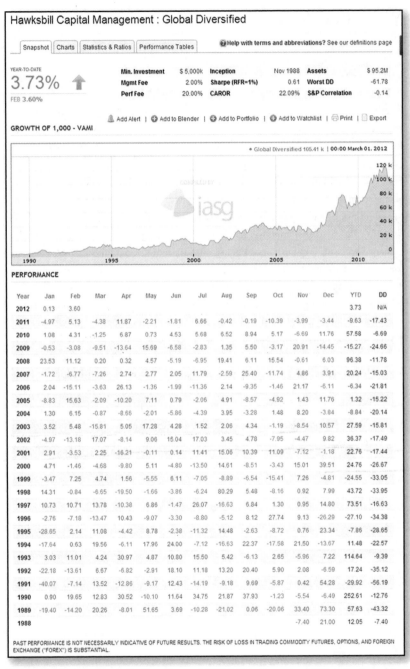

FIGURE 4.3 Hypothetically, if you invested $100,000 in November 1988, today it would be worth $13,560,306.49.

Source: Chart with permission from Iasg.com.

William Eckhardt

Eckhardt Trading Company
Began October 1991
CAROR 21.25 percent

Bill Eckhardt is considered by many in the industry to be the Trend Following Wizard. He was behind the Turtle Traders experiment with his high school friend, Richard Dennis. The two were trading partners in C&D. They had a bet to see if trading could be taught. The two disagreed whether the skills of a successful trader could be systematized into a group of rules. The Turtle program was overwhelmingly successful with novice traders ending up making $100 million. Eckhardt believed trading could not be taught and lost his bet with Dennis. After the closure of the Turtle program, Bill Eckhardt founded ETC in 1991. ETC manages over $700 million in managed accounts and both onshore and offshore funds. Eckhardt's managed account minimum is $10,000,000. Bill has been featured in various magazine articles as well as most prominently in *New Market Wizards* by Jack Schwager. He is the chief architect of ETC's system development and ongoing research. There was a recent article in *Futures* magazine with the title, "William Eckhardt: The man who launched 1,000 systems." He has traded futures professionally for over 31 years. Before he started trading he spent four years doing doctoral research at the University of Chicago in mathematical logic. He never lost his passion for mathematics and has even published in academic journals. Even with all of his experience, Eckhardt still had drawdowns and extended periods of elusive profits. His worst drawdown, which lasted for five months in late 1991, was 27 percent. He went through a 20-month drawdown in 2008 till 2010 of 15 percent. The point is that drawdowns and durations happen to every trader and cannot be avoided.

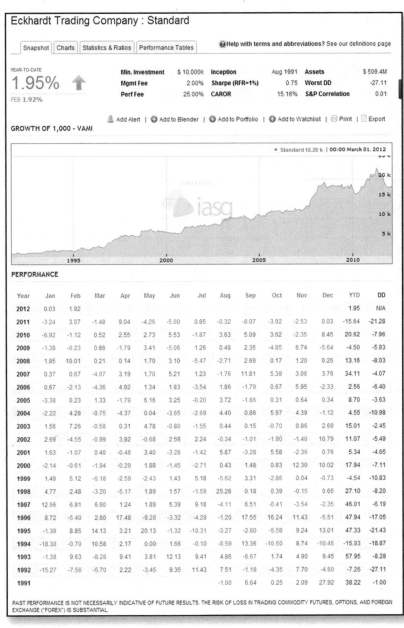

Eckhardt Trading Company : Standard

| Snapshot | Charts | Statistics & Ratios | Performance Tables | ⓘ Help with terms and abbreviations? See our definitions page |

YEAR-TO-DATE
1.95% ⬆
FEB 1.92%

Min. Investment	$ 10,000k	Inception	Aug 1991	Assets	$ 509.4M
Mgmt Fee	2.00%	Sharpe (RFR=1%)	0.75	Worst DD	-27.11
Perf Fee	25.00%	CAROR	15.16%	S&P Correlation	0.01

🔔 Add Alert | ➕ Add to Blender | ➕ Add to Portfolio | ➕ Add to Watchlist | 🖨 Print | 🗋 Export

GROWTH OF 1,000 - VAMI

● Standard 18.28 k | 00:00 March 01, 2012

PERFORMANCE

Year	Jan	Feb	Mar	Apr	May	Jun	Jul	Aug	Sep	Oct	Nov	Dec	YTD	DD
2012	0.03	1.92											1.95	N/A
2011	-3.24	3.07	-1.48	9.04	-4.26	-5.00	0.85	-0.32	-8.07	-3.92	-2.53	0.03	-15.64	-21.28
2010	-6.92	-1.12	0.52	2.55	2.73	5.53	-1.87	3.63	5.09	3.62	-2.35	8.45	20.62	-7.96
2009	-1.38	-0.23	0.86	-1.79	3.41	-5.06	1.26	0.48	2.35	-4.85	6.74	-5.64	-4.50	-5.93
2008	1.85	10.01	0.21	0.14	1.70	3.10	-5.47	-2.71	2.69	0.17	1.20	0.26	13.16	-8.03
2007	0.37	0.67	-4.07	3.19	1.70	5.21	1.23	-1.76	11.81	5.39	3.06	3.76	34.11	-4.07
2006	0.67	-2.13	-4.36	4.92	1.34	1.83	-3.54	1.86	-1.79	0.67	5.95	-2.33	2.56	-6.40
2005	-3.38	0.23	1.33	-1.79	6.16	3.25	-0.20	3.72	-1.86	0.31	0.64	0.34	8.70	-3.63
2004	-2.22	4.28	-0.75	-4.37	0.04	-3.65	-2.69	4.40	0.86	5.97	4.39	-1.12	4.55	-10.98
2003	1.56	7.26	-0.58	0.31	4.78	-0.80	-1.55	0.44	0.15	-0.70	0.86	2.69	15.01	-2.45
2002	2.69	-4.55	-0.99	3.92	-0.68	2.59	2.24	-0.34	-1.01	-1.90	-1.40	10.79	11.07	-5.49
2001	1.63	-1.07	0.40	-0.48	3.40	-3.28	-1.42	5.87	-3.28	5.58	-2.36	0.76	5.34	-4.65
2000	-2.14	-0.61	-1.94	-0.29	1.88	-1.45	-2.71	0.43	1.48	0.83	12.30	10.02	17.94	-7.11
1999	1.49	5.12	-6.18	-2.59	-2.43	1.43	5.18	-5.62	3.31	-2.86	0.04	-0.73	-4.54	-10.83
1998	4.77	2.48	-3.20	-5.17	1.89	1.57	-1.59	25.28	0.18	0.39	-0.15	0.65	27.10	-8.20
1997	12.66	6.91	6.60	1.24	1.89	5.39	9.18	-4.11	6.51	-0.41	-3.54	-2.35	46.01	-6.19
1996	8.72	-5.40	2.60	17.48	-9.28	-3.32	-4.28	-1.20	17.55	16.24	11.43	-5.51	47.94	-17.05
1995	-1.39	8.85	14.13	3.21	20.13	-1.32	-10.31	-3.27	-2.80	-5.58	9.24	13.01	47.33	-21.43
1994	-18.30	-0.70	10.58	2.17	0.00	1.66	-0.10	-8.59	13.36	-10.50	8.74	-10.45	-15.93	-18.87
1993	-1.38	9.63	-8.28	9.41	3.81	12.13	9.41	4.85	-6.67	1.74	4.90	9.45	57.95	-8.28
1992	-15.27	-7.56	-5.70	2.22	-3.45	9.35	11.43	7.51	-1.18	-4.35	7.70	-4.60	-7.26	-27.11
1991								-1.00	6.64	0.25	2.09	27.92	38.22	-1.00

PAST PERFORMANCE IS NOT NECESSARILY INDICATIVE OF FUTURE RESULTS. THE RISK OF LOSS IN TRADING COMMODITY FUTURES, OPTIONS, AND FOREIGN EXCHANGE ("FOREX") IS SUBSTANTIAL.

FIGURE 4.4 Hypothetically, if you invested $100,000 in October 1991, today it would be worth $5,718,955.18.
Source: Chart with permission from Iasg.com.

Howard Seidler

Saxon
Began November 1993
CAROR 21.65 percent

During the last Alphametrix trading conference in Miami Beach, I was fortunate to sit and chat with Howard Seidler. I have been watching his program, Saxon, for years. I was extremely impressed by Howard's returns in 2005–2006 when most commodity trading advisors suffered big drawdowns, but he did not. From September 2007 till the present Howard has not experienced any large drawdowns. I only invest when a manager who understands risk encounters a deep drawdown. I feel this lowers my risks to some degree when I invest with a commodity trading advisor. I discussed this with him at the Alphhmetrix convention, and he told me that he included a volatility filter to reduce trades. In prior years Howard would have some big swings in capital. In 1994 he made 142 percent. However, there were periods in which he had drawdowns of 65 percent in 1995–1996.

Howard graduated from Massachusetts Institute of Technology in 1980 with a B.S. in chemical engineering and management science. From June 1980 to July 1983 he was employed first by Putman, Hayes & Bartlett, and then by Industrial Economics as an associate. At about this same time in 1983 he began a full-time intensive study of the futures markets. In December 1983 he was hired and became one of the Turtles in the experiment of Richard Dennis and Bill Eckhardt. Upon the closure of the Turtle program in 1988 Howard opened his trading company, Saxon, in order to manage other accounts for multiple clients as a registered commodity trading advisor. He has a fund that is marketed by Gale Investments and his managed account size minimum is $2,000,000. He is managing approximately $170 million.

Howard is solely responsible for the trading decisions and strategies of Saxon and for directing its ongoing research and development of trading and money management principles. While a large portion of Saxon's trading program is based upon a mechanical application of Saxon's multiple systems, Howard exercises discretion and judgment over certain trades. Depending on market conditions, certain nonsystem trades may be taken and, conversely, certain system trades may not be taken.

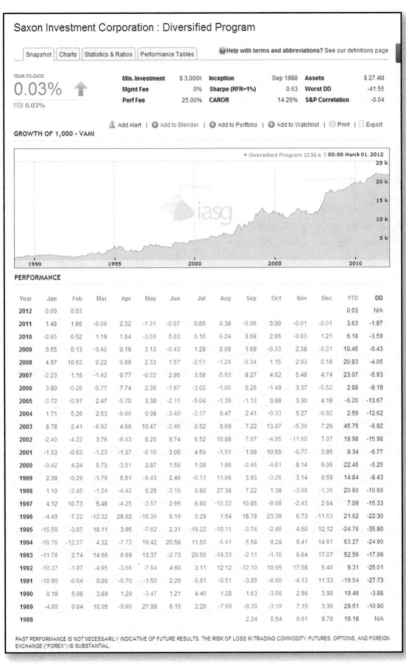

Saxon Investment Corporation : Diversified Program

| Snapshot | Charts | Statistics & Ratios | Performance Tables | ⓘ Help with terms and abbreviations? See our definitions page |

YEAR-TO-DATE

0.03% ↑

FEB 0.03%

Min. Investment	$ 3,000k	Inception	Sep 1988	Assets	$ 27.4M
Mgmt Fee	0%	Sharpe (RFR=1%)	0.63	Worst DD	-41.55
Perf Fee	25.00%	CAROR	14.26%	S&P Correlation	-0.04

⚠ Add Alert | ⊕ Add to Blender | ⊕ Add to Portfolio | ⊕ Add to Watchlist | 🖶 Print | ⬜ Export

GROWTH OF 1,000 - VAMI

• Diversified Program 22.95 k | 00:00 March 01, 2012

PERFORMANCE

Year	Jan	Feb	Mar	Apr	May	Jun	Jul	Aug	Sep	Oct	Nov	Dec	YTD	DD
2012	0.00	0.03											0.03	N/A
2011	1.48	1.86	-0.06	2.32	-1.31	-0.67	0.65	0.38	-0.99	0.00	-0.01	-0.01	3.63	-1.97
2010	-0.95	0.52	1.19	1.64	-3.59	0.03	0.10	0.24	3.69	2.96	-0.83	1.21	6.18	-3.59
2009	0.55	0.13	-0.42	0.19	3.13	-0.43	1.29	2.09	1.69	-0.33	2.38	-0.21	10.45	-0.43
2008	4.97	10.63	0.22	0.69	2.33	1.57	-2.51	-1.24	-0.34	1.15	2.03	0.18	20.83	-4.05
2007	-2.23	1.15	-1.42	0.77	-0.22	2.96	3.58	-5.93	8.27	4.62	5.48	4.74	23.07	-5.93
2006	3.80	-0.26	-0.77	7.74	2.35	-1.87	-3.02	-1.06	0.25	-1.49	3.37	-5.52	2.88	-9.19
2005	-3.72	-0.97	2.47	-5.70	3.39	-2.11	-5.04	-1.39	-1.13	0.89	3.30	4.19	-6.26	-13.67
2004	1.71	5.26	2.53	-6.66	0.08	-3.40	-3.17	0.47	2.41	-0.33	5.27	-0.92	2.59	-12.62
2003	8.78	2.41	-6.92	4.66	10.47	-2.46	0.52	0.69	7.22	13.07	-5.30	7.26	45.75	-6.92
2002	-2.40	-4.22	3.76	-8.43	8.20	9.74	6.52	10.88	7.07	-4.95	-11.60	7.07	19.98	-15.98
2001	-1.53	-0.63	-1.23	-1.37	-0.10	3.05	4.50	-1.51	1.09	10.50	-6.77	3.95	9.34	-6.77
2000	-0.42	4.24	0.73	-3.51	3.87	1.56	1.08	1.86	-0.46	-4.81	8.14	9.06	22.45	-5.25
1999	2.39	-0.29	-1.79	5.51	-8.43	2.46	-0.13	11.06	3.93	-3.26	3.14	0.59	14.84	-8.43
1998	1.10	-2.45	-1.24	-4.42	0.29	-3.19	0.80	27.38	7.22	1.38	-3.08	-1.36	20.60	-10.60
1997	4.12	10.73	5.48	-4.25	-3.57	2.65	6.90	-13.32	10.85	-9.68	-2.43	2.64	7.09	-15.33
1996	-4.49	-7.22	-12.32	28.02	-18.30	6.19	0.29	1.54	18.78	23.39	6.73	-11.53	21.62	-22.30
1995	-15.59	-3.87	18.11	3.95	-7.62	2.31	-19.22	-10.11	-3.74	-2.45	4.50	12.12	-24.78	-35.80
1994	-10.76	-12.57	4.32	-7.73	19.42	20.58	11.50	-6.41	5.58	9.28	9.41	14.61	63.27	-24.90
1993	-11.78	2.74	14.66	6.69	13.37	-2.73	20.50	-14.33	-2.11	-1.10	6.64	17.07	52.56	-17.06
1992	-10.37	-1.07	-4.95	-3.66	-7.64	4.60	3.11	12.12	-12.10	10.65	17.58	5.40	9.31	-25.01
1991	-10.90	-0.64	0.00	-5.70	-1.52	2.20	-5.61	-0.51	-3.89	-0.60	-4.13	11.33	-19.54	-27.73
1990	0.19	5.08	3.69	1.29	-3.47	1.21	4.40	1.28	1.63	-3.88	2.96	3.98	19.46	-3.88
1989	-4.80	0.04	10.05	-9.86	27.98	6.15	2.26	-7.69	-0.30	-3.19	7.15	3.36	29.51	-10.90
1988								2.24	5.54	0.61	9.78		19.18	N/A

FIGURE 4.5 Hypothetically, if you invested $100,000 in November 1993, today it would be worth $4,141,237.63.

Source: Chart with permission from Iasg.com.

David Druz

Tactical Investment Management
Began April 1993
CAROR 19.85 percent

David Druz started out as an emergency room doctor. He told me he became interested in the futures markets when a friend of his, another medical student, ran $2,000 into $500,000 in the soybean markets in the 1970s. For the next 20 years Dave worked in medicine while researching ideas for trading. Dave learned under Ed Seykota. He actually stayed in Ed's house and studied with him for an extended period of time, which was an intense learning process. This learning process was more self-introspection to learn trading indicators or systems. In 1981, he set up his first futures fund, Tactical, while practicing as an emergency doctor in Fairbanks, Alaska. He later gave up medicine and moved from Alaska to the Hawaiian island of Oahu. Tactical Investment Management manages one of the longest running commodity futures trading programs in the world. Since 1981 they have systematically traded futures and currencies for a small number of institutional and individual clients. One can consider Tactical a boutique commodity trading advisor. Dave runs the trading and has an assistant, Colleen Ann Haviland, who runs the back office. Both are a pleasure and I feel honored to be one of their clients.

Dave maintains a robust trading methodology. There is no second-guessing or optimization. More so the parameters are not changed or altered. All markets are traded under the same variables. This is the basis of a robust system. It works over many types of market conditions and over many time frames. The key to success is money management and risk controls. These, however, do not negate drawdowns.

Tactical has three different products and in total approximately $100 million under management. The returns range both on the upside as well as on the downside. Dave defines exactly what his system does: "My trading system captures the capital that hedgers use to defend positions." He has back-tested and quantified it, and so he knows and expects that his system will generate 30 percent drawdowns. But over time, he has achieved excellent results because he is focused, he understands his markets, he has good money management rules, and he has a realistic time horizon within which he plans his trading. In one particular fund, his Tactical Institutional Commodity Program, he has returned a CAR of 18.87 percent since 1993. I recently bought into his current drawdown, which is his worst. He is down as of this writing −32.94 percent. This drawdown started in May 2011 and is still continuing as of February 2012. I entered in February 2012. I have money with Dave in another of his products and used this point as an additional entry. I have no idea if the drawdown will worsen. I strongly doubt that I am buying in at the bottom. The only investors that do that are ones that have numerous drinks in them whom I have met at trading conferences. I am not recommending Tactical, rather demonstrating how I allocate to trend followers in my personal trading. Every trend follower is going to have drawdowns and ugly periods. These are the times to enter. Unfortunately, many feel much more comfortable buying when times are good. It is easier emotionally; however, I believe it enhances the inherent risks when allocating to trend followers. I am not recommending Dave and would suggest you conduct your own due diligence.

Tactical Investment Management : Tactical Institutional Commodity Program

Snapshot | Charts | Statistics & Ratios | Performance Tables

Help with terms and abbreviations? See our definitions page

YEAR-TO-DATE
1.85% ↓
FEB 0.43%

Min. Investment	$2,000k	Inception	Apr 1993	Assets	$105.4M
Mgmt Fee	2.00%	Sharpe (RFR=1%)	0.76	Worst DD	-32.94
Perf Fee	20.00%	CAROR	18.87%	S&P Correlation	-0.10

Add Alert | Add to Blender | Add to Portfolio | Add to Watchlist | Print | Export

GROWTH OF 1,000 - VAMI

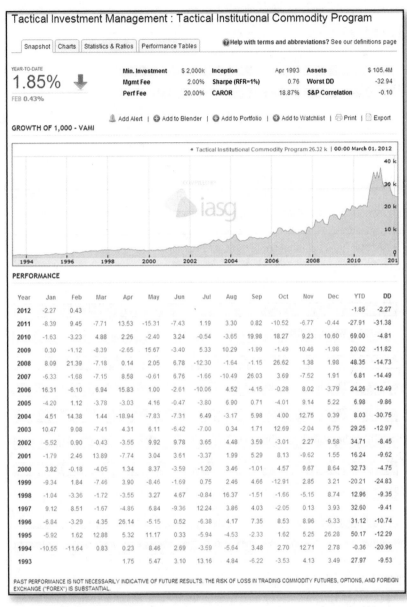

Tactical Institutional Commodity Program 26.32 k | 00:00 March 01, 2012

PERFORMANCE

Year	Jan	Feb	Mar	Apr	May	Jun	Jul	Aug	Sep	Oct	Nov	Dec	YTD	DD
2012	-2.27	0.43											-1.85	-2.27
2011	-8.39	9.45	-7.71	13.53	-15.31	-7.43	1.19	3.30	0.82	-10.52	-6.77	-0.44	-27.91	-31.38
2010	-1.63	-3.23	4.88	2.26	-2.40	3.24	-0.54	-3.65	19.98	18.27	9.23	10.60	69.00	-4.81
2009	0.30	-1.12	-8.39	-2.65	15.67	-3.40	5.33	10.29	-1.99	-1.49	10.46	-1.98	20.02	-11.82
2008	8.09	21.39	-7.18	0.14	2.05	6.78	-12.30	-1.64	-1.15	26.62	1.38	1.98	48.35	-14.73
2007	-6.33	-1.68	-7.15	8.58	-0.61	6.76	-1.66	-10.49	26.03	3.69	-7.52	1.91	6.81	-14.49
2006	16.31	-6.10	6.94	15.83	1.00	-2.61	-10.06	4.52	-4.15	-0.28	8.02	-3.79	24.26	-12.49
2005	-4.20	1.12	-3.78	-3.03	4.16	-0.47	-3.80	6.90	0.71	-4.01	9.14	5.22	6.98	-9.86
2004	4.51	14.38	1.44	-18.94	-7.83	-7.31	6.49	-3.17	5.98	4.00	12.75	0.39	8.03	-30.75
2003	10.47	9.08	-7.41	4.31	6.11	-6.42	-7.00	0.34	1.71	12.69	-2.04	6.75	29.25	-12.97
2002	-5.52	0.90	-0.43	-3.55	9.92	9.78	3.65	4.48	3.59	-3.01	2.27	9.58	34.71	-8.45
2001	-1.79	2.46	13.89	-7.74	3.04	3.61	-3.37	1.99	5.29	8.13	-9.62	1.55	16.24	-9.62
2000	3.82	-0.18	-4.05	1.34	8.37	-3.59	-1.20	3.46	-1.01	4.57	9.67	8.64	32.73	-4.75
1999	-9.34	1.84	-7.46	3.90	-8.46	-1.69	0.75	2.46	4.66	-12.91	2.85	3.21	-20.21	-24.83
1998	-1.04	-3.36	-1.72	-3.55	3.27	4.67	-0.84	16.37	-1.51	-1.66	-5.15	8.74	12.96	-9.35
1997	9.12	8.51	-1.67	-4.86	6.84	-9.36	12.24	3.86	4.03	-2.05	0.13	3.93	32.60	-9.41
1996	-6.84	-3.29	4.35	26.14	-5.15	0.52	-6.38	4.17	7.35	8.53	8.96	-6.33	31.12	-10.74
1995	-5.92	1.62	12.88	5.32	11.17	0.33	-5.94	-4.53	-2.33	1.62	5.25	26.28	50.17	-12.29
1994	-10.55	-11.64	0.83	0.23	8.46	2.69	-3.59	-5.64	3.48	2.70	12.71	2.78	-0.36	-20.96
1993				1.75	5.47	3.10	13.16	4.84	-6.22	-3.53	4.13	3.49	27.97	-9.53

PAST PERFORMANCE IS NOT NECESSARILY INDICATIVE OF FUTURE RESULTS. THE RISK OF LOSS IN TRADING COMMODITY FUTURES, OPTIONS, AND FOREIGN EXCHANGE ("FOREX") IS SUBSTANTIAL.

FIGURE 4.6 Hypothetically, if you invested $100,000 in April 1993, today it would be worth $3,119,771.09.

Source: Chart with permission from Iasg.com.

Jerry Parker

Chesapeake Capital
Began February 1988
CAROR 12.73 percent

Jerry Parker has been considered by some as the most successful of the Turtles. Jerry is a Turtle who trained under Dennis and founded Chesapeake Capital Management in 1988 after almost five years of trading his own proprietary capital. Jerry's approach is not as aggressive in seeking returns as some of his Turtle colleagues. This approach has made his trading more palatable for institutional investors as well as high net worth investors. At his peak Chesapeake in 2008 had a little under $2 billion of assets under management. Chesapeake encountered a rough patch in the markets in 2011 and so far in 2012. Assets plummeted to $766 million. Again, the institutional investors have done the wrong thing. After one has done due diligence, now could be considered a great time to invest with Chesapeake. I am not recommending; however, Jerry has been around with Chesapeake since 1988 and has returned a CAR of 12.62 percent. Considering how the stock market has done and at what volatilities, it is an interesting comparison. Chesapeake's investment portfolios are not biased toward long or short positions and, therefore, can profit in both rising and falling market environments. Chesapeake actively monitors, and has the potential to invest in, over 90 markets worldwide. Jerry, like most trend followers, patiently seeks trend breakouts. His Chesapeake system is a technical, trend following system. The system on average generates 200 trades per year, of which some six will pay for losses and generate returns, Jerry has stated. Quoting him, "One would not want to invest too much negative emotion in the 194 losers; you likely won't be around for the six big winners." This exemplifies what trend following really is. In a later section in my diary of trades, Jerry's statement is proven in my actual trades in my proprietary account.

Michael Covel is considered by many as well as myself as one of the best writers on trend following. He has a very select group of trend followers whom he considers his influencers and his mentors. Jerry Parker from Chesapeake is on the short list. This is a strong statement of support. It is ironic to me that some investors left Jerry after such a long and illustrious trading run. Probably a big mistake.

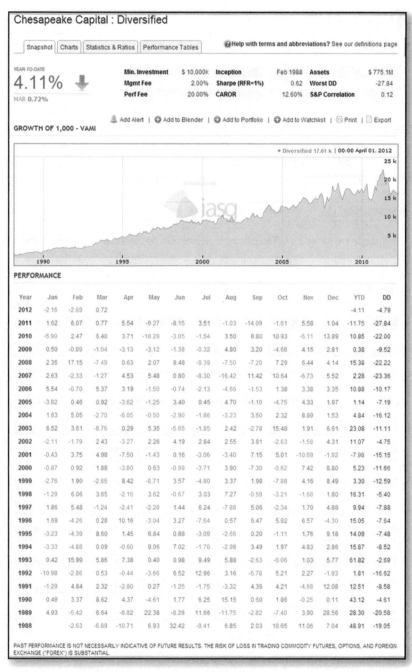

FIGURE 4.7 Hypothetically, if you invested $100,000 in February 1988, today it would be worth $1,642,892.48.

Source: Chart with permission from Iasg.com.

Michael Clarke

Clarke Capital Management Worldwide
Began January 1996
CAROR 14.14 percent

Michael Clarke, the principal of Clarke Capital, has been trading futures for client accounts since 1993. Michael was successful in his trading in the beginning, focusing on arbitraging equity options before he started trend following. His strategy was to be a disciplined buyer of volatility-sensitive options when they were extremely cheap and hedge them with overvalued options or stock. In the late 1980s the nature of the equity options business changed and it became less attractive to Michael. Starting in 1989, Michael started researching and verifying whether he could write computer algorithms that would be based on his knowledge and previous trading experiences in the markets. He questioned if he could actually make a living trading futures. Michael started developing a new career as a futures trader and eventually a CTA. He became a position trader using computer systematic algorithms to develop the entry and exit points. His earliest systems were profitable, yet they overtraded the markets and required too much risk to achieve their results. This would not have been attractive to clients. He developed techniques and various strategies over the period of 1989 to 1993. Michael spent a considerable amount of energy on the development of the software tools. Michael's testing was beyond extensive. He wanted to confirm the robustness of the systems. The systems had to be robust and were tested in over 100 markets with some containing data that dated back to 1945. Michael uses multiple trading systems. The systems had a synergistic and complementary effect by the fact that they were not all getting into or out of the same positions at the same time or at the same exit price. Additionally, when using multiple systems there were significant reductions in the length of drawdown periods as well as a smoothing of the equity curve. Remember our goal of building an equity curve. This is the way we compound money over time.

In order to diversify Michael has seven different programs: Worldwide with a minimum investment of $250,000, Orion with a minimum investment of $200,000, Millennium with a minimum investment of $1,000,000, Jupiter with a minimum investment of $3,000,000, Global Basic with a minimum investment of $50,000, Global Magnum with a minimum investment of $100,000, and FX Basic with a minimum investment of $1,000,000.

It was very smart on Michael's part to make all of these types of programs for investors. In this fashion he has made himself available to both institutional investors and smaller futures brokerage clients. Michael's programs are not immune to the inevitable drawdowns that trend followers face. His worst drawdown was in the Millennium program at 60.87 percent drawdown. He is currently in the drawdown from December 2008 till the month of this writing, February 2012.

Over the years Michael's hard work and efforts paid off. Michael has been awarded many accolades including:

- 1993 *Futures* magazine "Top Trader."

- 2000 *Futures* magazine "Top Trader."

- 2007 *Futures* magazine "Top Trader."

FIGURE 4.8 Hypothetically, if you invested $100,000 in February 1988, today it would be worth $829,862.02.

Source: Chart with permission from Iasg.com.

Paul Mulvaney

Mulvaney Capital Management
Began May 1999
CAROR 15.19 percent

Paul Mulvaney is the principle of Mulvaney Capital Management and is responsible for the Global Diversified Program. The Global Diversified Program is a long-term, systematic trend following program, covering all the major financial and commodity futures markets worldwide. Usually programs that are diversified provide returns that have historically exhibited low correlation to traditional stock and bond markets. The trading program is systematic and trend-based. Mulvaney Capital is operated out of London in conjunction with GNI Fund Management. GNI Fund Management seeded Mulvaney with a $5 million managed account in May 1999. Mulvaney's program is continually on the lookout for a market price breakout from a trading-range channel.

Mulvaney says his approach is totally systematic; he states, "The essence of trading comes down to psychological factors. What's really difficult is keeping emotions out of the equation. A completely systematic approach does that automatically." Mulvaney completely believes in mechanical trading systems that can be designed to exploit trends and produce acceptable risk-weighted returns. A fully computerized mechanical system can trade in many more markets than a discretionary trader could handle. He is a very big believer of reducing the risks inherent in the markets to remove the human element in trading process.

Mulvaney's program exploits price changes that occur over long periods. This is both a positive and a detriment. It has enabled large outsized returns as in 2008 when Mulvaney generated returns in excess of 100 percent. Yet there were periods of time such as in 2006 through 2007 when Mulvaney encountered 40 percent drawdowns plus. Mulvaney, like Dunn Capital, swings for the fences. He is looking to maximize his returns over time. Depending on the markets, it is not unrealistic to believe Mulvaney will achieve more 100 percent years in the future. However, with those types of returns, would I anticipate some steep drawdowns on the horizon?

Mulvaney is diversified across approximately 50 futures markets, many of which have no or low correlation with one another. Mulvaney's program attempts to capture long-term trends in all the major sectors of the global financial and commodity markets, and it invests 51 percent in financials and 49 percent in commodities. The rules of Mulvaney's trading strategy are simple: buy on strength and sell on weakness; run profits and cut losses short. "If you take our initial position and it starts to generate positive returns, then we'll increase it. If it starts to hurt the portfolio, then we'll reduce it and ultimately exit."

Mulvaney's initial commitment to any market is very small, on average 0.5 percent or less of account equity. His trading strategy is based on a piecemeal basis; if the trade seems to be working, he will scale in to a greater extent.

The program holds positions for 180 days on average, which is much longer than most. Mulvaney believes the way to beat the market and to garnish outsized returns is to have a longer time frame because psychologically participants seem to be too focused on the short term. Different from other commodity trading programs, it doesn't have to rush to market. Rather, the program can wait for a bigger breakout from a wider channel before taking a position. This is different from many other programs and the benefit is avoiding being caught by false breakouts. More so, the program, unlike many others, does not use a profit target. Mulvaney will hold a position until a trend reverses. There is never a free lunch when trading. There are always trade-offs.

FIGURE 4.9 Hypothetically, if you invested $100,000 in May 1999, today it would be worth $628,625.68.

Source: Chart with permission from Iasg.com.

Bernard Drury

Drury Capital
Began May 1997

Bernard Drury is the principle of Drury Capital. Drury Capital was founded in Illinois in 1992 as initially a fundamentally oriented grain trading program. Bernard focused on the grain markets from 1978 before shifting his focus to mechanical and algorithmic system development. While earning his M.B.A. from the University of Chicago, Bernard became interested in quantitative, systematic approaches to the futures markets. He was fascinated with the benefits that systematic trading could offer. This was a huge difference coming from a discretionary trading background. A computerized system offered consistency as well as diversification of different synergized models. This was the beginning for him to develop and refine his own trend following system. Bernard gained further trading experience at Louis Dreyfus Corporation, Commodities Corporation, and Goldman Sachs Princeton. His extensive research and development, along with his grain trading skills, served as a foundation for his trading career. In 1994, he joined Commodities Corporation in Princeton, New Jersey, where he further developed his systematic trend following trading system, operating as an independent entity within the firm. Through system testing Bernard became a firm believer that a systemic, rule-based approach to trading could give greater potential than discretionary trading in a single sector.

His systematic approach was thoroughly tested, researched, and applied robustly to a broadly diversified portfolio. He began trading client funds in the Drury Diversified Trend-Following Program in May 1997. Bernard's Diversified Trend-Following Program's trading methodology approach is built on elements of trend following and diversification.

The thoroughness of research and precision in execution was paramount to his models. The trading system has evolved over time to include additional systems and markets. Initially it only traded 30 markets and was only one system. By May 2008 he had increased the number of markets to 70 and included three other systems, making a total of four distinct systems. These enhancements on the methodology have reduced expected volatility from 25 percent to 18 percent. As far as risk per trade, there are a large number of small trades; the risk allocation to any given trade is very small. This is a common theme among successful trend followers.

The model is broadly diversified across six sectors, which are equally weighted, approximately. He maintains an exposure to 50 percent commodities and 50 percent financials. The portfolio emphasizes diversification by trading metals, agricultural products, foreign exchange, stock index futures, energy products, financial instruments, and softs such as cocoa and coffee. The speed of trading is slower than that of longer-term trend followers. As in most successful trend followers, the risk management system emphasizes the protection of equity. His unique methods of risk and money management result in different entry and exit points from other trend followers. His average hold period is four months and when trades are working, this can be up to eight months. Like most other trend followers, he exits losing trades quickly. Over a five-year time period, even with all of the inherent drawdowns, he has been profitable. His models do suffer as would most trend followers when there is a long period of broad nondirectional, high-volatility price behavior. Drury's minimum for managed accounts is $10,000,000. In addition to the managed accounts he maintains a fund in which an investor can gain access with a minimum of $100,000. He is currently managing approximately $400 million. He went through his worst drawdown in 2004 through 2006. He declined from his peak −32.52 percent. His second worst drawdown was in 2011 from February to October, −26.45 percent.

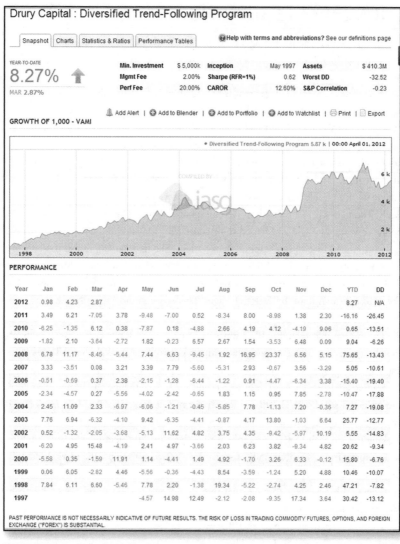

Drury Capital : Diversified Trend-Following Program

| Snapshot | Charts | Statistics & Ratios | Performance Tables |

🔘 Help with terms and abbreviations? See our definitions page

YEAR-TO-DATE

8.27% ⬆

MAR 2.87%

Min. Investment	$ 5,000k	Inception	May 1997	Assets	$ 410.3M
Mgmt Fee	2.00%	Sharpe (RFR=1%)	0.62	Worst DD	-32.52
Perf Fee	20.00%	CAROR	12.60%	S&P Correlation	-0.23

🔔 Add Alert | ⊕ Add to Blender | ⊕ Add to Portfolio | ⊕ Add to Watchlist | 🖨 Print | 🗋 Export

GROWTH OF 1,000 - VAMI

● Diversified Trend-Following Program 5.87 k | 00:00 April 01, 2012

PERFORMANCE

Year	Jan	Feb	Mar	Apr	May	Jun	Jul	Aug	Sep	Oct	Nov	Dec	YTD	DD
2012	0.98	4.23	2.87										8.27	N/A
2011	3.49	6.21	-7.05	3.78	-9.48	-7.00	0.52	-8.34	8.00	-8.98	1.38	2.30	-16.16	-26.45
2010	-6.25	-1.35	6.12	0.38	-7.87	0.18	-4.88	2.66	4.19	4.12	-4.19	9.06	0.65	-13.51
2009	-1.82	2.10	-3.64	-2.72	1.82	-0.23	6.57	2.67	1.54	-3.53	6.48	0.09	9.04	-6.26
2008	6.78	11.17	-8.45	-5.44	7.44	6.63	-9.45	1.92	16.95	23.37	6.56	5.15	75.65	-13.43
2007	3.33	-3.51	0.08	3.21	3.39	7.79	-5.60	-5.31	2.93	-0.67	3.56	-3.29	5.05	-10.61
2006	-0.51	-0.69	0.37	2.38	-2.15	-1.28	-6.44	-1.22	0.91	-4.47	-6.34	3.38	-15.40	-19.40
2005	-2.34	-4.57	0.27	-5.56	-4.02	-2.42	-0.65	1.83	1.15	0.95	7.85	-2.78	-10.47	-17.88
2004	2.45	11.09	2.33	-6.97	-6.06	-1.21	-0.45	-5.85	7.78	-1.13	7.20	-0.36	7.27	-19.08
2003	7.76	6.94	-6.32	-4.10	9.42	-6.35	-4.41	-0.87	4.17	13.80	-1.03	6.64	25.77	-12.77
2002	0.52	-1.32	-2.05	-3.68	-5.13	11.62	4.82	3.75	4.35	-9.42	-5.97	10.19	5.55	-14.83
2001	-6.20	4.95	15.48	-4.19	2.41	4.97	-3.66	2.03	6.23	3.82	-9.34	4.82	20.62	-9.34
2000	-5.58	0.35	-1.59	11.91	1.14	-4.41	1.49	4.92	-1.70	3.26	6.33	-0.12	15.80	-6.76
1999	0.06	6.05	-2.82	4.46	-5.56	-0.36	-4.43	8.54	-3.59	-1.24	5.20	4.88	10.46	-10.07
1998	7.84	6.11	6.60	-5.46	7.78	2.20	-1.38	19.34	-5.22	-2.74	4.25	2.46	47.21	-7.82
1997					-4.57	14.98	12.49	-2.12	-2.08	-9.35	17.34	3.64	30.42	-13.12

PAST PERFORMANCE IS NOT NECESSARILY INDICATIVE OF FUTURE RESULTS. THE RISK OF LOSS IN TRADING COMMODITY FUTURES, OPTIONS, AND FOREIGN EXCHANGE ("FOREX") IS SUBSTANTIAL.

FIGURE 4.10 Hypothetically, if you invested $100,000 in May 1997, today it would be worth $553,991.42.

Source: Chart with permission from Iasg.com.

Jeff Austin and Andy Silowitz

Blackwater Capital Management
Began July 2005

Blackwater Capital Management is managed by Jeff Austin and Andy Silowitz. Jeff started his career working on the floor of the Chicago Mercantile Exchange in 1994 taking care of the CTA business for Dean Witter. Andy traded spot forex and forex options. Jeff left the floor and gained further experience at Rotella Capital, a large commodity trading advisor. After that he started working at Eagle Trading Systems in Princeton, NJ, another large and successful commodity trading advisor. His focus of work at Eagle was research and system development. While at Eagle he met Andy. The two worked on system development at Eagle. The two partners got their pedigree while at Eagle and honed their skills. They decided to go out on their own and co-founded Blackwater Capital Management. The learning curve was passed from mentor to student. Eagle Trading's principal is Menachem Sternberg. Sternberg was the head trader for the Bruce Kovner fund, Caxton. Bruce Kovner was featured in the *Market Wizards* book by Jack Schwager. This is a common thread with successful traders.

The system that is run by Blackwater is a medium- to long-term pattern recognition program that trades 45 markets with strict profit targets. The model uses price and volatility patterns as well as some breakout elements. As do many other commodity trading advisors, they use multiple models. After launching the program in 2005 they added a second model that is longer term. Quoting Jeff, "It is two models and two signals. The second model is based on the same structure; the patterns that we are looking for are a bit bigger. ... Once we hit these profit objectives we are switching to a proprietary momentum indicator that tells us when we view the markets as stalling. If the markets are screaming we will stay with the trade until we see any kind of weakness." What is ironic to me is that they do not use trailing stops. They have profit targets and utilize wide stops.

The worst drawdown so far that Blackwater has experienced was in 2005–2006 of approximately 15 percent. I would believe that over time they will experience a much greater drawdown as your biggest drawdown is always ahead of you, not behind.

Blackwater Capital Management is currently managing approximately $500 million. Their minimum managed account size is $5,000,000.

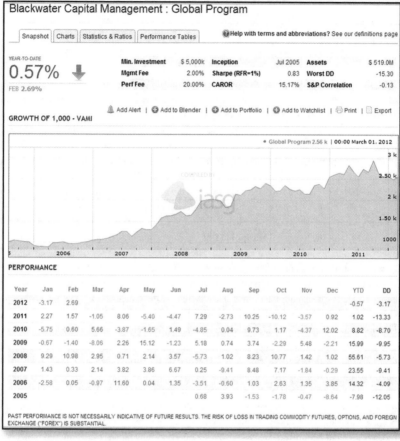

Blackwater Capital Management : Global Program

| Snapshot | Charts | Statistics & Ratios | Performance Tables |

🛈 Help with terms and abbreviations? See our definitions page

YEAR-TO-DATE

0.57% ⬇

FEB 2.69%

Min. Investment	$ 5,000k	Inception	Jul 2005	Assets	$ 519.0M
Mgmt Fee	2.00%	Sharpe (RFR=1%)	0.83	Worst DD	-15.30
Perf Fee	20.00%	CAROR	15.17%	S&P Correlation	-0.13

🔔 Add Alert | ➕ Add to Blender | ➕ Add to Portfolio | ➕ Add to Watchlist | 🖨 Print | 📄 Export

GROWTH OF 1,000 - VAMI

● Global Program 2.56 k | 00:00 March 01, 2012

PERFORMANCE

Year	Jan	Feb	Mar	Apr	May	Jun	Jul	Aug	Sep	Oct	Nov	Dec	YTD	DD
2012	-3.17	2.69											-0.57	-3.17
2011	2.27	1.57	-1.05	8.06	-5.40	-4.47	7.29	-2.73	10.25	-10.12	-3.57	0.92	1.02	-13.33
2010	-5.75	0.60	5.66	-3.87	-1.65	1.49	-4.85	0.04	9.73	1.17	-4.37	12.02	8.82	-8.70
2009	-0.67	-1.40	-8.06	2.26	15.12	-1.23	5.18	0.74	3.74	-2.29	5.48	-2.21	15.99	-9.95
2008	9.29	10.98	2.95	0.71	2.14	3.57	-5.73	1.02	8.23	10.77	1.42	1.02	55.61	-5.73
2007	1.43	0.33	2.14	3.82	3.86	6.67	0.25	-9.41	8.48	7.17	-1.84	-0.29	23.55	-9.41
2006	-2.58	0.05	-0.97	11.60	0.04	1.35	-3.51	-0.60	1.03	2.63	1.35	3.85	14.32	-4.09
2005							0.68	3.93	-1.53	-1.78	-0.47	-8.64	-7.98	-12.05

FIGURE 4.11 Hypothetically, if you invested $100,000 in July 2005, today it would be worth $258,318.06.

Source: Chart with permission from Iasg.com.

Justin Vandergrift

Chadwick Investment Group
Began July 2007
CAROR 21.37 percent

Chadwick Investment Group Inc. was formed by Justin Vandergrift in 2003. Justin's CTA is still small, approximately $11 million, however, with his firm grasp of trend following it would be easy to believe he could be an upcoming player in the commodity trading advisor world. He has the proverbial characteristics of a successful trend follower, passionate, hungry, and driven. Justin has contributed to the books *Trend Following,* 3rd edition, and *The Complete Turtle Trader,* 4th edition, written on the trend following method by Michael Covel. As well he was featured in Michael Covel's latest book, *The Little Book of Trading.*

Justin Vandergrift got his start at Futures Truth. I would assume his mentor at Futures Truth was John Hill Senior. John has been in the industry for decades. He has researched and developed thousands of trading systems utilizing a multitude of indicators. He has utilized his applied engineering and mathematical background to trading technology. John is well known in the industry due to his magazine that ranks 200 different 100 percent mechanical publicly offered commodity trading systems. With the name Futures Truth, he dispels the false holy grail claims of systems and gives an unbiased truthful approach to systematic trading. He has written several books on trading techniques and mechanical system trading. I spoke to Justin approximately two years ago and do not recall specifically what he did for Futures Truth. I found Justin to be extremely knowledgeable about mechanical trading systems and his focus on risk was impressive. He stated that future profitability is built on today's risk management. All of his trading decisions start with risk management, not charting patterns or technical indicators. This is a point I have tried to express throughout this book.

During my conversation with Justin he brought up the point that one of his original investors, a doctor, buys into his drawdowns. This was similar to my trading mentality. The doctor has been able to compound money at a greater rate by adding to his allocation during drawdowns. I recently invested with Justin. He was having a 22 percent drawdown at the time and thought it was as good as any time to invest with him. I am surely not buying in at the bottom nor do I have any plans to exit. I hope to invest with him over many years and compound money. I know that it could be a bumpy road as all trend followers experience draw downs.

Like many other successful trend followers, Justin's system looks for trading opportunities in 40+ global markets in the following market sectors: currencies, energies, grains, U.S.-based interest rates, international interest rates, meats, global soft commodities, and global stock indexes. He uses a quantitative trading system based on a statistical trading model created from research on historical price movements. He uses a money management system to limit the amount of exposure taken in one market. Trade duration can last from a few days to five months or more.

Justin has the ability to hit the ball out of the park. In 2008 he returned 82.60 percent for himself and his investors. His compound rate of return is approximately 19 percent. These returns are not without drawdowns, obviously. His worst peak to valley drawdown lasted for 16 months from December 2008 till April 2010. During this period he experienced a drawdown of −24.75%.

There are countless other CTAs and traders that have failed, however, and the previous results are not representative of those of all trend followers nor am I recommending any of them. My point is that compounding of money over long periods of time can bright about great wealth however, the reality is that there will always be drawdowns.

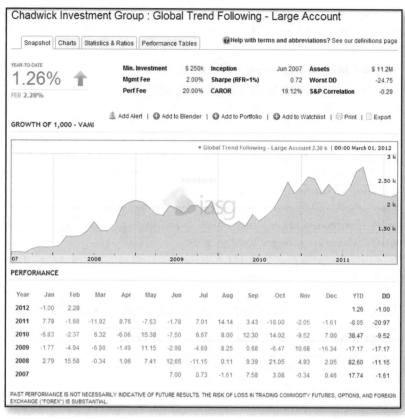

Chadwick Investment Group : Global Trend Following - Large Account

| Snapshot | Charts | Statistics & Ratios | Performance Tables | ❓Help with terms and abbreviations? See our definitions page |

YEAR-TO-DATE

1.26% ⬆

FEB **2.28%**

Min. Investment	$ 250k	Inception	Jun 2007	Assets	$ 11.2M
Mgmt Fee	2.00%	Sharpe (RFR=1%)	0.72	Worst DD	-24.75
Perf Fee	20.00%	CAROR	19.12%	S&P Correlation	-0.29

🔔 Add Alert | ➕ Add to Blender | ➕ Add to Portfolio | ➕ Add to Watchlist | 🖨 Print | Export

GROWTH OF 1,000 - VAMI

● Global Trend Following - Large Account 2.30 k | 00:00 March 01, 2012

PERFORMANCE

Year	Jan	Feb	Mar	Apr	May	Jun	Jul	Aug	Sep	Oct	Nov	Dec	YTD	DD
2012	-1.00	2.28											1.26	-1.00
2011	7.78	-1.68	-11.92	8.76	-7.63	-1.78	7.01	14.14	3.43	-18.00	-2.05	-1.61	-8.05	-20.97
2010	-6.83	-2.37	6.32	-6.06	15.38	-7.50	6.67	8.00	12.30	14.02	-9.52	7.00	38.47	-9.52
2009	-1.77	-4.94	-6.98	-1.49	11.15	-2.98	-4.89	8.25	0.68	-6.47	10.68	-16.34	-17.17	-17.17
2008	2.79	15.58	-0.34	1.06	7.41	12.65	-11.15	0.11	9.39	21.05	4.93	2.05	82.60	-11.15
2007						7.00	0.73	-1.61	7.58	3.08	-0.34	0.46	17.74	-1.61

PAST PERFORMANCE IS NOT NECESSARILY INDICATIVE OF FUTURE RESULTS. THE RISK OF LOSS IN TRADING COMMODITY FUTURES, OPTIONS, AND FOREIGN EXCHANGE ("FOREX") IS SUBSTANTIAL.

FIGURE 4.12 Hypothetically, if you invested $100,000 in July 2007, today it would be worth $239,056.79.
Source: Chart with permission from Iasg.com.

Gurus, Geniuses, and Legends Are Not the Way to Make Money!

There are always gurus, geniuses, and legends, but they are not the way to compound your way to wealth. Today we seem to have more gurus since the speed of information increases. The sad part is that even educated and intelligent investors follow gurus like a religion. The big difference, in my opinion, is that these gurus many times are false messiahs. I have seen numerous market cycles. It seems with each cycle there is a guru. These gurus have a hot streak and then in many cases blow up. In the 1970s there was Edson Gould with his famous rule of three steps and a stumble regarding the discount rate. Then along came Joe Granville who spoke to overflowing crowds with his wild antics, who later failed. Robert Prechter came to the spotlight in the 1980s with his Elliott wave theories.

There are even dead gurus such as W. D. Gann. There are Gann courses and Gann software that can even be purchased today.

All of these gurus pretty much have one thing in common. They were right at one point in their career, the media proclaimed them a guru and afterwards many of their followers lost money by investing blindly by their guidance.

We Have Our Legends As Well

In the last bear market some of the best-known mutual fund managers (legends) were deeply negatively impacted. My simple dumb question: as much as Warren Buffett is the poster boy for "buy and hold," why isn't everyone rich? Why didn't everyone just invest like Buffett?

> Warren Buffett, –43 percent
> Ken Heebner (CMG Fund), –56 percent
> Harry Lange (Fidelity Magellan), –59 percent
> Bill Miller (Legg Mason Value), –50 percent

Even Worse...Geniuses

Roger Lowenstein wrote the book *When Genius Failed* in 2000. The book discussed Long-Term Capital Management and how it imploded in 1998.

John Meriwether, a famously successful Wall Street trader, spent the 1980s as a partner at Salomon Brothers, establishing the best—and the brainiest—bond arbitrage group in the world. A mysterious and shy Midwesterner, he knitted together a group of Ph.D.-certified arbitrageurs who rewarded him with filial devotion and fabulous profits. Then, in 1991, in the wake of a scandal involving one of his traders, Meriwether abruptly resigned. For two years, his fiercely loyal team—convinced that the chief had been unfairly victimized—plotted their boss's return. Then, in 1993,

Meriwether made a historic offer. He gathered together his former disciples and a handful of supereconomists from academia and proposed that they become partners in a new hedge fund different from any Wall Street had ever seen. And so Long-Term Capital Management (LCTM) was born.

In a decade that had seen the longest and most rewarding bull market in history, hedge funds were the ne plus ultra of investments: discreet, private clubs limited to those rich enough to pony up millions. They promised that the investor's money would be placed in a variety of trades simultaneously—a "hedging" strategy designed to minimize the possibility of loss. At Long-Term, Meriwether & Co. truly believed that their finely tuned computer models had tamed the genie of risk and would allow them to bet on the future with near mathematical certainty. And thanks to their cast—which included a pair of future Nobel Prize winners—investors believed them.

From the moment Long-Term opened their offices in posh Greenwich, Connecticut, miles from the pandemonium of Wall Street, it was clear that this would be a hedge fund apart from all others. Though they viewed the big Wall Street investment banks with disdain, so great was Long-Term's aura that these very banks lined up to provide the firm with financing, and on the very sweetest of terms. So certain were Long-Term's traders that they borrowed with little concern about the leverage. At first, Long-Term's models stayed on script, and this new gold standard in hedge funds boasted such incredible returns that private investors and even central banks clamored to invest more money.

It seemed the geniuses in Greenwich couldn't lose. Four years later, when a default in Russia set off a global storm that Long-Term's models hadn't anticipated, its supposedly safe portfolios imploded. In five weeks, the professors went from megarich geniuses to discredited failures. With the firm about to go under, its staggering $100 billion balance sheet threatened to drag down markets around the world. At the eleventh hour, fearing that the financial system of the world was in peril, the Federal Reserve Bank hastily summoned Wall Street's leading banks to underwrite a bailout.

When LTCM Imploded Trend Followers Made a Fortune!

Futures get somewhat of a bad rap as being wildly speculative or dangerous. Most people are completely at ease with stocks and bonds. But in 1994 bond funds imploded. The Nasdaq stocks during the dot-com bubble imploded. The fact with stocks is that you leverage 50 percent and with futures this percentage is astronomically greater. It is not the leverage itself but the lack of planning and disregard for the leverage. The problem is the amount of leverage used when trading. There is nothing inherently different between Netflix stock and soybeans as far as volatility. Perceptions and beliefs on the future affect both examples. Netflix stock as well as soybeans can be volatile and risky (just ask anyone who purchased Netflix at $300). There are studies (which I do not give a lot of credence to) that the average annual price moments of stocks are greater than those of commodities.

Numbers can be manipulated and massaged. The reality is that anything from a stock share to soybeans to even gold can negatively affect your net worth if you do not have a plan.

Comparing the leverage of stocks and commodities is demonstrated below. First, consider stock trading. You put on margin at your broker $100,000 in cash and you buy XYZ stock. An alternative is that you can use margin and leverage your $100,000 that you have put up with your broker and utilize it as $200,000. If XYZ stock goes up 5 percent over the coming months, the investor who put up $100,000 has grossed $5,000. Another investor who put up $100,000 in cash and traded the account as if it was $200,000 and purchased XYZ stock grossed $10,000. He made a 10 percent return versus the more conservative trader who did not use leverage and made $5,000.

Comparing now to futures or forex. If one wants to trade the Japanese yen one needs to place initial margin of $4860 (this amount can change due to volatility) in order to control 12,500,000 yen or approximately $150,000. A 5 percent upside move when a trader is long is a tremendous profit for the trader. Conversely a 5 percent downward move when the trader is long is catastrophic. Traders are not aware that markets can go limit down or limit up. This means they cannot exit their trades. They get sucked down further into the abyss of losses. Traders blow up due to their lack of understanding the leverage at their disposal. Leverage is a double-edged sword. There are times when vast profits can be generated when one uses leverage and the trade works; however, more often the leverage destroys accounts. Traders do not believe it can actually happen to them nor do they understand the leverage. All those late-night commercials on TV that suggest you can control 100 ounces of gold for only $8,500 delude investors. MF Global blew up due to the leverage they used in their bet of European bonds. Out of panic they accessed client-segregated accounts in order to address their shortfall. MF Global leveraged their assets 30 times. Few traders or firms are truly prepared for dealing with 30–1 leverage. Worse is when there are those who do not even understand they are using that much leverage. Leverage can be compared to a Maserati that drives at speeds of 200 miles per hour. I know that I do not have that driving ability.

The sword of leverage cut off the head of MF Global. The management of MF Global did not have a cushion and were trading way too big. The complete lack of prudence is shocking. Jon Corzine, the CEO, wanted to transform the more than 200-year-old MF Global into a mini Goldman by taking on more risky bets on eurozone sovereign debt. Corzine was notorious for making big bets while he was at Goldman. The success of those leveraged bets gave Corzine negative reinforcement. There are times when even successful traders trade their egos. It is not just ignorance when one abuses leverage. They feel they have to be right. The only thing that is right is the market.

Given the size of your trading account and your personal tolerance of risk, you need to determine if leverage is for you or not.

Futures trading is a zero-sum game. When someone loses, someone wins. For every trader betting on higher prices there is an offsetting trader betting on lower prices. Trend followers have an edge and a plan. Everyone who takes on a position thinks they will win, but as in the case of LTCM there are losers as well. Trend followers are also losers at times and losses cannot be avoided. The goal, however, is to "try to keep these losses small."

When LTCM blew up in August 1998, in that one month:

Hawksbill made 80 percent.
Eckhardt made 32 percent.
Abraham Trading made 23 percent.

The Real Geniuses Were the Humble Trend Followers and Their Investors!

The irony was that some of the largest and smartest investors bought into the Long-Term Capital dream and lost countless millions.

How did the so-called smartest, best, and brightest traders who graduated from Harvard or Wharton with pedigrees do during the recent stock market rout in 2008? I will tell you: Many of them blew up while trend followers had a double-digit profitable year!

■ The Biggest Mistake Traders Make

The single biggest mistake traders make is thinking that investing and trading are "easy."

They allow themselves to fall for advertisements promising, "You can get rich by trading" or "Earn all the income you've ever dreamed of" or "Leave your day job forever and live off your day-trading profits." Trend following is not retirement in a box.

The actual tenets of successful trend following in their essence are basically simple and intuitive in nature. However, in practicality trend following is very difficult due to our greed and fears.

In order to succeed over time with trend following you will need to internalize these tenets and make them part of your trading.

It is imperative for your long-term success to always **cut losses short and take low-risk trades**. You will realize when you start trend following, if you haven't already, that many trades simply do not work. The fact that you will be taking low-risk bets and keeping losses manageable are the cornerstone of successful trend following.

The reality is that trading is inherently risky. If you were to engage in any highly risky activity other than trading, you would clearly spend some time considering how to protect yourself. It can be as mundane as riding a bicycle and wearing a helmet. I would assume before someone jumped out of a plane they would check their parachute. They probably have a backup parachute. In my trading I trade with a backup stop similar to a backup parachute, which I will detail later on in this book. There are those who trade and they do not even consider the concept of a parachute when they jump out of a plane.

These traders do not have stops. They do not know where a trade does not work. They believe they can fly like a bird. They believe the trade has to work, until they crash to the ground. Making one mistake while trading can be your last. The markets are unforgiving. Without even blinking several names come to mind of traders who have crashed. Dighton is one from 2011 as well as the famous trader Niederhoffer from 1997.

One of the first conferences I went to featured Victor Niederhoffer as a guest speaker. Niederhoffer was extremely successful and even managed money for George Soros. He had returned in the 30 percents for more than a decade. In cases such as this, he was showered with money. Investors only saw the 30 percent, not how he traded. They did not look at his daily equity curve. Within a month there can be tremendous volatility. Many times this is masked by the monthly numbers. Niederhoffer even wrote a bestselling book, *The Education of a Speculator*. During the Asian contagion he was hurt badly by his bet in Thai banks as well as his bet on the S&P 500. On October 27, 1997, the S&P 500 fell more than 7 percent or 554 points. Niederhoffer still felt his assumption was correct and the market was wrong. He thought the proverbial, that the market will bounce back! He had naked put positions on the stock indexes. As Murphy's Law would have it, he ended up being right but his timing was wrong. This was a fatal blow to Niederhoffer. He had to close his fund and left a $20 million debt at his broker.

As usual greed has a way of making people forget the past. After closing his fund in 1998 Niederhoffer traded his own account. However, in 2002 Niederhoffer came back and opened his Matador fund. He was returning 50 percent per year with his worst year at 40 percent. Again he was flooded with money and in 2007 at the onset of the credit and housing debacle, he closed the Matador fund after experiencing a 75 percent drop. Lightning struck twice with Niederhoffer.

Sadly, most traders, from the professionals who manage money to the vast majority of other traders, don't address money management until they have suffered an unexpected waterfall in their equity curve. Maybe it is human nature to focus on the positive, and the primary motivation of traders is clearly to make money. When traders put on a trade, why would they really risk hard-earned money if they think they can lose it? For this reason, many do not even consider it plausible to lose money. Only after time or a devastating loss they might wake up to the reality that success in trading is like in football: defense … defense and even more defense!

No one starts trading just to make 7 percent or 8 percent. I recall vividly when people were disappointed during the 1995 bull market that they only made 20 percent for three years in a row. The reason people seek trend following is to do better or achieve above-average rates of returns. These people have their priorities wrong, and preservation of capital should be one of their priorities at the onset. Many new traders are of the mindset that trading is "easy" and they can garnish riches. Thought processes like this are detrimental to one's net worth. I assume you are reading this book because you are truly looking to improve your results and have passed the gullible stage of thinking that trading is easy. Not to be negative, but fearing the market is good. I have a tremendous amount of appreciation of what the market can do to my financial situation. I would not say fear but respect. The lack of fear is what gets traders into trouble. I am a coward when a trade does not work. I do not try to prove anything or fight it, I exit quickly and stay in the marathon to fight another day with the hope that I can catch a nice trend. I want to be able to trade again tomorrow. I know that it is a useless effort to try to fight the markets. The markets are right. The trade did not work. Next, let's try another one and see what happens. The goal is to stay in this marathon without falling down or giving up. The way I know how to stay in the race is to manage my risks and to try to mitigate my losses. Doing so enables me to be available for those rare winning periods and rare big trades that work.

Trend following success can only happen if you trade **only in the direction of the trend**. There is no second guessing or debating. You do not let your opinions get in the way. You have an **exact plan** to follow trades that are working as well as an **exact plan** to exit quickly trades that are not working.

You follow the trend! Letting profits run without any fear or greed.

Simply detach yourself, see what is happening, and follow the exact plan. You will have an exact plan in which at every point in time you know exactly what you should be doing. When you are letting your profits run you will be exposed to profitable opportunities due to trending markets. You will not be in areas that are illiquid such as the housing bubble or on the wrong side of major trends such as the dot-com bubble or the 2008 October stock market meltdown.

This exact plan does not mean knowing the future. You do not need to know the future in order to succeed over time when trend following. Too often beginning traders **struggle to identify the direction of the market.** Beginning traders use very complicated formulas, indicators, and systems to identify a trend. They'll plot so many indicators on the screen that they can't even see the prices any more. They think that the more complicated a system is, the better it should "predict" the trends. As a result, they completely lose sight of the simple basic principle: Buy when the market is going up and sell when the market is going down if you can put on a low-risk bet. No one can ever tell when a trend starts or stops.

You will learn from my book and my mentoring how successful trend followers both approach the markets and think.

> You will have an exact plan. You will need to follow it exactly in order to succeed.
>
> You will take low-risk bets with the understanding that these trades do not have to work.
>
> You will immediately take losses when trades do not work without a second thought.
>
> You will allow profits to run when trades do work and not cut them short.
>
> You will have the proper mindset to overcome all the challenges, drawdowns, and durations of drawdowns.
>
> You will learn the proper mindset of patience and discipline.

CHAPTER 5

Managing the Risks when Trend Following

The only certainty in trend following is uncertainty. Due to this constant uncertainty it is imperative to manage the risks. We are surrounded by risks. Successful trend followers know that we do not know the future. Given the fact that we are dealing in uncertainty, we have no choice but to be extremely adamant in our risk and money management approach.

Larry Hite, a famous successful trend follower from the 1980s, put it very simply: Trend followers make bets when they trade. If you lose all of your chips, you can't bet!

In other words, you are out of business!

Many successful hedge funds teach their interns how to play poker. I invested in Green Light Hedge Fund with David Einhorn many years ago via a fund of funds that I was involved with. I was fortunate to meet David and learned another one of his talents besides trading was poker playing. David is not a gambler; however, he would make low-risk bets both in his trading and when he played poker. In 2006, Einhorn finished 18th in the World Series of Poker main event. Contrary to what some say, successful trend followers are risk adverse.

Trend followers are not cowboys. Every aspect of their trade is calculated with a well-thought-out exact plan. There is no second guessing. Every possibly outcome has been taken into account.

■ Risk of Ruin

The concept of risk of ruin tackles the issue regarding how much of your trading capital you may lose. You cannot recover from this drawdown or trade your way out. The size of your position is arguably one of the most critical elements of your success as a trader. Sound money management lets you survive the bad periods and gives you the potential to profit in the long run over time. There isn't a set-in-stone rule for position sizes even though I stress 1 percent. A lot of personal issues, such as the size of your account, your risk tolerance, and your experience, should all factor into how big a bet you should make. That said, risk of ruin or the possibility that you'll blow up your trading account when you encounter the inevitable rough patch increases dramatically when you increase your risk per trade. The risk of ruin does increase substantially as your risk per trade approaches 2 percent or less of your portfolio size. There is no perfect or ideal portfolio other than one that fits your personality and account size. You need to develop a portfolio in which you have funded adequately. If you trade too large for your account, you stand the distinct chance of ruin or blowing up. This is the worst case and on a lesser level you will experience deep drawdowns and swings in your portfolio. These wild swings can surely stop you from continuing to trade. This prevents you from building your equity curve and compounding money over time. Conversely, if you trade too small, you miss the opportunities the market can offer you. One needs to have a portfolio of markets and be diversified. As one market zigs another can zag. There are long periods when markets do not trend. When you trade a portfolio of markets you open your possibilities of not just trades but also success. The most practical aspect needs to be introspection of your account size. The more money you have in your accounts, the more markets you can trade. Clearly the less money you have in your account, the fewer markets you might/should want to consider or trade. In order to assist traders the exchanges have created mini contracts. Do not let the word *mini* mislead you. You make a mistake on one of these, and you can seriously hurt your trading account.

Those futures contracts are called minis. You have Mini S&P 500 and Mini NAS-DAQ versions of the larger size. The tick value of the E-Mini version of the S&P 500 contract is $12.50 a tick versus $25.00 on the full size. There exist mini contracts on the currencies such as the Mini Yen. The Mini Yen tick value is $6.25 versus the full size contract of $12.50.

There exists the direct possibility of encountering a series of consecutive trades that do not work and being forced to stop trading. Think of risk of ruin as bites out of an apple. If you are risking 1 percent of your account on a trade, you get to have 100 bites out of the apple. You can quickly fathom the possibility of having 100 trades in a row not working and losing money (not overly likely). If you are risking 2 percent of your account, you get 50 bites of the apple. Think about the possibility of having 50 trades in a row not working

Continuing our thought process, if you risk 3 percent of your account on any trade, you get approximately 33 bites out of the apple. If you risk 5 percent, you get 20 bites out of the apple, or 20 trades in a row not working. One last example: If you are risking 10 percent of your account, you only get 10 bites out of the apple. I can promise I have had close to 10 trades in a row not work over the years. Basically you risked too much and your trading account is ruined. The concept of risk of ruin accentuates the reason why I suggest you take approximately 1 percent risk per trade.

The actual calculation takes into account the probability of winning, the probability of incurring losses, and the percentage of an account at risk. I know I oversimplified my apple idea, but I am sure you get the point. You need to believe that anything can happen. There is a six sigma event out there that can prevent you from continuing to trade. I vividly remember the stock market crash in 1987. More than just the stock market, I remember the move in eurodollars. Believe that anything can happen. I have been trading since 1994 and have executed over the years a large number of trades. Over this period of time I have personally seen long losing periods (much longer than I would have liked). The longer you expose yourself to trading, as I have, the more likely you will see these events, and they are not unexpected. If you trade frequently, it is really only a matter of time before you experience a run of four, five, or even more losers in a row. Consider that this can be not just losing trades but also losing weeks or even months. You need to be able emotionally, psychologically, and financially to get through these inevitable periods. You can't be so overleveraged that a normal statistical run of losers ruins your account. Many traders talk about maximum drawdown, as if there is a maximum limit. Your worst drawdown is always ahead of you.

Following is the math formula of risk of ruin:

$$R = e \char`\^ (-2 * a/d)$$

Where: R = risk of losing one standard deviation
         e = 2.71828, the base of the natural logarithm
         a = average, or mean return
         d = standard deviation of returns

You can play with the numbers, but the reality is that if you risk more than 1 percent on any trade, you will surly encounter pain in your trading account at some point.

I have seen traders lose 10 percent in a couple of days without proper risk management. My day is filled with speaking with traders as well as testing trading ideas. I even heard a story of how a professional trader lost 50 percent of his account over a period of several short days. He was an ex–mutual fund manager and during the volatility in 2008, he froze. He did not follow his plan. Even with all of his experience he did not accept the risk and felt the market would come back.

■ The Exact Elements of Risk Management

The elements of risk management relate to one of the most important topics in trading: stop-loss orders. A stop-loss order or money management stop is a protective stop that needs to be placed immediately upon entry. There are those who think they are comfortable with "mental stops." However, in the thick of trading these "mental stops" are not activated. I have heard the excuse that if I place my stop, traders on the floor will run the stop. I find this an excuse for blaming. Blaming does not make you money and the market does not care for excuses. In the heat of the moment the mental stop order must be placed and I have seen traders freeze. They wait, they rationalize, and they convince themselves with a myriad of reasons why not to take the trade. This is one of the most common issues I have seen traders blow up. I do not think you want to be one of the 90 percenters (failed traders). Just one bad trade can implode a trading account that took years to build. Mental stop-loss orders are an accident waiting to happen.

The only time I would agree that mental stops might be used is if a large number of shares or contracts are purchased or sold. However, this is not reality for most readers, and I strongly suggest once your orders are filled you put in your protective stop. The stop loss is a protective stop you have placed in the market if your open trades reaches or exceeds this stop level. The stop-loss order's purpose is to protect you against large losses. It is prudent to take a small loss. The stop loss is only an attempt to mitigate a loss to a preset amount. However, in the real world there exist gaps and limit days, which can and will exceed your stop-loss order. There are absolutely no guarantees with stop-loss orders. Large losses can be detrimental to both one's financial account as well as emotional makeup.

I promise you there will be many times your stop losses are hit and the market completely turns around again. This is reality. The only way to avoid situations like this is not to trade. If you get stopped out, you need the mental fortitude to put the trade back on if you get a signal. If you don't put the trade back on, you will feel terrible if this trade becomes the trade of the year. You need to be consistent and accept the risks and that you will have countless losses.

Worse than trying to put in mental stops, there are traders who believe they do not need to use stops at all. This is the scariest of all. These nonstop traders believe they have a winning strategy or system. If they have a winning technique, why would they bother? These nonstop traders soon wake up after a devastating loss in which they let a small loss compound into a nightmare.

Risk per Trade

Risk management starts on the trade level. Too many traders and even experienced traders miss the point on how much to risk on a trade. They think in terms of risk management via a fixed dollar amount or based on their overconfidence of a trade succeeding. Neither of these are traits of successful trend followers.

Overconfidence   The greater the confidence, the bigger the risk they are willing to take. A recent example is John Paulson. He made huge bets in regard to the housing crisis and benefited substantially. Paulson made billions of dollars. However, in 2011 his huge bets worked against him and he encountered a drawdown close to the 50 percent range.

As in the example with John Paulson, this way of thinking can lead one to failure or big drawdowns. Successful trend followers have internalized that any trade is 50/50 and has no guarantee of success.

Fixed-Dollar-Amount Risk   The idea of having a fixed dollar amount per trade would be saying you are willing to risk a fixed $1,000 per trade. The mistake traders make when they risk a fixed dollar amount per trade is that there will be times they will benefit less or even lose more when risking a fixed dollar amount per trade due to lack of position sizing. This is wrong. There are times when you might be able to put on a greater position due to a low-risk trade. At times when these trades work even greater returns can be generated due to position size. Position sizing will be further discussed shortly.

Successful trend followers are methodical. Very little is left to their personal opinions. Therefore considering this, successful trend followers risk the same amount percentage risk on every trade.

Consistency is achieved when trading with an exact plan.

Position sizing is one of the key components in successful trend following.

Exactly how much to buy or sell is based on the dollar size of the trading account and the volatility of the issue. The volatility is the dollar risk from entry signal to the initial hard stop exit in case the trade does not work. (Further on I will discuss how to determine the hard stop.)

The concept of position sizing is shown in the following examples.

You have an entry signal of Buy of share XYZ at $20.00. Your worst-case exit signal or hard stop protection is $17.00; you are risking $3.00 to see if the trade works. If you have a $100,000 account size and you are willing to risk 1 percent or $1,000, you can put on approximately 333 shares. You divide your 1 percent risk on your account size or $1,000 divided by $3, which is 333 shares.

You have an entry signal of Buy of share ABC at $15.00. Your exit signal or hard stop protection is $13.00; you are risking $2.00 to see if the trade works. If you have a $100,000 account size and you are willing to risk 1 percent or $1,000, you can put on approximately 500 shares. You divide your 1 percent risk on your account size or $1,000 divided by $2, which is 500 shares.

As we have already discussed, any trade is 50/50; however, if share XYZ moves $2.00 you can profit $666. Contrarily, if your share ABC moves that same $2.00, you make $1,000. This is what can make trend followers who think in terms of position sizing much more successful than others. The goal of position sizing is to attempt to limit drawdowns and prevent them from becoming so large that it causes you to stop trading. You need to be both financially and mentally prepared for the magnitude of drawdowns you are likely to experience. Your greatest drawdown is always ahead of you, not behind your portfolio.

Changing the Percentage Risk Changes the Equation   You have an entry signal of Buy of share XYZ at $20.00. Your exit signal or hard stop protection is $17.00; you are risking $3.00 to see if the trade works. If you have a $100,000 account size and you are willing to risk 1 percent or $1,000, you can put on approximately 333 shares.

The difference on percentage risk per trade is increased if you are willing to risk 2 percent, and since you are risking $2,000 of your $100,000 account you can put on 666 shares. If share XYZ moves $2 you profit $1,332 versus $666 on the same $2 move. However, you took on more risk (potential loss of $2,000), and taking larger risk per trades can increase drawdowns dramatically.

As I have presented to you, most trades do not work with trend following, therefore you are more apt to lose $2,000 versus the $1,000 initial risk. Deciding on how much to risk per trade is a personal choice. Many times with new traders greed or a sense of false security kicks in and they are more apt to risk more per trade. However, after going through drawdowns, this hubris subsides and they learn risking 1 percent can help them achieve their goals of compounding money over time. There is a trading period when if you go through a drawdown that is too steep, it can put you out of business.

This is the essence of position sizing and seeking low-risk trades.

One needs to determine one's personal comfort level with risk per trade percentage. The bigger the risk per trade percentage, the greater potential returns; however, there will be bigger drawdowns.

The problem with drawdowns is there is a drawdown out there that can stop your trading.

I have seen traders take on too much risk, enter a severe drawdown, and stop trading. I am personally less concerned about the return on investment and more concerned about how much risk I will have to tolerate to achieve my goals of reasonable returns over time.

I personally risk .75 to 1.25 percent basis points versus my core equity (dollar account size not including open trade equity) on one of my managed account models, and on my other managed account model I risk a maximum of 1.25 percent of my total core equity size.

To quantify risk per trade, for example on a $100,000 account, on one model I am only willing to risk $750 on a trade and on the other model a maximum risk of $1,250. Core equity is the equity of all my closed positions and my cash positions. Core equity does not include any open profits. If I were to include my open trade equity I would distort to the upside my true account balance and possibly take on more risk.

That is it! I have and believe over time I will be able to continue to generate reasonable returns only risking these amounts.

If there is more risk than the .75 percent of my core equity and 1.25 percent of my core equity, I pass on the trade.

I know that most of my trades will not work, therefore in order to try to mitigate inherent drawdowns I simply pass on these trades. I have no fear of missing out or any greed to think to chase a trade.

Big profits can be pulled out of the markets by taking low-risk bets. Most traders do not realize this, and that is why they overbet. It is the same mistake that traders make thinking that they need a complicated system or methodology in order to make money.

In the upcoming section I will delineate exactly the entry signal and initial exit signal. From the difference from these two attributes you will able to calculate your exact risk per trade.

My simple proprietary robust ideas have the propensity over time to compound money.

Risk per Sector

Earlier in my career I had no idea of sector correlation. Only through big drawdowns and losses did I learn the importance of this rule. There is a statistical function of correlation called the *correlation coefficient*. Markets that trade exactly the same would have a correlation of 1. Conversely, markets that trade completely the opposite would have a correlation of -1. In today's world it seems when we look at our charts on strong directional days we see a preponderance of a sea of either green or red. This means even many of the markets that we think are not correlated actually are correlated.

There are severe limitations with the correlation coefficient. It only looks at past performance and the markets are always in flux. Actually I wrote an article for *Futures* magazine demonstrating the fallacy of past correlations. Correlations change and what occurred in the past is not written in stone. However, it would be fair to say that within a particular sector there are correlations. For example, when gold seems to start trending it is not unreasonable to see silver start trending. Another example could be easily found in the grain complex. When you see a move in soybeans, you might see a run with corn and wheat. In the stock market correlations within sectors are also prevalent. When the tech sector is strong, you can anticipate the majority of the shares in that sector will move in unison. Contracts and shares all rise and fall together. When you trade them all in the context and time and if you are long this is great. On the other hand and in reality, you will find this to be the opposite and you are increasing your risk. At times you may achieve nice profits, but in the context of risk control you will expose your portfolio to increased volatility. There will be sharp swings both up and down. At times these swings might be too great to handle. There is always a point at which one goes through a drawdown that is too painful to continue. This is the reason we must be aware of correlations in sectors. When I first began, I would get a signal to buy or sell in the interest rate sector or the grain sector. I would buy five-year bonds, 10-year bonds, 30-year bonds, gilts, bunds, and name it. The same could occur in the grains. I would buy soybeans, bean oil, bean meal, corn, and wheat.

What actually happened to me was there were times these trades worked well, but when they didn't it was a disaster. Even though I thought I was taking low-risk trades with small percentage risks of my account size, these trades were heavily correlated and I was not taking a low-risk bet.

I woke up some mornings and all of these trades went against me and I faced a heavy draw-down. What I learned from these incidents was to cap my sector risk. Today part of my risk plan is that I will only allocate 5 percent of my total portfolio to any sector. Any sector means any stock sector such as tech, retail, and so on, or in the commodities interest rates, energies, grains, metals, and so forth. Putting it in clear terms: If my total account size were $100,000, I would have the total number of positions not exceeding a risk of 5 percent or $5,000 in that particular sector.

Personally, I am not only concerned about the return on investment but how much risk I will have to tolerate to achieve my goals.

Risk per sector is a personal issue. There are others who are comfortable taking on more risk. They are willing to risk more per trade as well as risk more per sector level. However, everything has a price. I might generate lower profits but I will have fewer drawdowns. Contrarily there are those who will generate greater profits and have greater drawdowns.

There is no free lunch when we trend follow.

Consider when you trade a diversified portfolio of 10-year bonds, corn, Australian dollars, and crude oil, it could be expected for them to be somewhat independent of each other as opposed to just trading 10-year bonds, five-year bonds, and 30-year bonds. At times it would be expected that the diversified portfolio would have elements rising, some falling, and some actually doing nothing. When one of the elements trends, it can offset the inevitable losses in the other elements and you smooth out your equity curve. As I stated above there is no free lunch. All we are trying to do is smooth out our equity curve and "trying" has a lot of limitations.

What I have seen firsthand is that when traders actually go through the drawdown they are in shock and can't handle the drawdown both financially and emotionally. This is why I want to maintain a more stringent risk approach.

Overall Risk on the Portfolio

Another overlooked aspect of risk management is overall open trade risk on a portfolio. The more open trade risk, the more potential for increased drawdowns. More so, your biggest drawdowns will probably be after one of your biggest run ups. For this reason when I invest with other trend following money managers I will only try to buy their drawdowns. I will not buy their highs and sell their lows like so many traders who do not have a plan.

I have seen this way too often.

Investors, probably out of greed, will invest with a trader when he or she has a good run. They believe it is almost safer to invest in this fashion. As trend followers do the untraditional, I look to buy successful trend followers when they have a steep drawdown. It is as if I am buying on sale. Every manager will have a drawdown and this is the time to jump on board.

Open trade equity is my open profits at any one time. I am constantly monitoring this. As I stated earlier, I let my profits run and cut my losses short. The greater the profits I have on open trade equity, the greater the risks I am allowing. I compare my open trade profits/open trade equity to my core equity. My core equity is really the true value of my account. Core equity includes my cash equity as well as closed positions. Open positions are not really mine until I close them. If I measure my risks against my core equity and my open trade equity, I am enhancing my risks. Some traders are OK with this; however, as I stated earlier, I am looking to achieve realistic returns over time, all the while controlling my risks to a manageable level.

I cap my total open trade equity versus my core equity at 20 percent of my core equity. When at times I get to that level I stop taking new positions or trades.

This mitigates to some degree the potential of drawdowns. Putting this in simple terms, considering if I have a $100,000 account size (closed equity plus core equity) and my open trade profits are $20,000, I stop taking new trades. That simple!

Additional Risk Measures When Commodity Trading and Forex Trading

Margin to Equity   Due to the leverage involved in commodity trading, I use additional levels of risk management. Margin to equity is how much margin money I need to put up versus how much equity I have in my account. I am constantly managing and monitoring my margin to equity every day. The greater the margin to equity, the greater the potential risk. My comfort level is not to surpass 15 percent margin to equity. The same holds when I invest with other trend followers. I do not like to surpass 20 percent.

The higher the margin to equity, the more positions and more potential risk!

Dollar Risk per Contract   Over the years I made one mistake after the next. I learned to risk only approximately 1 percent of my account, I learned to cap my sector risk, I learned to cap my open trade equity as well as to cap my margin to equity, but I still made a mistake. What happened was that when my account was relatively small, $100,000 or $200,000, I would risk a maximum of $2,000 a trade. The issue became apparent as my account grew over time. A 1 percent risk on a $200,000 dollar account size is $2,000 and 1 percent risk on a $500,000 account size is $5,000 for a one-lot trade.

Bearing in mind that most trades do not work, I learned that it was not prudent to risk $5,000 on a one lot. After making this mistake I added the filter to my models that I am not willing to take a trade if I am risking too much on a dollar level risk per contract. In one model of my managed accounts I cap my dollar per contract risk at $2,000 a contract and on my slightly more aggressive managed account model I cap my dollar per contract risk at $2,500.

This approach can be applied to stock market trading. You can look at not just the percentage risk but also the dollar per share risk. As there is a tremendous variance in the stock market, you need to come up with your own dollar max per share risk. My personal preference is $20 a share.

I have learned over the years that that biggest percentage trades that work come from quiet markets and from position sizing.

The smaller the risk per trade, the more shares or contracts that I can put on. The example is that for the same $1,000 risk on one trade I might put on 300 shares and on another trade I might for the same $1,000 risk put on 600 shares. Given the fact that I did not increase my total dollar risk, if the 600 shares move in the direction of the trend, I can make much more money. This is the key to position trading.

Our job as successful trend followers is to try to manage the only thing we can manage and that is the risk!

Profits take care of themselves.

I have learned over the years that anything can happen and actually will happen.

■ Choose Markets to Reduce Risk

We have boundless choices of what to trade. There are thousands of stocks and numerous currencies and commodities. Even when we have a well-thought-out plan with exact entries and exact exits it can be confusing. If we change our time frame this even offers more options.

Too many options become confusing and my goal is to simplify the trading process.

We know we cannot trade everything.

Do not trade the wrong markets!

Trade a market that is MOVING, either up or down, if you can put on a low risk. You know you should buy when the market goes up and sell when the market goes down. It is very obvious. So stay away from a market that is choppy or just moving sideways, and start trading a market with nice trends.

What I learned many years ago from Ned Davis Research, an advisor to many large hedge funds, was to look to buy the strongest trending markets and look to sell the weakest trending markets. What I learned over the years, however, was that I could not just buy the strongest or sell the weakest. I could only buy the strongest or sell the weakest if I could put on a low-risk trade. We have already discussed what a low risk trade is . . . but . . . the question becomes what is a strong or weak market?

The only way to approach it has to be quantitative. There has to be no guessing or interpreting.

The simple way I learned to do this was to look at a rate of change. Another word for rate of change is momentum. We look to measure momentum and identify a potential universe that I am open to trade. This approach is tactical. Almost like how a shark identifies the weakest of its prey. A shark does not look to attack the strongest in a pack of seals. The shark looks for a sick, frail, or young cub that is potentially an easier target. The lion also gets its prey this way as well. In a pack of bison he identifies his target. We as trend followers identify our target.

The strongest markets with the possibility they will get stronger and the weakest markets with the possibility they will get weaker.

It is just a possibility. There are no guarantees and every trade regardless of anything is 50/50.

■ We Are Dealing with Uncertainty!

As I learned over the years: **Keep it simple and stupid**. In order to determine the momentum, a simple formula is calculated between the differences between two periods. The rate of change calculation compares the current price with the price n periods ago. Depending on your degree of sensitivity you can choose that period. The rate-of-change indicator is momentum in its purest form. It measures the percentage increase or decrease in price over a given period of time.

The problem is that if you look at just one period it can distort. I prefer to look at an average of the rate of change and even look at three periods and average them. Working in this fashion, each market is assigned a numerical value. Depending on your platform or simply in Excel you can quickly identify the strongest markets and the weakest. When I am trading on a daily time frame, I look to the higher time frame of weekly markets. I use several different weekly periods to smooth out the noise.

In Metastock this is a simple code to use an indicator or it can be easily done in Excel.

```
Inputs: Price(Close), Length1(2),Length2(5),Length3(7);

Plot1(RateofChange(Price, Length1) + (RateofChange(Price, Length2)
    + (RateofChange(Price, Length3))/3));
```

Place this code on a chart. If you are looking at a group of stocks or currencies you can rank them in order to determine the strongest and the weakest components. As far as commodities they need to be nominally adjusted.

Once you determine the strongest and the weakest, this becomes your tactical portfolio or the portfolio in which you look for a signal for entry for either a long or a short.

In regard to stock investing, I use the IBD50 as a basis of stocks to look at and within this group rank the stocks by a smoothed rate of change. The IBD50 are the strongest momentum stocks based on *Investor's Business Daily* parameters based on CANSLIM[1], which mostly includes fundamental aspects but is a great place to start identifying strong stocks.

More so I look on a daily basis on 52-week new highs and new lows. This is another area of interest. In conjunction with that I look at all-time new highs and all-time new lows.

This simply becomes a general universe, and then I rank the stocks based on a smoothed rate of change. I will not try to short a stock if it is below $20 and suggest you pass as well. More so I would not look to buy stock if it is under $10. The volatility can kick up in these shares. Another area that needs to be paid attention to is volume. Make sure there is enough volume. Otherwise you can get into a very negative situation.

As another layer of risk management, even though I have risk per trade, risk per sector, open trade equity risk, and margin to equity, I look to cap my number of positions both long and short. I know that having overlapping risk management should help me in my goal of mitigating some of the inherent drawdowns. I cap the number of markets that I trade in each direction. For example, I will not trade more than 10 markets on the long side and no more than 10 markets on the short side. Again, you can determine how many depending on your risk tolerance. This is a personal preference.

As far as the S&P 500 I look to go long when the S&P 500 is above the 200 exponential day moving average. When the S&P 500 is below the S&P 200 I would be more apt to be out of the market or short.

Clearly, when one looks at some of the past big trades that worked from the IBD50, long trades can go much further to the upside while short trades have a floor. Bull markets seem to creep up over time, however, bear markets crash with thunder at times.

That is why it is very important to be aware of the 200 exponential moving average at all times.

If you are above the 200 exponential moving average the coast is clear. If you are below . . . look out and be careful!

■ Note

1. CANSLIM stands for:

   C —Current quarterly earnings per share have increased dramatically from the same quarters' earnings reported in the prior year.

   A —Annual earnings increase over the last five years.

   N —There is something new or innovative in the company such as new products, new management, and other new issues. More so it is to be noted that the company's stock has reached new absolute highs.

S —There is a small supply and large demand for a this particular stock which creates a large demand as well as there is a positive environment in which stock prices can run. Additionally look for low debt-equity ratios.

L — Look for leaders versus weaker stocks within the same industry. Use the relative strength index as a guide. Buy Strength!

I — Look for stocks with institutional support as well as that those institutions have above average performance.

M — Determining market direction by reviewing market averages daily or in my personal opinion verify that the averages are above a 200 day moving average.

CHAPTER 6

Your Complete Robust Trading Plan

Should I enter this trade?

Should I wait?

I made some money; should I take it?

I think the market will come back; I am not going to exit now with my loss!

I am sure the market will continue rising!

Shoot . . . What do I do now?

A trader with a complete robust trading plan will not ever say—or even *think*—these questions or statements. You MUST have a solid trading strategy. Having a trading strategy is probably the single most important thing you can do in order to succeed with trading. Having a trading strategy means having a predefined set of rules that you have developed or accepted for your trading. It means knowing what you're doing instead of just gambling. Too many people start off trading without a strategy, which means that they're completely unprepared.

When you have a complete, well-thought-out trading plan, you mitigate the emotional roller-coaster.

You will know exactly what you need to do! It is your job to follow the plan. **If you can't follow the plan, I strongly suggest you do not start trading.**

First, I want to be very clear that this is exactly how I approach trend following. It is not magic in any way whatsoever. It simply appeals to me as well as many others. There are other ways to trend follow besides the breakout and retracement strategies that I use. My goal is to share with you exactly what I do every workday. When a market does trend, various methodologies can work such as moving average crossovers, Bollinger breakouts, channel breakouts, or even stochastic. There is not one that is better than the other.

There is no holy grail system; rather, there is one that fits your personality.

There is no magic or perfect parameter. Be careful not to try to curve fit or make parameters something they are not. What is more important are the risk measures and the mental plan.

When you trade with a plan, you never have to worry about missing a trade. You only want to try to put on low-risk trades. If you miss a trade, it was not supposed to happen as you would be putting on too much risk.

When you trend follow with a plan, there is no fear that the U.S. dollar will crash, gold will go to $5,000, or the stock market will crash. You stand the possibility somewhere along the line of being able to put on a low-risk trade in which you should not risk more than approximately 1 percent.

I use two approaches in order to attempt to catch and ride trends. They both attempt to put on low-risk trades in the direction of a trend and have various similarities.

■ Trend Breakout and Trend Retracement

Trend Breakout

How to determine what to buy or sell. This is the key to determing the universe to trade.

Step 1: Identify the Universe

When using the trend breakout approach, I liken the thought process and trade process to the idea of a conveyor belt. All potential trades are on a conveyor belt. The first filter I use in my attempt to put on low-risk trades is to identify our universe of potential trends. This is completed by ranking all potential markets by a smoothed rate of change. This was discussed in an earlier section. We look at three rates of change periods on a higher time frame and average them together. We smooth them in order to be free of noise from sudden spikes. All markets that we look at are ranked from strongest to weakest. We want to only focus on the strongest markets with the hope that they will continue to trend and be strong, and vice versa we only want to focus on the weakest markets with the hope that they will continue to trend and be weak.

Step 1 is about identifying the strongest markets and the weakest markets.

Step 2: Look for a Trend Breakout

The idea of the trade breakout was devised by Richard Donchian decades ago. Countless trend followers have based their methodology on Richard Donchian's thinking. Some famous trend followers that have used Donchian's work are William Eckhardt and Richard Dennis from Turtle Trading fame.

The basis of this robust idea is simple: Buy the X day high and sell the Y day low.

Donchian made it very simple: Buy the 20-day high and sell the 10-day low. Richard Donchian lost virtually all of his money during the Great Depression. After analyzing what he did wrong, he came to the conclusion that he would trade with the trend breakout approach. He traded in this exact fashion for decades. I want to reiterate: DECADES!

However, trend following is not easy in any aspect, and repeatedly throughout my career over the last 18 years I have heard that trend following is dead. Even my wife at times has asked me if trend following is over. There will always be periods in which profits are elusive. Some of these periods are longer than we are comfortable with and people give up. I have seen drawdowns lasting greater than two years.

In the 1980s Richard Dennis and William Eckhardt furthered their use of the trend breakout concept when they made a bet that trend following can be taught. This real event was the basis of the movie *Trading Places* with Eddie Murphy. Richard Dennis and William Eckhardt taught a select group of traders the trend breakout approach and called them Turtles or Turtle Trading. These traders all received the same education and rules from Richard Dennis and William Eckhardt. **The learning curve only lasted two weeks.** What is most ironic is the difference in returns of the Turtles. They all had the same education, yet they invariably had different returns. There was only one reason why: how they thought and their mental processes.

Trend breakouts are simple yet extremely effective!

Remember, simple does not negate profit potentials!

A proper trend following mindset is more important for success than any methodology!

The trend breakout approach can use a multitude of variables. Richard Donchian as well as the Turtle Traders used a 20-day high with a 10-day low as the breakout for a buy and vice versa for a sell, a 20-day low with a 10-day high as the protection. The actual variable is subjective and depends on the trader. Shortening these parameters will lead to more false breakouts and extending them lessens false breakouts but gets you into trades later. There are always trade-offs when trend following.

Going back to our risk parameter, risk per trade, one measures the dollar risk from the breakout high X to the Y period low to ascertain the risk (the distance from X to Y and what each tick is worth). The trade should be passed if the dollar risk as a percentage of core equity exceeds approximately 1 percent. The idea of 1 percent is my personal opinion. There are others who are willing to entertain more risk and benefit from greater potential reward. However … I want to point out in the strongest of terms that many think they can handle the risk until they go through the inevitable drawdown. When going through this drawdown they go into shock. This is the reason I always look at how much risk I must take on in order to generate reasonable returns.

The signal is the breakout buy of X high with the risk to the Y low. The signal for a breakout sell is vice versa.

In order to calculate the 1 percent risk, you calculate the difference between the X day high to the Y day low. For example, you decide you want to use the breakout parameters of buying the 20-day high and selling the 10-day low. Remember, there are no magic number parameters, and the smaller the parameters, the more trades and more false breakouts. More so, remember that most breakouts do not work and you might be increasing the likelihood of more trades not working. Contrarily, if you use a lower parameter, you will enter earlier and have greater potential profits. Again, there is no free lunch. To further present, for example, the 20-day or X day high you decide on is 20 and the 10-day low or Y low is 16, the difference is 4. You do not want to risk more than 1 percent. For example, you have a $100,000 account and you want to risk only 1 percent or $1,000; therefore you can put on 250 shares. Another point to consider: I would pass if the per share risk was too high. Again, that is a personal decision and there is no exact parameter. It is a number you are comfortable with. More so, in many trading platforms this calculation can be automatic.

In Step 2, you confirm the breakout risk is not more than 1 percent of your core account size; if it is, go to the next step.

Step 3: Trade in the Direction of the MACD

In virtually every trading program or Internet chart software there is a momentum indicator called the MACD. As part of our conveyor belt of trading ideas, I will only consider taking the buy or sell if I am trading in both in the direction of the trend of the MACD. For a buy, I want the MACD to be above the zero line and positively increasing. For a sell, I want the MACD to be below the zero line and negatively decreasing.

Figure 6.1 depicts Google. In this chart, we are buying an X period high, and this is confirmed in the MACD by being above the zero line and increasing.

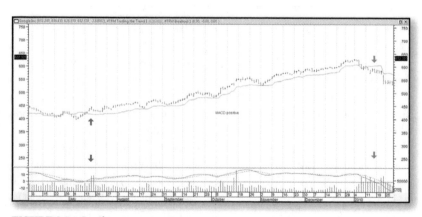

FIGURE 6.1 Google
MetaStock®. Copyright© 2012 Thomson Reuters. All rights reserved.

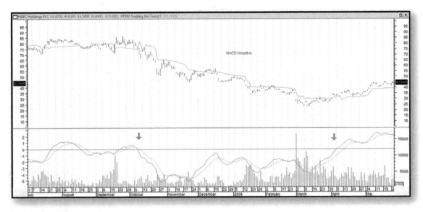

FIGURE 6.2 HSBS

In Figure 6.2, showing HSBC, we would be selling an X period low. We are confirming with the trend that we are currently in a downtrend by the MACD being negative and below the zero line.

In Figure 6.3, showing Leucadia, the downtrend is confirmed by the MACD being below the zero line and decreasing. We would have sold the X period low and follow the trend.

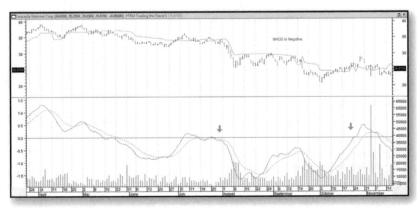

FIGURE 6.3 Leucadia

Figure 6.4 shows a chart of Netflix, in which we are trading with the trend confirmed by the MACD above the zero line and increasing. We would have bought an X period high to see what would happen.

FIGURE 6.4 Netflix

Step 3 is about trading only in the direction of the MACD. If long, confirm you are above the zero line. If short, confirm you are below the zero line.

Step 4: Limit the Number of Trades in Each Direction

As another filter in order to attempt to mitigate some of the inherent drawdowns, I limit the maximum number of positions I will have at any one point. I have overlapping levels of protection. Again, the number of positions of longs and shorts is subjective. I personally do not want more than 10 longs or 10 shorts at any time. The more positions, the more risk. Going down my conveyor belt idea, I will not take the trade even if the other prior parameters hit if this upcoming trade will put me over 10.

So for Step 4, do not exceed more than 10 longs and 10 shorts. Now on to Step 5.

Step 5: When Trading Commodity Futures Contracts Limit the Maximum Dollar Risk per Contract

As another layer of risk management, limit your total dollar risk per contract. What I experienced was that as my account size grew, 1 percent of $200,000 is a $2,000 risk per contract. However, when my account grew over the years, 1 percent risk on a $500,000 account became a $5,000 risk. As we know that most trades do not work, in my opinion that was too much risk to take. Therefore, I limit my dollar risk per contract. If the risk exceeds my levels, I do not take the trade.

Step 5 says not to take a commodity trade if the dollar risk exceeds $2,500 a contract, regardless of account size.

Step 6: Maximum Risk per Sector

Over the last 18 years I have made repeated mistakes. One of the most glaring mistakes has been allocating too much to a particular sector. Regardless, if I am only taking a small risk per trade when they are concentrated I open myself up to increased risks. What happened was that I would get a signal in the interest rates. They all seemed low risk with risk per trade of approximately 1 percent. However, due to their concentration, I ended up with big drawdowns. I limit my exposure per sector to a maximum risk of 5 percent of my portfolio.

I will not take a trade if I surpass this risk per sector. Sectors are prevalent in the stock market as well as the commodity markets. To further clarify, I will not take another trade in tech stocks, for instance, if my total risk in tech stocks was 5 percent, or if I had an exposure to the grains—wheat, corn, soymeal, soybeans, and so on—that was 5 percent, I would pass on the trade that would put me over this threshold.

Do not take the trade if you have already allocated 5 percent of your account in that sector.

Step 7: Maximum Risk on Total Portfolio

Before I take a new position I verify that I will not surpass a total open trade risk versus my core equity. The reason for this is that the more open positions, the more risk I am taking on.

I have learned over the years that my biggest drawdowns are during periods in which I have the greatest amount of open trade profits. When I get to a point when I have 20 percent open trade profits compared to my core equity, I will take a new trade. This is an attempt to mitigate big drawdowns.

This is very easy to calculate. I simply divide my open profits by my core equity. My core equity is my original equity and closed profits. For example, if I have a current account size of $100,000, I would not let my open trade equity or open equity increase more than $20,000. One could tighten the stops by adjusting the ATR volatility stop or take profits. There is no wrong or right answer. The answer is dependent on your risk tolerance.

Do not take the trade if you have already have 20 percent of your total core equity in open profits.

Quick review of the seven steps to take before entering any trade:

1. Identify the strongest markets and the weakest markets. These should be the only markets in which you look for a trade.

2. When you get a breakout signal, confirm that the breakout risk is not more than 1 percent of your core account size; if so, go to the next step.

3. Trade only in the direction of the MACD. If long, confirm you are above the zero line. If short, confirm you are below the zero line.

4. Do not exceed more than 10 longs and 10 shorts.

5. Do not take a commodity trade if the dollar risk exceeds $2,500 a contract regardless of account size.

6. Do not take the trade if you have already allocated 5 percent of your account in that sector.

7. Do not take the trade if you have already have 20 percent of your total core equity in open profits.

If you have passed all of these criteria, then you can take the trade and see what happens. Do not expect the trade to work.

Any trade is 50/50.

Now that you are in the trade you need to protect yourself and follow the trade if it works.

Stops

You need to protect yourself since most trades do not work. I do this by the usage of two stops. My first stop is my hard stop or initial stop.

If I am long my predefined risk is the Y period low, and if I am short my predefined risk is the X period high.

As an example, if I use parameters such as a 20-day high and a 10-day low, my initial hard stop is the 10-day low. I count back 10 bars and that is my maximum risk level. I do not vacillate! Most trading programs include this feature (lowest low for Y periods or highest high for X periods). The Y day low stop is immediately entered into the market once I have been filled. I do not change it if the price gets close to it. This stop is set in stone. If the stop is hit, then I exit with a small loss and move on to the next trade, no big deal!

On another tangent one can offset these stops slightly by a small parameter, but this is a personal preference and not totally necessary.

An important point from an earlier section is that the last trade has no bearing on the upcoming trade. Every trade is 50/50 and statistically independent. You must take every trade—you cannot pick and choose because you do not know the future!

■ If the Trade Starts Working

If the trade starts working, meaning it starts moving away from my initial hard stop, then the next following or trailing stop kicks in: the ATR trailing stop. There is no perfect indicator; however, I prefer the trailing ATR stop as a trailing stop method.

The ATR stop is based on average true range. Average true range was developed by J. Welles Wilder as an indicator that measures volatility. Welles Wilder developed his concept called true range (TR), which is defined as the greatest of the following:

- Method 1: Current high less the current low.

- Method 2: Current high less the previous close (absolute value).

- Method 3: Current low less the previous close (absolute value).

For those of you who would like to understand the background of the ATR trailing stop, the basic premise is in measuring the distance between two points, not the direction. If the current period's high is above the prior period's high and the low is below the prior period's low, then the current period's high-low range will be used as the true range. This is an outside day that would use Method 1 to calculate the true range. This is pretty straightforward. Methods 2 and 3 are used when there is a gap or an inside day. A gap occurs when the previous close is greater than the current high (signaling a potential gap down or limit move) or the previous close is lower than the current low (signaling a potential gap up or limit move).

Figure 6.5 shows examples when methods 2 and 3 are appropriate.

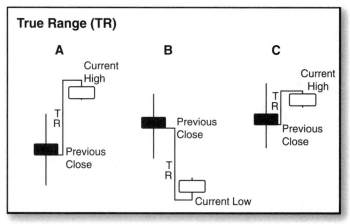

FIGURE 6.5 True Range

Example A: A small high/low range formed after a gap up. The TR equals the absolute value of the difference between the current high and the previous close.

Example B: A small high/low range formed after a gap down. The TR equals the absolute value of the difference between the current low and the previous close.

Example C: Even though the current close is within the previous high/low range, the current high/low range is quite small. In fact, it is smaller than the absolute value of the difference between the current high and the previous close, which is used to value the true range.

■ The Calculation of Average True Range

Basically, the average true range (ATR) is based on X periods, which can be calculated on any period such as intraday (for day traders), a daily, weekly, or monthly basis. For this example, the ATR will be based on daily data. Because there must be a beginning, the first true range value is simply the high minus the low, and the first 14-day ATR is the average of the daily TR values for the last 14 days. After that, Wilder sought to smooth the data by incorporating the previous period's ATR value. The ATR value as well as breakout highs and lows are subjective. I personally like to look at a much longer period. I use a 39 period. I give the trade more room with this parameter, but again there is no magic number.

Most charting packages have average true range and average true range stops built in so there is no need to manually calculate either the average true range or ATR stop.

The trailing ATR stop continually makes adjustments to make sure that the stop is moved in your favor. The ATR stop trails the progress when there is a trend yet gives the trade enough room to work. The ATR trailing stop is one way to limit losses and protect profits. A stop-loss order is set a multiple of the average true range (ATR) away from the current price. If the price moves in the trade's favor, the stop follows along. As with all trailing stops, the ATR trailing stop never exits at the high or a low of a trade. You will always give back some of the profits.

Only liars get out at the highs or lows of a trade.

Giving back part of your profits is reality and nothing to fear.

The real hard part of using an average true range stop is where the need for a proper mindset is paramount. One needs both the patience and discipline to see what happens and let the trade unfold both with a potential profit as well as a potential loss. Many traders get nervous when a trade does not start to work and simply exit.

They did not follow the plan.

To their astonishment after they exit, the trade starts trending. Then there are those who see open profit and cannot contain themselves and want to grab that profit. The problem with that is possibly the trend continues and they did not follow their plan. You need these rare big winners to offset all the small losses you will encounter. You need to believe in the plan. As simple as it is, it is robust and can give you the power to compound money over time.

Simple proprietary robust ideas that I use in my daily trading with a strong measure of risk as well the proper mindset are the pillars of successful trend following.

Trend Retracement Rules

The concept of trend retracement can be applied in various ways. There are times when for numerous reasons you are not in a trade, you prefer the trend retracement to the trend breakout, or you want to increase your position by pyramiding. There is no right or wrong and each has its own set of rules. The basis is the same; you are **trading with the trend and you are only taking low-risk trades.**

The reality is also the same that you will have many trades that simply do not work. You will have small losses, small profits, and rare big winners. This is trend following. For aggressive traders you even want to pyramid. Pyramiding is adding to positions. This is a personal issue and left to the discretion of the trader. Greater profits can be created as well as greater drawdowns. It is important to bear in mind that there is a drawdown out there that can stop you from trading.

Just Do It

I know many aspiring traders who have read countless books, have learned or developed their own trading strategies, and who have analyzed a number of markets; but they've failed to pull the trigger when it comes to real-time trading. As you know, part of your education is your knowledge and your experience. If you want to make money with trading, then eventually you have to take the plunge and get started.

CHAPTER 7

Trend Breakouts

R emember that hypothetical trades have severe limitations and are used for educational purposes only. The following examples are hypothetical and should not be utilized to provide historical data or make real-life predictions.

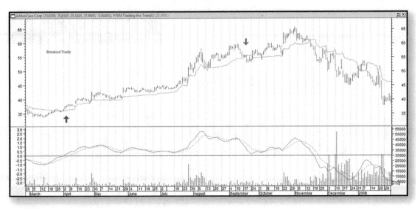

FIGURE 7.1 ArthroCare Corporation

MetaStock®. Copyright© 2012 Thomson Reuters. All rights reserved.

■ ArthroCare Corporation

ArthroCare Corporation was a high-momentum stock that was one of the strongest at the time of the signal (Figure 7.1). Going through the conveyor belt of checklist items, it hit all the criteria.

Review

1. Strongest via smoothed rate of change.

2. Not more than 1 percent risk of total account size.

3. MACD positive and above zero line.

4. Not more than 5 percent of the portfolio was allocated to health care and medical appliances.

5. Did not have 20 percent open trade equity versus core equity.

6. Experienced a breakout trade of X days.

7. No more than 10 longs at the time.

8. After entry the shares started to progress and the hard stop of Y days ago was replaced by the average true range stop. This trade worked; however, as discussed repeatedly, most trades will not work.

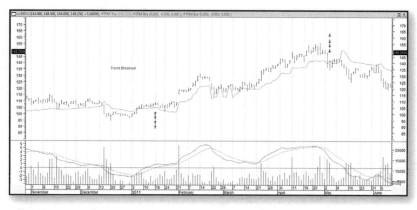

FIGURE 7.2 Baidu

MetaStock®. Copyright© 2012 Thomson Reuters. All rights reserved.

▉ Baidu

Baidu (Figure 7.2) is a Chinese Web services and search engine company that is often likened to Google.

Review

1. Strongest.

2. Not more than 1 percent risk of total account size.

3. MACD positive and above zero line.

4. Not more than 5 percent of the portfolio was allocated to China or Internet.

5. Did not have 20 percent open trade equity versus core equity.

6. Experienced a breakout trade of X days.

7. No more than 10 longs at the time.

8. After entry the shares started to progress and the hard stop of Y days ago was replaced by the average true range stop. This trade worked; however, as discussed repeatedly, most trades will not work. The reason I wanted to present this idea was to show the patience that is needed in order to succeed. Those who were not patient or disciplined and did not let the trade work would lose. The average true range stop is not perfect as any methodology is not perfect but does a very good job keeping you in trades when they work. More so, the average true range also is good to get you out of trades that do not work.

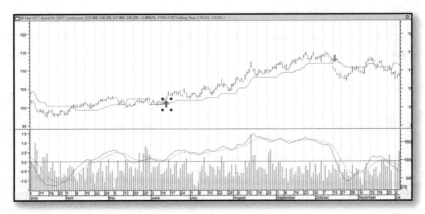

FIGURE 7.3   30-Year U.S. Government Bond
MetaStock®. Copyright© 2012 Thomson Reuters. All rights reserved.

■ The 30-Year U.S. Government Bond

Typically, U.S. government bonds (Figure 7.3) are considered safe long-term investments.

1. Strongest via smoothed rate of change.

2. Not more than 1 percent risk of total account size.

3. MACD positive and above zero line.

4. Not more than 5 percent of the portfolio was allocated to interest rates or government bonds.

5. Did not have 20 percent open trade equity versus core equity.

6. Experienced a breakout trade of X days.

7. No more than 10 longs at the time.

8. We have an additional check when trading futures that the dollar risk per contract does not exceed $2,000.

9. After entry the contract started to progress and the hard stop of Y days ago was replaced by the average true range stop. This trade worked; however, as discussed repeatedly, most trades will not work.

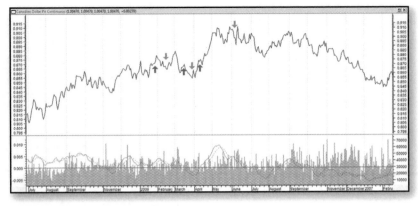

FIGURE 7.4 The Canadian Dollar

■ The Canadian Dollar

I selected this example to exemplify the reality of trend following. In the prior examples I presented many trades that worked. However, in the real world this is not the case as there will be many trades in which you will have small losses, small profits, and on rare times big profits. Figure 7.4 is a great presentation for this.

You will see the first trade was a loss (dashed lines). The second trade also was a loss. However, the third trade was a profit. Successful trend followers take every trade. They have no idea if the trade will work or not. They just keep on putting on low-risk trades and then see what happens. They have the patience to let the trades work over time as long as they are working.

1. Strongest via smoothed rate of change.

2. Not more than 1 percent risk of total account size.

3. MACD positive and above zero line.

4. Not more than 5 percent of the portfolio was allocated to currencies.

5. Did not have 20 percent open trade equity versus core equity.

6. Experienced a breakout trade of X days.

7. No more than 10 longs at the time.

8. We have an additional check when trading futures that the dollar risk per contract does not exceed $2,000.

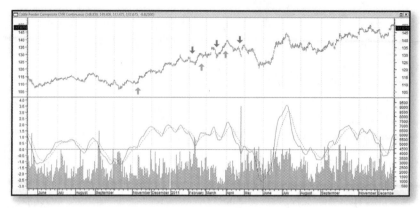

FIGURE 7.5   Feeder Cattle
MetaStock®. Copyright© 2012 Thomson Reuters. All rights reserved.

■ Feeder Cattle

Feeder cattle, shown in Figure 7.5, is an interesting example. The first trade worked and there was a profit. What I have seen from inexperienced traders is that they would debate taking the next signal thinking that possibly the trade couldn't go higher. They could have been reinforced with this wrong thinking when the trade did not work. It did not work not just once but twice! Two small losses followed. However, on the next trade the feeder cattle trade started working. *The point here is that we must be disciplined 110 percent when trend following. We must take every signal. We do not know the future. Anything can happen.* The only thing in our control is how we approach risk. This is why risk management is so important.

Reviewing the trade thought process . . .

1. Strongest via smoothed rate of change.

2. Not more than 1 percent risk of total account size.

3. MACD positive and above zero line.

4. Not more than 5 percent of the portfolio was allocated to meats.

5. Did not have 20 percent open trade equity versus core equity.

6. Experienced a breakout trade of X days.

7. No more than 10 longs at the time.

8. We have an additional check when trading futures that the dollar risk per contract does not exceed $2,000.

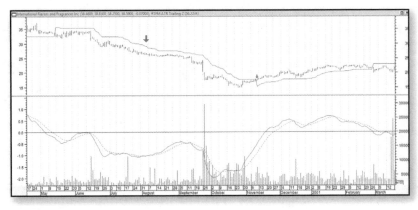

FIGURE 7.6 Short Trade Example

International Flavors and Fragrances

Figure 7.6 is an example of a short trade.

The concept I want to show is that money can be made both in bull markets and bear markets. It does not matter. The key is to put on low-risk trades. Have the discipline and patience to put the trades on when you have a signal, and when/if they work, have the patience to follow them via the average true range stops. This trade was for 70 bars or days. Too often greed sets in and traders want to take the quick profits. However, as Jesse Livermore pointed out, the greatest profits are made by doing nothing and being patient.

Another point is that it does not matter if you are trading daily bars or hourly bars. The concepts that I have presented are viable on all time frames.

1. Weakest via smoothed rate of change.

2. Not more than 1 percent risk of total account size.

3. MACD negative and below zero line.

4. Not more than 5 percent of the portfolio was allocated to specialty chemicals.

5. Did not have 20 percent open trade equity versus core equity.

6. Experienced a breakout trade of X days.

7. No more than 10 shorts at the time.

8. After entry the shares started to progress and the hard stop of Y days ago was replaced by the average true range stop. This trade worked; however, as discussed repeatedly, most trades will not work.

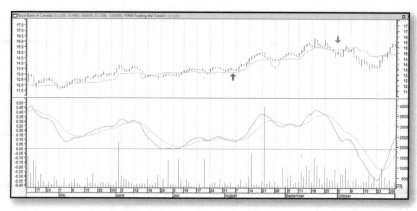

FIGURE 7.7 Royal Bank of Canada

▆ Royal Bank of Canada

Figure 7.7 is another stock example, this time examining the Royal Bank of Canada.

You never know how long a trade will continue. You need to be flexible in expectations and rigid in your rules. This hypothetical trade lasted for 36 bars. When the trades work, we want to be taken out only by the average true range stop. If the trade does not work, we have our hard stop, which is our Y day's stop, which protects it, and if the trade does start working, we simply follow it and follow our rules. The rules are very simple yet robust and powerful.

1. Strongest via smoothed rate of change.

2. Not more than 1 percent risk of total account size.

3. MACD positive and above zero line.

4. Not more than 5 percent of the portfolio was allocated to banking sector.

5. Did not have 20 percent open trade equity versus core equity.

6. Experienced a breakout trade of X days.

7. No more than 10 longs at the time.

8. After entry the shares started to progress and the hard stop of Y days ago was replaced by the average true range stop. This trade worked; however, as discussed repeatedly, most trades will not work.

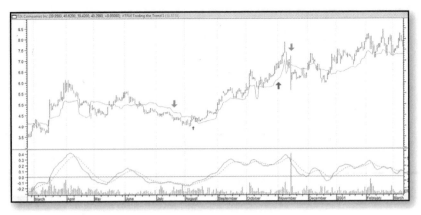

FIGURE 7.8 TJX Companies

■ TJX Companies

The TJX Companies trade is a great example of being flexible and still having trades not work. As you can see, there was a short. This short trade did not work and a small loss was incurred. Luckily the short was covered as the shares rallied and big losses could have been incurred. Several months later a buy signal was received. As Murphy's Law would have it, the trade did not work after a short period of time. Traders at this point would have experienced two small losses in a row and frustration could set in. There is nothing to get upset about.

This is the trend shown in Figure 7.8. You will have countless losses. If you can't take the losses, you should not trend follow. The most important reason for your potential success is how you think or your mental state. You have to just keep on putting on the trades and follow the plan. Hopefully at this point you have internalized that anything can happen. You will have rare big profits at times. You need to have the patience to let them work. These big rare profits more than make up for ALL the losses you will incur. This is why the losses need to be kept small.

Successful trend following boils down to having a simple and robust plan, strong discipline, and the patience to let it work over time.

There will be long periods when you do not make money. At this point you will question yourself and ask yourself if trend following does not work anymore. I can tell you from my own personal experience, I have been there, but the years of successful trading have reinforced me. In addition, there have been generations of successful trend followers. Richard Donchian trend followed for decades.

If Richard Donchian can do it,

If the dentist can do it,

So can you!

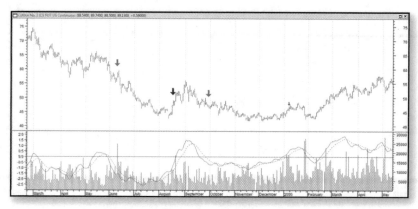

FIGURE 7.9   Cotton Trade Example

■ Cotton Trade

You can see in Figure 7.9 there are two short trades. Initially on the first short one could have gotten nervous. The short was entered and almost immediately the trade reversed. An inexperienced trader or a trader who is not following the exact plan could have panicked and closed the position. However, the trade soon reversed and started moving in the direction of the short. When we are trend following in the proprietary methodology I am teaching, you have two seatbelts to protect you, so there should not be any fear. When you drive a car you wear a seatbelt and do not have fear! You need to believe in the viability of the plan and mostly understand this is not a get rich quick overnight plan.

It is truly a marathon and takes a great deal of endurance to get through all the periods that are very tough and all the trades that do not work.

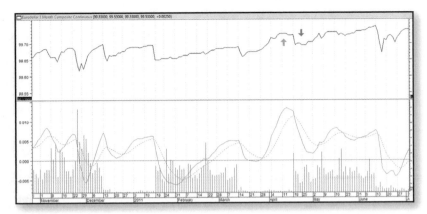

FIGURE 7.10 Eurodollar Chart

■ Eurodollar Chart

Figure 7.10 is interesting. The question can come up why the trade seemed to have occurred late. It would have seemed that the trade hit the X day high yet the trade was hit.

This is a hypothetical example but there will be many reasons in the real world. It could have been that you had more than 10 longs at the time and you did not have permission to take the trade. Maybe one of those longs exited and you had a slot open. Another reason could have been that you exceeded your sector risk of 5 percent. You were allowed to take this trade because another trade in that sector dropped out. Another possible situation could have been that you had too much open trade equity versus your core equity. (Do not take trades when you have 20 percent OTE versus your core equity.)

The irony could be that once you finally do enter, almost immediately the trade does not work and incurs a loss. This is trend following. We do not know the future. Most trades do not work! We take low-risk bets and put ourselves in a position to be carried in when trades do actually work. Forget about the concept of win percentages. What is critical for your success is the profit percentage when the trades do work.

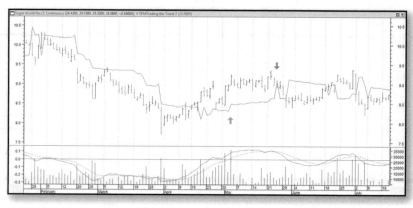

FIGURE 7.11 Sugar Example

◼ Sugar

See Figure 7.11 for a commodity example dealing with sugar.

Many times when we are trend following we will have initial profits. However, we give the trade enough room to work via the average true range stop we utilize. In the real world, there will be countless times when you have some small initial profit; however, you end up giving up some of it and, at best, having a small profit. The other reality, however, is that in the real world there will be times that these small open profits even turn into small losses. This is the price we as trend followers have to pay in order to put ourselves in a position over time to compound money.

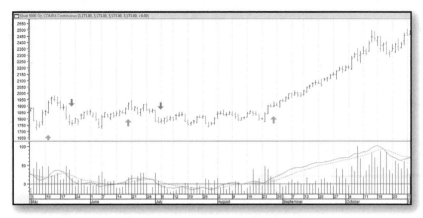

FIGURE 7.12 Silver Example
MetaStock®. Copyright© 2012 Thomson Reuters. All rights reserved.

■ Silver

An interesting example of the necessity of taking every trade is exemplified with the silver chart shown in Figure 7.12. As you can vividly see, you had two small losses one after the other (green vertical lines). If you had not followed the plan and taken the third trade, you would have beaten yourself up. This is why you need to take every trade without question. Neither you nor I know the future. Forget about all the so-called analysts and gurus. They do not know the future either. The only thing we know is that we will have numerous small losses, numerous small profits, and at rare times big profits of trades that surpass our expectations.

With my help as your mentor you will be consistent. Consistent does not mean every trade has to work. Consistent means you follow the plan and let the odds work over time.

CHAPTER 8

Trend
Retracements

As for trend breakouts, there are seven basic rules you must follow for trend re-tracements.

1. Identify the strongest markets and the weakest markets via a smoothed rate of change. These should be the only markets where you look for a trade.

2. When you get a trend breakout signal, confirm the breakout risk is not more than 1 percent of your core account size; if so, go to the next step. In most cases I risk even less personally.

3. Trade only in the direction of the MACD. If long, confirm you are above the zero line. If short, confirm you are below the zero line.

4. Do not exceed more than 10 longs and 10 shorts.

5. Do not take a commodity trade if the dollar risk exceeds $2,500 a contract regardless of account size.

6. Do not take the trade if you have already allocated 5 percent of your account in that sector.

7. Do not take the trade if you have already have 20 percent of your total core equity in open profits.

We have some additional parameters that I have added. Throughout my career many trend followers have used the concept of multiple time frames. Trend followers from David Harding from Winton to Don Steinitz to Alexander Elder are proponents of multiple time frames. *You want to be in sync with a time frame one step higher.*

For example, if you are trading daily bars, you want to look at the weekly bars direction. If you are day trading and trading hourly bars, you want to look at daily bars to determine trend direction.

Don Steinitz's Approach

Don Steinitz's approach, discussed in "Improving the Odds by Trading Multiple Time Frames" article, is very clear. He presents the laws of multiple time frames, as outlined below:

- Every time frame has its own structure.

- The higher time frames overrule the lower time frames.

- Prices in the lower time frame structure tend to respect the energy points of the higher time frame structure.

- The energy points of support/resistance created by the higher time frame's vibration (prices) can be validated by the action of lower time periods.

- The trend created by the next time period enables us to define the tradable trend.

- What appears to be chaos in one time period can be order in another time period.[1]

Alexander Elder's Approach

Elder's approach is similar. He looks for retracements within the larger trend. His methodology is called the triple screen and is a good basis for a trend follower to use as well as his Force Index for retracements.

However, in order to complete the whole trading plan, I strongly suggest adding the risk management rules that I have been referring to throughout thisbook.

Step 1: Identify the Trend on the Higher Time Frame

One of the easiest ways to identify the trend on the higher time frame is to use the weekly MACD. You can see, quantitatively or numerically, the increase or decrease in the MACD. As well, you can also use a 20-period exponential moving average. Either way, it is your personal preference. The premise is to easily identify the trend on the higher time frame. It should be easily visible.

Examples of Trend Retracement

An Example of Trend Retrecements are demonstrated in this weekly crude oil chart.

Weekly Crude Oil   On the weekly chart shown in Figure 8.1 you see, even from a distance, a strong downtrend.

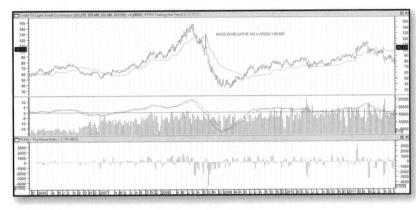

FIGURE 8.1   Strong Downtrend in the Weekly Chart
MetaStock®. Copyright© 2012 Thomson Reuters. All rights reserved.

The MACD is negative and below the zero line. The trend is down.

Daily Crude Oil   On the daily crude chart in Figure 8.2, you will notice the MACD is below the zero line and negative. Highlighted with the red arrows are points in time when crude is retraced. On the second pane is an indicator called the Elder Force Index. This oscillator demonstrates the pullback. These retracements become potential entry points to get in with the trend if these pullbacks fail and the trend continues negatively.

Weekly Yen   As you can see, from late 2005 till 2007 the yen was in a strong downtrend (Figure 8.3). This is evidenced by the MACD being below zero.

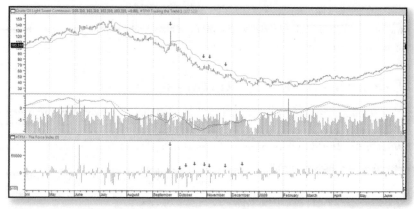

FIGURE 8.2 Daily Crude Oil

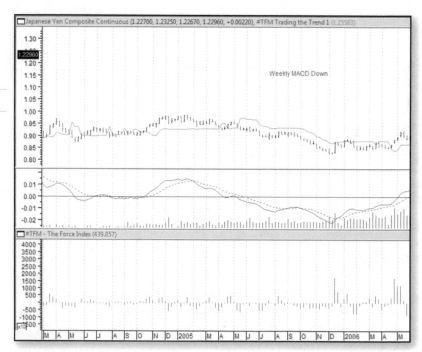

FIGURE 8.3 Weekly Yen

Daily Yen You will notice on the daily chart in Figure 8.4 that in June, July, and September there were some strong upward retracements on the weekly charts. These are potential entry points. It is not known if the trend is ending or if this was a retracement. These retracements can be used for possible trend short entries.

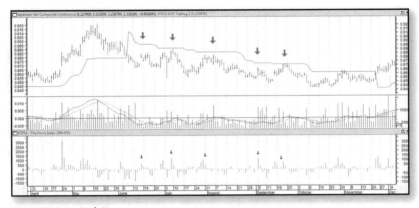

FIGURE 8.4 Daily Yen

Weekly Royal Bank of Canada You can see from Figure 8.5 that in 2011 there was a strong downtrend noted by the MACD.

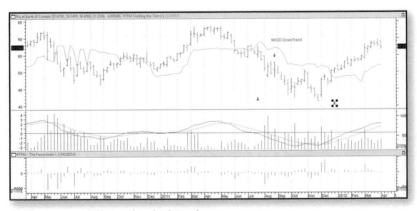

FIGURE 8.5 Weekly Royal Bank of Canada

Daily Royal Bank of Canada   You will notice within the downtrend there were some retracements as noted by the down arrows (Figure 8.6). Furthermore, you can look at the middle retracement oscillator indicator for moves above the zero line. These were potential entry points to go short.

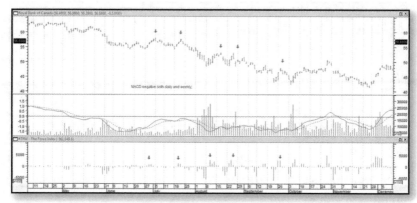

FIGURE 8.6   Daily Royal Bank of Canada
MetaStock®. Copyright© 2012 Thomson Reuters. All rights reserved.

Weekly Sugar   Sugar was in a strong uptrend as evidenced by the weekly MACD, shown in Figure 8.7.

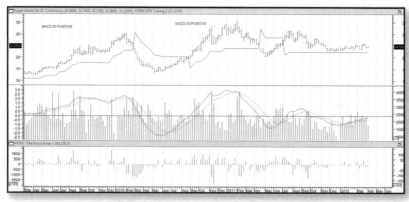

FIGURE 8.7   Weekly Sugar
MetaStock®. Copyright© 2012 Thomson Reuters. All rights reserved.

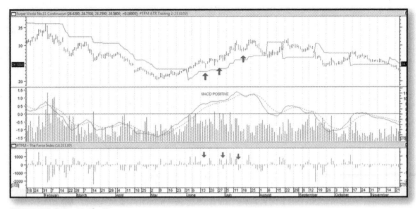

FIGURE 8.8   Daily Sugar

Daily Sugar   As noted by the up arrows in Figure 8.8, there were pullbacks on a daily chart. Note on the retracement oscillator points in which it fell below the zero line (August and October). These were potential points at which to start looking for a long trade.

■ Step 2: Identify the Retracement/Pullback

The basis is that if you are looking for a **long trade,** you want to see that on the higher time frame it is trending positively, yet on the lower time frame there is a pullback and slight downtrend. This retracement is identified by the Oscillator Rec indicator crossing the zero line and becoming negative.

Identify Long Buy Potential

Look for a weekly MACD that is positive and above the zero line.

Daily there is a pullback via the retracement oscillator when it crosses below the zero line.

Identify Short Sell Potential

Look for a weekly MACD that is negative and below the zero line.

Daily there is a pullup via the retracement oscillator when it crosses above the zero line.

The concept is similar to waves at the seashore. Within the tides you have big waves and then inside of them smaller counterwaves or tides. We want to trade with the trend and look to enter on these retracements with a low-risk trade.

These are the indications you look for in a retracement trade due to the pull-back for a long and pullup for a short. You never know if it is just a retracement or if it is a change in trend. **No one ever rings a bell to tell you there is a change in trend.** You need to ask yourself how much you are willing to lose to see if the trade will work.

■ Step 3: Putting the Trade On

As we do not know if the trend is reversing or retracing, we want to be pulled into the trade *if* it starts retracing back in the direction of the trend as identified on the higher time frame.

For Buys

We put in a buy stop one tick or .001 percent above the high of the prior two bars. We want the market to show us it wants to continue back in the direction of the higher time frame. If prices continue to fall, our buy stop will not be filled. If we do not get filled, then on the next bar put the buy stop one tick or .001 percent above the high of the prior two bars. We continue lowering our buy stop at each bar until either we are stopped in or if on the higher time frame the MACD reverses and our buy stop is cancelled.

Baidu   Baidu was in an uptrend on the weekly bars, yet there was a pullback on the daily toward the end of February (Figure 8.9). Note on the Retracement Osc indicator

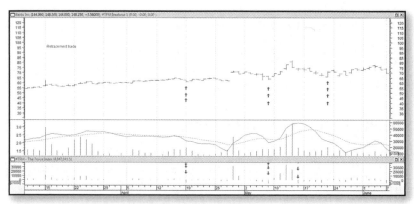

FIGURE 8.9   Baidu Shares Retracement Buy
MetaStock®. Copyright© 2012 Thomson Reuters. All rights reserved.

toward the end of February the Retracement Osc turned negative as noted from two red bars. For two consecutive days we tried to enter the trend. Eventually, when the trend resumed, we were pulled into the trade.

Sugar Sugar was in an uptrend on the weekly bars yet had a pullback (Figure 8.10). We were looking to go long. We kept on moving the buy stop until we were pulled back into the trade.

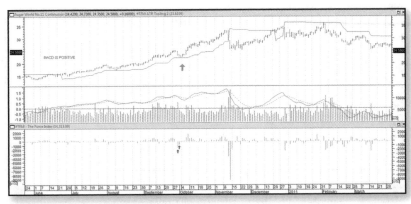

FIGURE 8.10   Sugar Buy
MetaStock®. Copyright© 2012 Thomson Reuters. All rights reserved.

CMG CMG was up on the weekly (Figure 8.11). CMG had a pullback on the daily bars toward the end of July as noted by the Retracement Osc indicator. We looked to go long and set up our buy stops until filled.

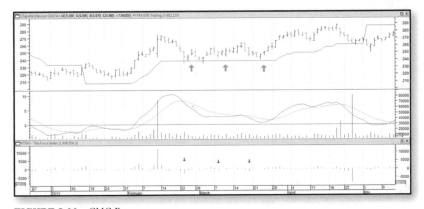

FIGURE 8.11   CMG Buy
MetaStock®. Copyright© 2012 Thomson Reuters. All rights reserved.

Gold Gold was in an uptrend on the weekly bars (Figure 8.12). There was a pullback on the daily bars around the beginning of May. We wanted to see if we could go long. We kept on lowering our buy stops until we were pulled into a trade. There were other points if we wanted to pyramid our positions (put on additional contracts); however, this increases both our risks and our drawdowns.

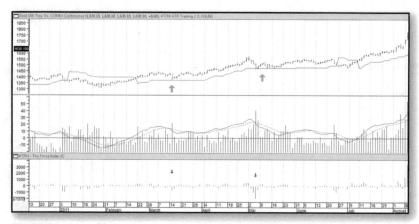

FIGURE 8.12 Gold Buy
MetaStock®. Copyright© 2012 Thomson Reuters. All rights reserved.

130

THE TREND FOLLOWING BIBLE

Netflix Toward the end of February Netflix started to pull back on the daily bars (Figure 8.13). The weekly was up and we wanted to put on a long trade. We noted the Retracement Osc turned negative and looked to jump in. We were taken long by the noted arrow.

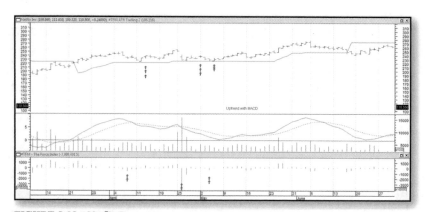

FIGURE 8.13 Netflix Buy
MetaStock®. Copyright© 2012 Thomson Reuters. All rights reserved.

For Sells

We put in a sell stop one tick or .001 percent below the low of the prior two bars. We want the market to show us it wants to continue back in the direction of the higher time frame. If prices continue to rise, our sell stop will not be filled. If we do not get filled, then on the next bar put the sell stop one tick or .001 percent above the low of the prior two bars. We continue raising our sell stop at each bar until either we are stopped in or if on the higher time frame the MACD reverses and our sell stop is cancelled.

Netflix   Netflix was in a severe downtrend on the weekly (Figure 8.14). There was a retracement as noted in the Retracement Osc turning positive around November with one bar. We started looking to go short. We kept on moving our sell short stop until we were pulled into the trade.

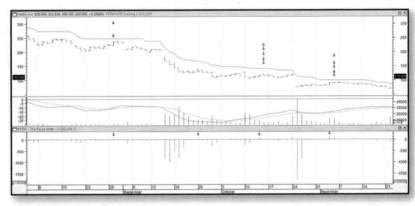

FIGURE 8.14   Netflix
MetaStock®. Copyright© 2012 Thomson Reuters. All rights reserved.

Crude Oil   In the fall of 2008 crude was in a huge selloff. On the weekly charts the trend was down; however, every time the Retracement Osc crossed the zero line to the upside a potential short trade was available (Figure 8.15). The actual short entry was a sell stop at the one tick below the two bars low.

Eurodollar   The trend on the Eurodollar on the weekly was negative (Figure 8.16). As evidenced by the Retracement Osc indicator when it crossed the zero line, we had a potential short trade. We would sell one tick below the low of a two-day bar. As you can see, this was a choppy period in which several of the trades did not work.

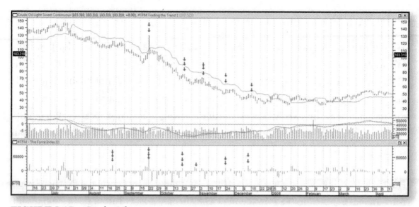

FIGURE 8.15 Crude Oil

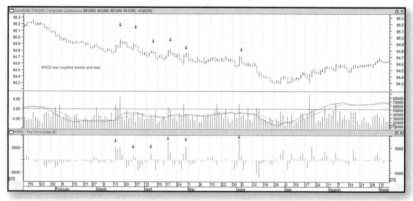

FIGURE 8.16 Eurodollar

Royal Bank of Canada   On the weekly chart RY was in a downtrend as evidenced by the weekly MACD (Figure 8.17). On the daily there were retracements as evidenced in the Retracement Osc that crossed the zero line. Each of these times a potential sell short was presented. A sell short was put at one tick below the two day low.

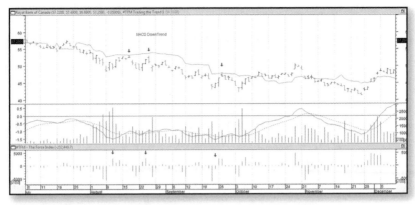

FIGURE 8.17   Royal Bank of Canada

■ Summary

The summary of our discussion on trend retracement trades is as follows:

- ■ Identify the strongest markets and the weakest markets via the average rate of change. These should be the only markets in which you look for a trade.

- ■ Trade only in the direction of the higher term MACD to determine the trend. If the higher term MACD is above the zero line and increasing, you want to be long. If the higher term MACD is below the zero line and decreasing, you want to be short.

- ■ For long trades look at the lower time frame bar that on the Elder Force–Retracement Osc bars fell below the zero line and are negative. For short trades look at the lower time frame bar that on the Elder Force–Retracement Osc bars rose above the zero line and are positive.

- ■ For long trades put in buy stop orders at one tick or .001 percent above the two-bar high. Keep on raising your buy stop orders at each following bar until you are stopped in or until the higher time frame MACD turns negative and cancel the buy stop. For short trades put in sell stop orders at one tick or .001 percent below the two-bar low. Keep on lowering your sell stop orders at each following bar until you are stopped in or until the higher time frame MACD turns positive and cancels the sell stop.

- Do not exceed more than 10 longs and 10 shorts.

- Do not risk more than 1 percent on any trade as determined by the hard stop.

- Do not take a commodity trade if the dollar risk exceeds $2,500 a contract regardless of account size.

- Do not take the trade if you have already allocated 5 percent of your account in that sector.

- Do not take the trade if you have already have 20 percent of your total core equity in open profits.

■ Protect Yourself

Now that you are in the trade, you need to protect yourself.

As in the case of the trend breakout we use two stops for our protection. We use a hard stop and if the trade starts working, we replace it with the average true range Stop, which adjusts for volatility.

For Buys

For buys the hard stop is one tick or .001 percent above the two-bar low. I prefer to use the parameter two-bar as if the trade is going to work I will be pulled into the trade. I have tried the one-bar and it has resulted in many whipsaw trades. It is too sensitive. In order to determine the position sizing we measure the entry price to one tick or .001 percent below the two-day low divided by our account size.

To determine how many shares to trade: As an example, our two-day low is $50, the buy stop is $52.10, and we are trading a $100,000 account, so we can risk 1 percent or $1,000 − $52.10 − $49.95 = $2.15 − $1,000/$2.15 = 465 shares.

If the trade starts working we have open trade profit, and we switch our stop to the trailing average true range stop. We hold our hard stop until the average true range stop is less than our hard stop. We trail the trade and have patience and discipline to see what happens.

For Shorts

For shorts the hard stop is one tick or .001 percent below the two-bar high. If the trade starts working we have open trade profit, and we switch our stop to the trailing average true range stop. We hold our hard stop until the average true range stop is less than our hard stop. We trail the trade and have patience and discipline to see what happens.

To determine how many shares to trade: As an example, our two-day high including the .001 percent is $36.80, the sell stop is $34.10 including the .001 percent, and we are trading a $100,000 account, so we can risk 1 percent or $1,000 − $36.80 − $34.10 = $2.70 − $1,000/$2.70 = 370 shares.

■ Note

1. http://www.tradingmarkets.com/.site/forex/how_to/articles/trading-with-the-trend-on-multiple-time-frames-81828.cfm.

CHAPTER 9

The Trend Follower Mindset

There's more to trading than just having a strategy.

There are countless trading strategies for you to choose from. The most important aspect of a trading strategy is that it matches your personality and risk thresholds. You can find hundreds of books with different trading strategies, along with countless websites that offer trading strategies for free. In trading magazines as well as websites that list trading system results, they all seem to highlight "the trading strategy of the month."

If it were as simple as buying one of these systems, you would have retirement in a box.

With all of these trading strategies available, why isn't everyone rich?

The sad reality is that most traders fail. There are estimates that only 3–5 percent of all traders are successful over time.

The problem is that strategies do NOT make a good trader.

There's more to trading than just having a strategy. Only time, knowledge, experience, and guidance can make you the trader you want to be.

You are your biggest enemy because of your emotions, fear, and greed!

In order to develop the right mindset, you need to know what to expect when trading. Many traders mistakenly believe that trading will result in a consistently rising account balance, like having an ATM in their office. But you already know that losses are a part of our business as traders. There will be some days and weeks when your trading exceeds your expectations, but more likely there will be periods when your trading results are far worse than you expected.

It's essential that you maintain a long-term perspective. That is why I commonly say trend following is a marathon. Too many traders and even investors in traders focus on short-term results and lose their perspective. I am asked all the time how I did last month or last year. The reality is, that is meaningless. If I had a great month or year, does that mean I will have a great month or year following? Probably not! I am at the mercy of the markets trending. If they do not trend, I will not make any money. They do not have to do anything. I like the analogy: If there are fish, I believe I stand a good chance to catch them. (If there are no fish . . . I'm probably going to eat pasta that day.)

After experiencing a loss or a bad week, too many traders give up and start looking for or start trading a different strategy. And while the trading strategy they just abandoned is recovering from the drawdown, the new trading strategy may result in yet more losses, so again, they start looking for another. It becomes a vicious cycle.

You need to be convinced that trend following is right for you. Truthfully, it might not be. It might too boring or too slow. You have to believe that over time you stand the potential to grind out profits. If you do not really believe or internalize this, you will quit at the first steep drawdown. I promise you . . . there is a drawdown out there that can stop anyone from trading.

The biggest single mistake beginning traders make is that they believe that trading is easy.

Successful trading has to be the hardest thing to achieve. My goal is to enlighten you and teach you what it took me decades to truly learn.

You will learn to have an exact plan with exact entries, exact exits with both profits and losses, and exact quantities to buy or sell. My goal is to teach you to manage the uncertainty and risks in the markets. We are dealing in the unknown and uncertainty; this is why trading is full of tremendous risks.

You will learn to take losses easily and quickly because you will know exactly where the trade does not work. You will learn that if you do not exit you will cause yourself tremendous financial and emotional damage.

You will learn that trend following is a marathon, that any trade or month really does not mean anything.

You will learn to trust your trading plan.

You will learn to take responsibility for all of your trades.

You will learn to be objective. You will not become emotionally attached to your trades.

You will learn that you do not need to be right all the time in order to make money! You need to have an exact plan as well as the discipline and patience to let it work over time.

Luckily for me, my mentors instilled in me that it was more important how to think than to find that elusive magical system or indicator. Richard Dennis and William Eckhardt from the Turtle legend also emphasized this when they taught their Turtle protégés.

In 1983 William Eckhardt and Richard Dennis made a bet that trading can be taught. The bet was lost by William Eckhardt. He believed that trading was a skill not easily taught. His colleague Richard Dennis differed and believed that trading could be taught. They called their students Turtles. Not all of the Turtles succeeded even though they were all taught exactly the same. Why did some of the Turtles succeed and continue till today compounding money? Simple answer, how they thought!

William Eckhardt and Richard Dennis raised a generation of trend followers. Today the offspring of those trend followers are making a mark for themselves. The entire training of the Turtle program was two weeks long. There was very little in the secret sauce learning. Most of the learning was how to think and how to deal with the psychology of trading. Sadly, this is the least interesting to most beginning traders but the most important.

■ Make It Second Nature

How to think like a successful trend follower hopefully will be ingrained in you.

One of my mentors learned under Ed Seykota and Van Tharp. He would constantly remind me of many of their statements and how to think. As well, one of my mentors is a big admirer of Mark Douglas, who is well known in the trading psychology field. Mark Douglas left a big impression on him and I was constantly reminded of many of Mark Douglas's thoughts in our countless conversations. Imagine 18 years of speaking to someone virtually every day, the correct trading mentality resonated.

There are the greed and fear aspects you will learn to overcome. When trading, these two emotions are constantly present: greed and fear. If your trade goes well, a possible natural inclination will be to trade even more, opening yourself up to significant loss. And if your trade goes wrong, fear will torture you. Fear of loss or fear of a further loss makes traders scared. Greed and fear are destructive emotions, and all traders are influenced by them; they're a natural part of every trader's psychology. Greed and fear can make traders act irrationally: they may know what they should do, but they simply can't do it. The bottom line: If you're scared or greedy, and you can't control your emotions when day trading, then you'll have a very difficult time being profitable.

You will learn it is not about being smart or trying to prove something to anyone. There will be no need to try to pick tops and bottoms. You will learn to accept the truth when the trade did not work and there is no need to hold on.

Do not allow yourself to get caught up in positive or negative emotions. Understand the psychology behind trading and not just know that no trade is guaranteed but also internalize the fact. Work on your mental state. If a trade goes wrong, try to work out why it did and learn from it. Executing a trading method with discipline is the only way to overcome destructive emotions. Whether you're a day trader or an investor, and whether you trade in commodities, stocks, or currencies, the fact is that your trading psychology WILL influence your results. If you miss a trade, another one will be just around the corner. Practice patience and discipline.

You need to control your emotions by having a specific plan to follow. Having the correct trading psychology is just as important as having a robust trading strategy.

The more you are prepared mentally for trading, the better you will trade.

You will learn to negate impulsive behavior in which you might buy or sell without following a plan or thinking that you need one. Impatience or boredom is another pillar of failure. There are those who are seeking action or simply adrenaline.

It all boils down to—Do you really want to succeed?

If you truly want to succeed—you need a well-thought-out plan and you need to follow it exactly!

I am giving you my plan that I use every day when I trade. You can use it exactly as I do or use pieces of it that match your personality.

I know people that are overweight, yet they have been on a diet for years. They will drink the Diet Cokes and not eat cakes in front of others; however, in their kitchens they will devour the whole cake. The fact is, these people want to be slim, yet they are overweight for years and nothing changes.

Amazon lists thousands of books on "Weight Loss" as well as thousands of books on "Exercising and Fitness." There is always this fad diet and that fad diet.

I like to keep things simple . . . KISS. I had a discussion with one of the executives of Reuters/Metastock who is an avid sports enthusiast regarding triathlons and dieting. We concurred that if one wrote a book on weight loss, it would be very, very short:

- Eat less.

- Exercise more.

Come on, it's simple: We all know that we can lose weight if we just follow those two rules. We reduce our calorie intake and we do some aerobic exercises at least three times a week for a minimum of 30 minutes.

The sad reality is no one wants "simple."

The more complicated, the better!

Simple works! Robust ideas on trend following work over time!

As in trading, the more complicated, the so-called better!

Why do people keep buying these books and magazines that promise a new diet or a new way to lose weight? In my opinion it is a lack of discipline.

It is almost how beginning traders buy new courses or constantly seek gurus. They believe there is a holy grail or someone knows something more than they do. Either they were never taught robust trend following ideas or they went through an inevitable drawdown and thought to find another method. They gave up on their patience and discipline.

I am not a therapist but it would seem that the short-term pleasure outweighs the long-term benefit of healthy eating. This is exactly like traders who want to be successful, yet they keep on making mistakes in the markets. They are impulsive or they simply do not follow their plan. They are seeking short-term pleasures or profits. They do not have the patience when the trade works. They seek to ring the cash register.

There are millions of books on dieting, yet people are overweight. There are millions of books and courses on trading, yet most people are not successful and lose money. I want to instill in you the methodologies I have used every day for the last 18 years and how to deal with your mind.

I will give you the knowledge, but you have to have the motivation.

They blame the plan: "It's too hard," "It's impossible," "It doesn't work." This isn't true. The ideas I am sharing with you are simple and robust. These beginning traders didn't succeed because they were simply too lazy, or they didn't have the discipline to execute the plan. But instead of working on the true problem—the execution—they think can change the plan itself, hoping that there's an easier way. Successful traders realize that their problem doesn't lie in the plan, but in the execution.

Here's what you can do in order to ensure your own motivation and discipline when it comes to executing the plan:

It's important to focus on the big picture.

> **Your money will be made over a series of many trades.**
>
> **No single trade means anything.**
>
> **No month or any year means anything.**

Thinking in these terms will help you greatly execute the plan.

The concept that trading is easy is very dangerous to the financial stability of a trader.

When beginners make money on a trade, they feel like a genius and invincible. Then they can take wild risks and lose everything.

Many beginner traders delude themselves and fall for advertisements promising "You will get rich by day trading," "Earn unlimited income," or "Forget about your day job and trade for a living."

■ Trend Following and Trading Is Not Retirement in a Box!

The average person wants to be told exactly which stock to buy or sell. They want a little bit of excitement or fun. The average person does not really want to work. The average person will risk hard-earned savings on stock tips with less thought than what to eat for dinner. This is why most fail in the investment world.

You need to be self-reliant and believe in yourself.

When you believe in yourself, you are in the right direction of success.

Nothing ever changes in the markets.

Fear and greed never subside.

Jesse Livermore, a market wizard from the beginning of the last century, stated, "Wall Street never changes, the pockets change, the suckers change, the stocks change, but Wall Street never changes because human nature never changes."

If you truly want to change your reality when trading, I am here to help you!

The answer is within you!

You have to learn to think like a successful trader. I will help you but cannot guarantee your success. It is all about you. I will give you all the tools that I have used on a daily basis for the last 18 years! You will have to internalize what I am teaching you, use it as part of your mental framework when trading, and not quit when you hit a drawdown or rough patch. What I guarantee you is that you will go through an ugly drawdown and your worst drawdown is always ahead of you. There will be no surprises from what I teach you and when you actually trend follow under my plan.

Successful trend followers are simply playing the game to win and to compound their way to wealth. And they are enjoying every moment of it. Successful trend followers are humble and low key. They do not need to impress others.

There only exists a small group of consistently successful trend followers and traders. Most traders experience varying degrees of frustration in various degrees including extreme exasperation, wondering why they can't create consistent success. Many look for the holy grail and all types of magical indicators. Successful trend followers do not waste their time in searching for the holy grail.

Hopefully I will instill this in you!

I joined a brokerage in order to learn firsthand who was making money and who wasn't. I was told about the most successful client in the firm. My first reaction was that this "successful client" was one who was "in the know" or maybe a financial professional like someone from Goldman Sachs or Morgan Stanley.

When I was told he was a dentist, I thought he was kidding!

The dentist started in 1979 and has been compounding money ever since. He started with $200,000, understandably a lot of money in 1979, but today he has a $5,000,000 trading account, plus accounts for his kids, and he has taken $12,000,000 out of the markets. He is an example of one who has compounded his way to wealth. As you read on further you will realize this is not a get rich quick or an instant millionaire trader story. Rather it is one where you compound your way to wealth over many long years full of steep and drawn-out periods of losses. The dentist had countless losses. He strived to keep them small and he had the discipline, patience, and focus to get through all the inevitable losses he encountered and draw downs to stay in the marathon of trend following. You can also do this if you truly want it!

■ What Makes a Successful Trend Follower?

Is it intelligence or simply that successful trend followers work harder? Do successful trend followers have better trading systems or computers? Why do the vast majority of beginning traders fail? One has to take into account that most beginning traders are successful in their own right. Many unsuccessful traders include professionals such as pilots, engineers, doctors, and wealthy retirees. More interesting is that most analysts are also not profitable traders. In short, intelligence is not the only answer to successful trading. Actually a greater intelligence can be detrimental. Too often an intelligent person wants to know why a market did whatever it did. There are always a myriad of possible reasons but the simple answer is that it does not matter WHY. The market moved, that is it, and we have a choice to figure out why or try to ride the trend and hopefully make some money. Intelligent people try to analyze things much more than the general populace. I have a colleague who has a sign on his door, *Don't think, It will cost you MONEY!* In trading there is a lot of merit to this statement. One needs to react and follow one's plan. This is what makes trading so hard. This is a dichotomy from our human existence. We are taught not to be rash or too quick to make a decision. In trading we have to be as we are in the thick of it and postponing a decision such as an entry or exit can be costly.

Reacting in trading means following your plan explicitly.

Your plan needs to be meticulously developed in order that you are not being rash but rather decisive.

This really sums up having confidence and the realization that it is not about being smart. It is about being disciplined and having faith in one's actions.

The reality is that the markets will do whatever they want. There is really no easy way or any way to figure them out. The markets do the unpredictable. A stock goes down with a positive earnings report. Bernanke speaks, which would seem would be positive news, and the markets sell off in a rage. There can be a statement from an official that can set in motion a major bear market. After a speech by Treasury Secretary Jim Baker in 1987, investors began to fear that the weak U.S. dollar would cause further inflation. The Dow dropped about 200 points or 9 percent in the first hour and a half. Prior to the waterfall drop the stock market had been doing great for the first nine months of 1987. It was up more than 30 percent, hitting new highs. The prior two consecutive years had had gains of 20 percent+.

One can rationalize or try to find the reasons why the market sold off. Intelligent people live for reason. If they cannot find a reason, they invest a great deal of emotional energy in analyzing. There is no reason to analyze. Markets do whatever they want. Our job is to follow (trend follow) without wasting time looking for reasons. The intelligent populace wanted a reason for the 1987 stock market crash. Maybe the market needed a rest. Maybe investors panicked. For whatever reason, which does not matter, fortunes were lost and some fortunes were made. Traders that were trend followers made fortunes. One of these traders was Marty Schwartz. His exploits during 1987 are a great lesson to trend followers. Schwartz uses very simple indicators such as a 10-period moving average. In his book *Pit Bull*, Marty states that one needs to be consistent and trade within one's means. Even with the stock market crash in 1987, that was one of the most profitable years for Marty Schwartz. At the onset of the crash he lost $315,000. He did not sulk or try to figure out why. The "why" is the normal or human reaction. Trying to figure out the "why" instead of reacting can be lethal to one's trading account. Schwartz did not try to figure out the "why"; he followed his plan and took his loss without any hesitation. As he later said, if you did not take the $315,000 loss it could have morphed into a $5,000,000 loss. Compare Schwartz to other traders who were frozen or thought the market would come back. Schwartz was a Marine. His Marine training came into play. They taught him never to freeze when under attack. One of the tactics in the Marine Corps officer's manual is either go forward or backward. Don't just sit there if you are getting the hell beat out of you. Even retreating is offensive, because you are still doing something. It is the same thing in the market. The most important thing is to keep enough powder to make your comeback. Let Marty Schwartz's experience serve as a lesson on how to be a trader. No opinions, follow the plan, cut losses immediately, and realize that if you run out of money, you cannot keep on trading. Very powerful lessons that I hope you internalize. I was lucky to have met Marty at a dinner in Boca and was very impressed by him as a person. I suggest you pick up a copy of his book, *Pit Bull*.

The answer regarding intelligence and reasons why markets move, however, is much closer at hand.

Internalize this statement by William Eckhardt: "I haven't seen much correlation between good trading and intelligence. Average intelligence is enough. Beyond that, emotional makeup is more important."

The way one thinks when trend following is critical to one's success.

It all boils down to attitude. We as trend followers are faced with the dilemma of how to be and remain confident in spite of adverse conditions such as drawdowns and extended periods when we do not make money. If you really think about it, when a trade does not work, we are wrong, and to make matters worse we lose hard-earned money. Clearly trading is risky.

No trade ever has a guaranteed outcome regardless of all the analysis or anything. On every trade one stands the definite risk of losing money.

The funny thing I learned over the years was that most traders truly believe that the trade has to work. They believe they are not taking a risk. They do not fully internalize that they can lose money.

Contrarily, when I put on a trade I ask myself how much this is going to cost me to see if it works. Losses do not cause me any anguish or emotional discomfort. The markets will at times inflict pain or cause frustration. This is the reality of trading. The only way to avoid this pain or frustration is not trade. Our job as traders is to take both the pain and frustration in stride. The markets do not care about you or me. The markets are going to do whatever they will do. You cannot avoid losses or avoid the pain. You need to accept it as a reality of trading. What you need to do is control how you react to the situation. The situation is just the event. Our reactions are what are detrimental to our psyche. When you have a well-thought-out plan that you follow exactly, you build to some degree immunity to your personal reactions. We have accepted the risks that are inherent in the market. There is no fear, greed, or ego that inhibits us.

I have accepted the risk of the trade even before I put it on.

I know that I cannot avoid losses. All I can do is define what I am willing to lose on a trade and let the probabilities work out over time. There is no sense in trying to avoid something that is unavoidable. I have absolutely no fear or hesitation. Fear is immobilizing and works to the contrary; I simply go with the flow. I ask myself, "How much is this going to cost to see if this trade will work?" Using the wording *will work* is a lot different than saying *make money*. Everything is in how you think.

I have heard these words countless times from my mentors: Remain confident in the face of constant uncertainty.

The reality is that one needs absolute trust in one's abilities as well as one's trading plan. Without these two attributes success will never be achieved.

Too many traders assume the more indicators, the better.

Many traders start for all the wrong reasons. They are bored, or they are seeking adventure or challenge.

I have a simple reason for trading. First, I love it and it is my passion. Second, I need to support a wife, three children, and two dogs.

My goal is to compound money over long periods of time.

The more analysis, the better, so say the masses!

The more CNBC or Bloomberg or other financial news you take in, the better! However, I am a proponent of keeping it simple. Everything is represented in price. My trading plan is solely based on that with strong measures of risk.

■ Sweet Simplicity

My goal is to get you into this mindset. Learning the proper attitudes and mindset are critical for successful trend following. When I put on a trade, all that I can expect is that something will happen. There are only four possibilities.

- ■ A big loss.

- ■ A small loss.

- ■ A big profit.

- ■ A small profit.

These are the only possibilities. Immediately I put my stop in without any hesitation, so in essence I avoid the big loss (except there will be times of gaps that I can't control). It is very rare that on any given day the markets will open exactly at the price at which they closed the day before. Most times the opening range of prices is above or below the prior day's close. This is called an opening gap. There are traders that specialize only in trading these opening gaps. Most times these opening gaps are not large. However, when we are dealing with trading, the only certainty is uncertainty. There are times, as rare as they are, in which there are huge opening gaps. The implication to traders can be adverse. Many times this happens in the currency markets when there is government intervention to support or depress currencies. Last year trend followers got hit with both the Swiss franc and the Japanese yen. Late on Sunday night the central banks went into actions to suppress their currencies. Trend followers who were long these currencies got whacked. I was one of these unlucky traders. The magnitudes of these moves were intense. Thousands of dollars per contract were vaporized within minutes. Every trader that was long these currencies going into the weekend encountered a huge hit at the commencement of trading.

Situations like these, even as six sigma as they are, need to be included in the trading plan.

Before the first Gulf War the general consensus was that the prices of crude would go through the roof at the onset of war. As usual you had the predictors on Bloomberg and CNBC calling for crude to exceed $200 a barrel. Traders bought into the story, counting their profits beforehand. On my mother's birthday on January 16, 1991, crude closed at $30.29 a barrel. After the initial bombing of Iraq, it became clear to the world that the United States and its allies had clear superiority. On January 17, 1991, crude opened down $7.50 a barrel or $7,500. All the traders who bought into the fear were shocked. They woke up $7,500 a contract poorer. There are limits in the markets but they can get locked (limit locked). You cannot exit markets like this. The good news with markets with daily price limits is that you can only lose that fixed amount in any one particular day. However, there is a tomorrow and you might experience another day in which you are locked and cannot exit. This scenario is reality and can cause you much greater losses than you could have ever anticipated. There is no way to predict or know or even prevent being on the wrong or right side of such dramatic moves. There is no certainty. We are dealing with the unknown. For the inherent risks in the markets it is strongly suggested to undertrade. Always calculate your risks on all levels. Risk per trade, risk per sector, and risk on the open trade level always needs to be calculated on a constant basis, as shown in Figures 9.1, 9.2, and 9.3.

Sym	P.	Qty	Entry Date	Entry Fill	Profit	%	Exit Date	Exit Fill
C	S	2	2009-09-02 Day	348.000	$-2,275	-0.8%	2009-09-15 Day	369.250
W	S	1	2009-09-02 Op...	791.500	$163	0.1%	2009-10-08 Day	786.750
JY	L	1	2009-09-03 Op...	1.0974	$575	0.2%	2009-10-22 Day	1.1078
BO	S	1	2009-09-04 Op...	41.98	$-693	-0.2%	2009-10-12 Day	43.01
ND	L	1	2009-09-08 Day	1624.25	$330	0.1%	2009-10-30 Day	1644.50
EC	L	1	2009-09-09 Op...	1.4438	$1,025	0.3%	2009-11-03 Day	1.4614

FIGURE 9.1   Examples of Small Losses and Small Profits
Source: TradingBlox.

Sym	/	P.	Qty	Entry Date	Entry Fill	Profit	%	Exit Date	Exit Fill
EC	L		2	2008-07-14 Op...	1.5735	$-4,038	-0.8%	2008-07-29 Day	1.5424
EC	L		1	2008-09-23 Op...	1.4686	$-2,588	-0.6%	2008-09-29 Day	1.4284
EC	S		1	2009-04-22 Op...	1.2878	$-2,494	-0.5%	2009-04-29 Day	1.3265
EC	L		1	2009-07-20 Day	1.4088	$3,263	0.7%	2009-11-03 Day	1.4622
EC	S		1	2010-03-02 Day	1.3458	$-1,744	-0.4%	2010-03-12 Day	1.3725
EC	S		1	2010-03-22 Day	1.3444	$6,356	1.4%	2010-06-21 Day	1.2415

FIGURE 9.2 Another Example of Small Losses and Small Profits
Source: TradingBlox.

Sym	/	P.	Qty	Entry Date	Entry Fill	Profit	%	Exit Date	Exit Fil
CT	L		2	2009-11-11 Op...	29.82	$-3,190	-0.7%	2009-11-12 Day	26.78
CT	L		2	2009-11-20 Day	30.49	$-450	-0.1%	2010-01-05 Day	30.19
CT	L		2	2010-02-12 Day	30.75	$3,930	0.9%	2010-04-08 Day	34.83
CT	L		2	2010-04-21 Op...	39.54	$-4,210	-0.9%	2010-05-05 Day	35.48
CT	L		2	2010-08-02 Op...	35.21	$42,740	9.6%	2010-11-22 Day	78.10
CT	S		1	2011-12-12 Day	91.02	$-2,280	-0.4%	2012-01-03 Day	95.43

FIGURE 9.3 Examples of Small Losses With a Rare Large Profit
Source: TradingBlox.

I also know as a trend follower that most of my trades will not work (they will lose small money). **Big deal!** It is not that I did something wrong or negative; rather, the fact is that the majority of trades when trend following are not profitable.

I laugh when I hear that trend following is not a viable strategy or that trend following is over. Yes, you will go through periods in which you do not make money as well as periods of extended duration in which you will have losses.

In reality, what has happened to me over the last 18 years is that I have had a lot of small losses, small profits, and some rare big profits, which more than make up for the effort that will enable me to compound my money over time.

Another way to think when putting on a trade is how much this is going to cost me to see if the trade will work. I know I have said it already but I really want to reiterate it! Thinking in this manner forces me to take low-risk bets. I know that the majority of the trades will not work and I know exactly what I am risking.

■ Think Probabilities

When one thinks in this mindset, it becomes easy to put on trades. What also lets one put on the trades effortlessly is trust in a robust methodology and knowing that over time one will make money. Sometimes it is easier said than done when one goes through the inevitable period in which eight or more trades do not work in a row (I promise you it will happen and as long as you have small losses it will not matter). Many times I have seen traders that think the market is wrong, it will come back.

The market is never wrong. Do you want to be right or do you want to make money over time? Trend following success is more dependent on discipline than any pure academic achievement.

When you have three or four trades in a row that are profitable, is it easier to put on the next trade? In most cases yes, but it should not be that way. So why should trades that don't work impact you? Every trade has its own statistical outcome and should not cause you any fear, greed, or pain.

Successful trend followers are focused on executing every trade flawlessly. This is what you need to internalize. They are relaxed as they let the probabilities work over time. Every trade is statistically independent from the next trade.

The people who run casinos do not try to predict or know in advance the outcome of any particular hand of cards; however, they know over time they anticipate to make X percent.

Otherwise they would not have all of those wonderful modern casinos. You need to think like the owner of a casino. Take small risks; realize that any trade or any month does not mean anything. Realize that you will make your money over long periods of time, and if you really convince yourself of this, you are on your way to compounding money and wealth.

Professional gamblers as well as the casinos know and understand probabilities. They know that they need a large series of hands to be played and that there will statistically reliable outcomes over time. Ask yourself how many traders think like this. Not many, that is why most traders fail. I want to help you be one of the successful trend followers!

Believe in Uncertainty ∨ √

Believe in the uncertainty and unpredictability of every single trade.

Any trade, any month, and even any year really does not mean anything. There will be flat years, flat periods, bad periods, and exceptional periods. This is the reality. Trend following is not a get rich quick plan to wealth. It is a compound your way to wealth over long periods of time plan.

Losses are simply the cost of doing business or the amount of money I need to make myself available for eventual big winning trades.

Successful trend followers are in the "Just Do It" mode in which there is no fear or stress. When you get in your car and start driving are you stressed? Probably not as you have a seat belt and you understand the concept of defensive driving. There is no fear or stress when you trade because they have a well-thought-out plan and there is nothing at risk other than their small bet that you are willing to spend to see if the trade will work. There is no being right or trying to avoid a loss. Basically they are not trying to prove anything other than to make themselves available for potential profitable trades and compound money over time.

Accept the Risk; Stick to the Plan

Successful trend followers accept the risk, follow their plan, and have reasonable expectations without fear or stress.

The pillar of successful trading is accepting the inherent risks, accepting the uncertainty, accepting that you will have countless losses. You must keep the losses small. You do not need to adversely affect your lifestyle. I know this is easier to say than do. My broker gave me a suggestion one day after I was complaining about my trading. I thought he was crazy, but later saw he wanted to teach me to accept the risk. He suggested that I withdraw $5,000 in single bills. Go to the top of a building and throw the money off. Watch the money fall and watch the lucky people on the ground pick up my money. Afterwards be introspective and ask myself how I feel and move on.

This is trading. You do something without a plan, the 10 percenters pick up your money. You need to accept the risk and the uncertainty. If you can learn something from this exercise, you are starting your learning curve about trading. You are both emotionally and financially prepared to trade. You have internalized what is at hand. You must be able to lose money. You must be able to move on and dust yourself off.

Successful trend followers know that most trades will not work, yet they know that they have an edge and know that there will a random distribution of trades that work and those that don't.

Remember, a trade does not have to work.

It will be a random outcome.

This brings us to believe that **anything can happen when we put on a trade, and there will be an uncertain outcome**. This makes us do several things in order to be a successful trader including immediately putting in your stops to protect. By doing so you are following your plan exactly because you expect that virtually anything can happen.

Think of all of those investors who in their wildest dreams would never have expected the NASDAQ to fall as it did or all of the dot-com investors who watched all of their profits evaporate.

Expect Anything

Any market can do virtually anything at any time.

Once you truly grasp this, you realize the utmost need to have stops both for losses and to follow trades that work beyond our expectations. Successful trend followers cut their losses without any hesitation when the trade is not working. Successful trend followers have an exact plan, are organized and systematic, and have determined their risk thresholds.

Successful trend followers have eliminated costly trading errors caused by fear or greed.

Successful trend followers have internalized that they do not need to know the future in order to be profitable and know to expect the unexpected.

Salem Abraham, one of the most successful trend followers since the 1980s, through his long work has instilled in me the idea that trend following is a marathon, grinding it out over the years, and the following statement:

Plan for the Unexpected

I have an unshakable belief that anything can happen and will happen.

Basically the only certainty in trading is uncertainty.

You define your risk in advance because you know there will be uncertain situations and things can go to extremes.

My goal is to eliminate the emotional baggage when trading. This methodology of thinking will help you, as it did me.

One thing that helped me to eliminate the emotional baggage was to mitigate my expectations. I have no expectation that any trade will work. I mitigate my expectations of profits.

I believe that I will make money over time, but I never know in which market or stock or when. There are no guarantees as we do not know the future.

Most people when they put on a trade expect it to be profitable or otherwise why would they put on the trade? Successful trend followers know that they will make money over a long series of trades. They have an edge but never expect that any one particular trade has to work.

In order to compound money over time we need to force ourselves out of the unrealistic expectation mode. Every trade is a random event. Because the last X number of trades did not work, who says that trade Y will not be the trade of the year?

Trade Y could be the trade when you sit back and say to yourself, Wow, I would never have expected that to happen.

This leads to the understanding that anything can happen and will happen, trades can go to extremes. Since we know trades can go to extremes, this reinforces why we immediately have stops to protect to the negative and why we have trailing stops that follow big winners to lock in profits for the positive.

Use the NASDAQ chart in Figure 9.4 as an example. No one ever believed the NASDAQ could fall from approximately 5,600 down to below 1,000 and stay down now for more than 13 years.

Markets can go to EXTREMES!

Many are not aware of the action of the Japanese stock market from the late 1980s to the present. In the 1980s Japan was an economic superpower. They were buying real estate throughout the world, especially in the United States.

The Japanese stock market reached a high in 1989 of approximately 39,000. Today, 20+ years later, the Japanese stock market is hovering around 8,500 (Figure 9.5). Can you imagine buying and holding?

Things can and will go to extremes!

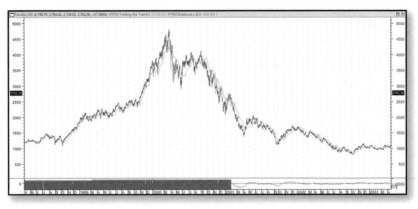

FIGURE 9.4 Nasdaq Stock Crash

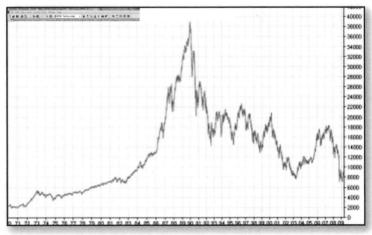

FIGURE 9.5 Japan Stock Market Crash

The majority of investors never considered the cotton market as an area to invest in. Cotton went from a low of approximately 6 to a high of 180 on a back-adjusted basis. Fortunes were made and lost with cotton.

Cotton was one of the reasons in 2010 I made close to 40 percent in one of my managed accounts. I entered in the end of July 2010 and was able to stay with the trade until the end of November 2010. You will note that cotton continued to climb but the volatility and risk were too great to take on (Figure 9.6).

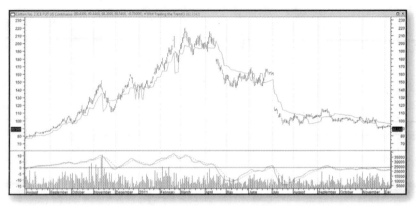

FIGURE 9.6 Cotton Massive Rally

Do you remember what you were paying for gas in 2008 when everyone was calling for peak oil? There were calls that gas would go over $7 a gallon or even more. Crude oil got up to approximately $147 a barrel to crash down to the $34 dollar a barrel range (Figure 9.7). Where were the experts? They were wrong. Trend followers made money as crude oil went up as well as down. Fortunes were made and lost. T. Boone Pickens, the oil guru, lost a fortune while his neighbor Salem Abraham (whom I invest with), the trend follower, made a fortune.

Since we know (or I hope you will learn) that anything can happen, what makes you think you can predict it?

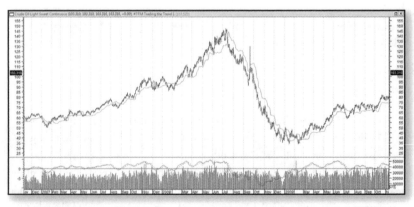

FIGURE 9.7 Crude Oil Rally and Crash

Predicting is a complete waste of time. One does not need to know the future in order to make money. All we need to do is take low-risk bets and stumble into trends. The market will do whatever it wants; it is not about you or me. The market does not care.

Successful trend followers know that they do not know what will happen.

They think in terms of probabilities and possibilities. Once one thinks in terms of probabilities one becomes more confident, less stressed, and less fearful.

We are programming our minds to be successful trend followers. In order to be a successful trend follower we need to trade without fear or overconfidence. We must see what the market is offering us, take action on this, and make ourselves available for opportunities.

When one is in fear, opportunities are blocked. For example, your last trade did not work, so you do not take the next trade?

If you do not take that trade, you had fear of losing money.

To make matters worse and to beat yourself up, that next trade could have made up for all of the other small losses or been the big rare winner of the year.

■ Traders Lose Because of Fear

Accept the fear!

Accept that fact that most trades will not work!

Big deal, you are taking low-risk bets that are between .5 percent and 1.5 percent of your whole account size. You are able to take many small losses. Small losses do not ruin your mental state or at least they shouldn't. Be extremely wary of system sellers who claim their system or methodology has a high win rate. You will experience losses in a row multiple times. This is why we attempt to keep losses small. However, you will see in Figure 9.8 that one trade we incurred -1.9 percent loss. This loss was much more than we target however this loss was probably due to a gap up/down or limit days. These type of losses can't be avoided.

Sym	P.	U.	Qty	Entry Date	Entry Fill	Profit	%	Exit Date	Exit Fill
C2	S	1	1	2012-03-08 Day	575.700	$-1,431	-1.0%	2012-03-12 Day	604.325
SXE	L	1	3	2012-03-08 Day	2,413.65	$-2,707	-1.9%	2012-04-03 Day	2,345.45
DX2	L	1	1	2012-03-09 Day	81.063	$-1,613	-1.1%	2012-04-03 Day	79.450
FCH	L	1	1	2012-03-09 Day	3,376.5	$-1,872	-1.3%	2012-04-04 Day	3,234.0
BL2	L	1	2	2012-03-15 Day	199.28	$-270	-0.2%	2012-05-03 Day	197.23
C2	S	1	1	2012-03-22 Day	580.250	$-153	-0.1%	2012-05-18 Day	583.300

FIGURE 9.8   Losses Greater Than We Anticipate Due to Gaps or Limit Moves

Stay focused and "just take the trade if it fits your trading plan." You have a plan, you follow the plan, you take low-risk bets, you have realistic expectations, and you compound your way to wealth over time.

▪ It Is All Perception

Take the threat of fear or pain out of your market information.

Successful trend followers don't feel anything painful nor do they experience fear about putting on a trade. **They "Just put the trade on!"**

Successful trend followers have internalized that there is an endless stream of opportunities and that many of these trades will not work. I even say to myself, " How much will this trade cost me to see if it will work"!

Internalize and start truly believing in the following statements. If you need to write them down and put them next to your computer.

> **There is abundance in the markets.**
>
> **There are always oppurtunities**
>
> **Successful trend followers are objective in their trading.**
>
> **They just flow with the markets without trying to control or predict anything.**
>
> **Successful trend followers will go long or short and never try to impose their opinions or belief systems on their trading.**
>
> **They are focused on opportunities and follow their plan flawlessly!**
>
> **They perceive opportunities!**
>
> **They know what an opportunity looks like.**
>
> **The markets are constantly offering us opportunities!**

We are surrounded by potential abundance and opportunities, not pain or fear. Fear is irrational and almost stupid when one is the "Just do it" mode. Successful trend followers know when they are in the "just do it" mode.

▪ Just Take the Trade Mode

Each trade is a probable event. Statistically it is independent from every other trade, and investors should simply follow their plan. They perceive the opportunities as a way to compound their way to wealth over time.

There is no threat of pain or fear.

The Key Is to Be Consistent

Successful trend followers are consistent in their plan and execution. They do not have any magical indicators nor are they gurus. In simple terms, they have a plan and focus on executing the plan. In contradiction, the novices put on trades without any plan. Sometime they work and they make a lot of money. These trades empower them and at times lead them to trade recklessly. This reckless trading leads to large unexpected losses.

This is why is trading is so hard to master.

In order to be consistent one must first have a well-thought-out plan and even more so follow it meticulously.

There is no fear, greed, boredom, or even having fun. Trend followers with a plan "Just Do It," trend followers focus on execution.

Successful trend followers trade in order to compound money over time. They are not looking for action or seeking to relieve boredom.

They are consistent.

They do not have to try to be consistent, they are consistent. It all comes naturally. It just flows. Being consistent is not something that you can try to be, you must be consistent. You take every trade that your methodology presents you. You do not second guess your methodology. You don't try to get anything from the market; rather, you make yourself available for the next opportunity. You take advantage of what the market is offering you at any particular time.

You stay in the moment and be consistent.

You have accepted the risks when you are consistent.

There Is No Fear or Pain

Basically fear will cause you to make more errors and cost you more money. One cannot avoid losing trades. They are as natural as breathing. You take responsibility for your actions when you are consistent. There are no limitations or expectations when you are consistent. You are just putting trades on and saying to yourself "Let's see what happens." I promise you there will be numerous losing trades. As long as you keep them small, they mean nothing.

One of the overriding issues that I gleaned from the *Market Wizards* book by Jack Schwager was not only the profits these unique traders made but the fact that all the successful traders stressed the need to cut losses and keep all losses small. Sadly, most traders do not get this message. Many traders are confused about using tight stops or wide stops or even no stops. There is no exact right answer except the exit stops need to be thought out ahead of time before one trades. Once one commences trading one needs to have the stops in place and needs to stick to one's exact plan and not move the stops.

Stops are used to protect your trading capital. Stops are the basis of risk control. Risk control is what gives you the strength to stay in the marathon of trading. Taking small losses is a lot easier on the pocket and the emotions.

Some traders are blinded by greed and only look at the profits. You will not have profits if you do not manage the risks. On one level I can understand. No one wants to hear bad news. However, cutting losses is not bad news, it is rather a necessity for success over time. It is hard to accept losses. No one likes to lose money especially when they follow their plan and they are rewarded with a loss. I personally have no problem taking losses as I feel if I do not exit, the situation can morph into a situation in which I lose more money and worse, affect my mental state. Trading is not about being right or having an ego. Trading is about not being too wrong and letting a loss morph into a big loss, which impacts the trading account and the psyche. This is what makes trading so hard; we put on trades and we hope or expect profits. Otherwise why would anyone risk his or her hard-earned money? The problem arises when a trader encounters a trade that is not working and takes it personally. This type of trader has a major issue accepting that the trade has not worked and they are "wrong." I check my ego before I start my day. There is no wrong or right. The trades either work or they don't work. My day starts with the firm belief that anything can happen and I need to be humble. Otherwise I will probably be out of business. I know that the safest thing for me is to take a small loss and move on to the next trade, otherwise this small loss can have extreme consequences for both my trading account and my emotional state.

There is no wrong, losing, missing out, second guessing, or any other mental baggage when you are consistent when following your trading plan. You do not look to avoid anything or any pain. You let the market do its own thing and unfold and let yourself be available for the opportunity flow. The market is going to do whatever it wants. The market does not care about you or me.

Don't Try to Control It

No one can control the market. No one knows where any market is really ever going for sure. You do not need to know where a market is headed in order to make money. Why even try to think about it?

Accept the risk!

Define the risk!

Once you do this there is no struggle or pain. **You are in the "just do it" mode.** You will not perceive anything that the market can do as threatening. There is nothing to fear. It's all about taking responsibility for your trading.

Sadly, most traders have an issue taking responsibility. It is easier to blame the broker, the data, the system, or the market rather than themselves. It is hard to put into practice taking responsibility. However, those who want to play the blame game will never be successful trend followers.

In order to reach this elusive level of success you must take responsibility. Successful traders take responsibility for all of their actions. They trade without any fear or anxiety.

When they are trading their exact plan, they are aware of not being reckless and every potential outcome has been thought out.

They have restraint, patience, and discipline.

I have seen countless traders who would spend hours planning their trades and instead of just putting them on and seeing what happens they freeze and don't put them on. They watch something on CNBC or a friend gives them a tip contrary to their plan and they do not execute their plan. It is like Murphy's Law, they do not take the trade, and these trades could have been the big winner.

Trend followers need these big winners to succeed over time.

It Is All About Attitude

I have personally seen this occur repeatedly with traders.

I have been investing with commodity trading advisors since 1994. I have seen commodity trading advisors and even my dentist colleague with simple, robust, and even mediocre trading techniques that have the correct tools as far as mindset outperform other more astute traders. Some of the better or astute traders might have better analysis or systematic trend following methodologies; however they lack the proper mindset. They hesitate, they pick and choose their trades, and they jump the gun or simply pass on trades they do not like. Some of these traders are simply brilliant; however, they do not make money. They operate out of fear while the less brilliant trader follows his or her plan and compounds money over time.

Attitude separates success and failure.

Ideally we would want both and in actuality you need both. With a robust methodology that trades all markets and all time frames the same with proper money management and proper mindset, you are on your way to compounding money. Sadly, most traders think they need to read every article in the *Wall Street Journal* or figure out what will happen in the world to make money.

The truth is much further than that.

Once you start believing in your trading methodology and following it exactly to the plan, you will realize that no one knows anything more than you, nor is there anything to predict. Really, no one knows where the dollar is going or where gold is going. If you can internalize that, anything is possible. Gold can go to $3,000 or $300 and you do not care.

The Dow can go to 20,000 or 2,000. You do not care nor are you at the mercy of the markets.

Think Like an Olympic Athlete!

Get in the Nike "Just do it" mode!

World-class athletes have the winning attitude. They envision themselves in the now moment. They envision that they have already won. They do not beat themselves up after making errors, they keep going. World-class athletes just do it, as Nike says. It is almost the same when we drive a car. We just do it. We learned how to learn, we wear a seat belt, we have our cars checked, and then we just drive.

It is the same with trading. You can be confident, not overwhelmed with fear or greed, not afraid to miss out, you just flow with the markets.

You have a positive and reasonable expectation of yourself and your trend following. More so, you accept whatever results you get as an indication of where you are and what the market gives you. No matter how brilliant you are, if there are no trends depending on your time frame, you will not make money. My simple analogy, I tell traders, is that if the fish are not out, you will not catch any fish no matter how good your fishing rod is.

No Way to Avoid a Loss

Losses are as natural as profits. When you try to avoid them you will put yourself in a position to lose even more. There is no holy grail or any guru. Losing is a natural outcome of trading. Trading patterns and trends repeat themselves but not every time. When they do not repeat, we have losses. Do not expect the market to fulfill your expectations. Be pleasantly surprised when a trade works because it does not have to. As I stated earlier, take responsibility for all outcomes. There is an endless stream of opportunities. You are responsible for your success and failure as a trend follower. No one else! If you do not follow your plan, you will be destined to failure. Perceive the endless flow of opportunities. Enter, exit trades without fear, criticism, or regret and let the plan work over time. Be consistent, patient, and disciplined. Once you enter this mode of attitude, you flow with the markets without anger, fear, betrayal, disappointment, or despair. I know this sounds very pink but it is doable. It took many years of trend following to get into this mode. That is why you purchased this book and hopefully you will use my services to help you become a better trader and compound money over time.

Basically, you need to be relaxed when trading. You can't try to be relaxed; it just has to be not stressful. It just flows. Have a carefree state of mind. It is similar to driving. You have a carefree state of mind without worry or fear. You just drive.

When you have numerous trades working you are the most susceptible to making mistakes, overtrading, putting on too big of a position, breaking your plan or rules. Basically, you might feel invincible. This defies common sense and will bring on disastrous results. Cockiness is the antithesis of successful trading. The markets are humbling.

The reality is that only a small handful of trend followers are long-term successful. When I say small handful I would assume less than 10 percent.

Besides my own trend following I have been investing with other commodity trading advisors since 1994. There are thousands of them to choose from. However, there are only a small number of CTAs that I have invested with and compounded money with. I chose them not just by their record, rather by how they think and approach risk.

The irony is that countless professional traders do not approach risk in the appropriate way. Now if you take into account nonprofessional traders who do not address risks, the failure rate skyrockets. Many traders go through boom and bust cycles. Either they do not have rules or they ignore them. The boom and busters make money and then end up losing more. Their equity curves look like a roller-coaster ride.

There is another group of traders that are the antithesis of the consistent compounding of successful trend followers. All of this has nothing to do with years of trading or methodologies. It all boils down to attitude, patience, discipline, and following a well-thought-out plan based on risk and money management. But these traders are full of fear and greed. Successful trend followers check those attributes at the door. I have heard repeatedly from brokers that their job is to keep their client traders from terminally damaging themselves. It is just a matter of time until they quit.

■ This Will Not Be You

My goal is to help you compound money over time. I had a mentor who taught me how to think. My mentors taught me that there is no holy grail. My mentors taught me my money would be made over a long series of trades. My mentors taught me that the market does not care about me. I cannot get revenge on the market. My mentors taught me to take responsibility for my attitudes and my perspectives.

This thought sticks out with a definition of a winning attitude:

A positive expectation of my efforts all the while accepting my results are a reflection of where I am at in my learning and development as a trend follower. I have gotten to the point of just doing it! I have no fear or hesitation. I have developed a winning attitude. I am solely responsible for my winning attitude. I do not expect or demand anything from the markets. I do not expect that markets will do anything special for me or simply give me anything. The markets have a life of their own.

If I can learn this, so can you!

I did not go to Harvard!

I did not work for a large hedge fund.

Some of the most successful trend followers do not have large staffs or trading floors. Rather, they work out of their house or small offices. Bill Dunn, an extremely successful trend follower, started in the 1970s out of his house. At his pinnacle of success Bill Dunn was running in excess of $2 billion out of a small office. Another example is David Druz, who is currently managing $100 million and works only with a compliance worker who runs his office. Trend followers do not have large infrastructures in place.

You will not need it either. After you have done the proper mental work, the actual trading does not take much time from your day. Within 30–60 minutes a day you can complete all of your trading.

CHAPTER 10

My Trading Journal

To give you the full realistic picture of trend following, I am including my proprietary trading results in a diary fashion. I do not trade that often. A good trading day is a day in which I do not put on a trade. On average in both models I only trade 100 times a year. This keeps my slippage and commissions to a minimum. My trading programs are systematic without any discretion used and tested over the years. Prior to the fall of 2009 I primarily had one account and all of my trading programs were put in this one account. I decided to segregate my trading in order to build my proprietary track record. Even though I have been trading the same methodologies over the years, I have added filters based on my experiences and mistakes. I was not searching for the holy grail; rather, I have added risk filters over the years.

I have been trading in real time two models that are very close to being identical in the rules and thought processes of the trading plan I have presented above. These trading programs are based on unit sizes.

One unit is based on an account size of $150,000 Global Diversified and the other account size is $300,000 Diversified. Both accounts trade the liquid futures markets. I believe when we trade the futures markets we trade and make ourselves available for every aspect of our human existence. What I mean by this is, we wake up in the morning. We eat cereal, wheat. We drink coffee. We get dressed, cotton. We get in our cars to go to work. We put gas in our cars. We pay for the gas with a credit card (interest rates). We invest in the stock market (stock indexes). We heat our homes, heating oil. We eat chocolate, cocoa. You get the concept. Each and every one of these is a market. They go up and they go down. Some of the time they trend. I look to ride these trends in these various markets.

Some of the markets in which I look to take trades are the following:

Australian dollar	Eurodollar	Soybeans
Soybean oil	Gold	Sugar
British pound	Copper	Swiss franc
Corn	Heating oil	Silver
Cocoa	Japanese yen	Soymeal
Canadian dollar	Lean hogs	S&P 500
Crude	Live cattle	10-year bond
Cotton	Nasdaq	Wheat
Dollar index	Natural gas	30-year bond

They are all liquid and highly traded. I have no opinion on any of these markets. As in the rules I delineated in the prior chapters, I look to buy the strongest based on the average rate of change and sell the weakest based on the average rate of change. The difference between the two models is the risk I am willing to take, anticipated returns, and anticipated drawdowns. The $300,000 Diversified unit model size is built to be less volatile (at least try to be) with lower returns and lower drawdowns. The $150,000 Global Diversified unit model size is slightly more aggressive, anticipates greater drawdowns, and trades fewer markets due to its size. These models are based on the rules expressed in the prior chapters. I have been researching and testing with my passionate programmer for approximately one year to come up with a model in which the returns are very modest and with lower volatility than the current two models. The attempted goal is not how much we can generate but with the focus (attempt) to keep the draw downs, very low.

The $150,000 Global Diversified model takes on slightly more risk. It risks 1.25 percent maximum on any trade. However, many of the trades end up losing less than this. In reality, as we are dealing in uncertainty, some trade losses have exceeded 1.25 percent. There are a few trades in which even though I had stops in the market, which were placed immediately upon my entry, the price gapped above or below. More so, there are periods when there will be limit moves in which one cannot exit. We are dealing with risk and uncertainty. I have accepted the risk and try to mitigate as much as possible, but it is not completely possible. Another slight variance of the model is that I am willing to take on only a maximum risk of $2,000 per contract regardless of total account size on the Global Diversified unit. What is ironic to investors is that these slight differences have produced dramatically different real-time results. It truly exemplifies the realities of what I have expressed.

The $300,000 Diversified unit size model maximum risk is .75 percent. This is less than 1 percent. I built the model in order to try to smooth out returns. Future results will be interesting to see if this is the case. As we all know, past performance is not indicative of future performance. More so, I am willing to risk $2,500 per contract.

I will chronicle the real-time results of both starting from January 2010 to March 2012. I will demonstrate the realities of what possibility you might encounter.

Figure 10.1 shows what transpired with the $300,000 diversified unit model.

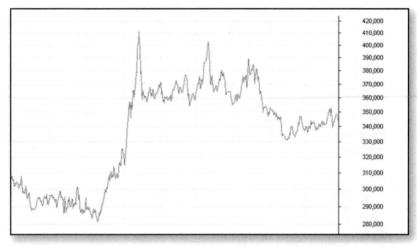

FIGURE 10.1   Equity Curve

Right off the bat I started experiencing a drawdown. As I stated I opened the separate proprietary account in the fall of 2009. Actually from that point all I experienced was a drawdown. At the end of July 2010 while I was on vacation with my family, for whatever reason several markets started to move. I did not do anything special other than make myself available and they took off. My account for this unit jumped to the $410,000 range in approximately October 2010. That is the good news. The reality is that I have been in a drawdown since then, 17 months and no profits. This is the reality of trend following. Do not think this is easy or retirement in a box. One trade after the next I have put on. I have been waking up at 5 a.m. every trading day and not seen a profit for 17 months. I have not nor will I quit. This is trend following. Trend following is a marathon.

For My Proprietary Account: $300,000 Diversified:

   2009 (September–December) –2.73 percent net of fees

   2010 +11.64 percent net of fees

   2011 –2.10 percent net of fees

My $150,000 Global Diversified unit model equity curve in Figure 10.2 is from January 2010 till March 2012, the time of this writing.

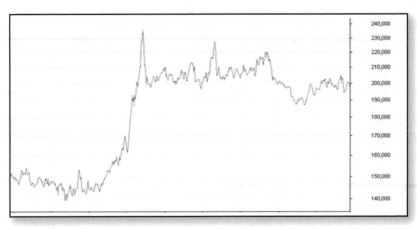

FIGURE 10.2   Real Time Equity Curve of Diversified Program

What you need to notice is the long periods when nothing has happened. Nothing has to happen when trading. I had a very short run up and then for 17 months I have been in a drawdown. Welcome to the reality of trend following.

For My Proprietary Account

2009 (November–December) –1.12 percent net of fees

2010 +34.27 percent net of fees

2011 –11.46 percent net of fees

There are only 4 possibilities when trading. One can have big losses, small losses, small profits, and rare large profits. The above demonstrate this. In my $300,000 unit size, Figure 10.3 shows some of the trades.

Sym	P.	Qty	Entry Date /	Entry Fill	Profit	%	Exit Date	Exit Fill
C	S	2	2009-09-02 Day	348.000	$-2,275	-0.8%	2009-09-15 Day	369.250
W	S	1	2009-09-02 Op...	791.500	$163	0.1%	2009-10-08 Day	786.750
JY	L	1	2009-09-03 Op...	1.0974	$575	0.2%	2009-10-22 Day	1.1078
BO	S	1	2009-09-04 Op...	41.98	$-693	-0.2%	2009-10-12 Day	43.01
ND	L	1	2009-09-08 Day	1624.25	$330	0.1%	2009-10-30 Day	1644.50
EC	L	1	2009-09-09 Op...	1.4438	$1,025	0.3%	2009-11-03 Day	1.4614

FIGURE 10.3   Example of Small Losses and small profits

Actually all that transpired for the first several months were small losses and small gains up until the end of March 2010 (Figure 10.4). I had a Eurodollar breakdown trade. Ironically the immediate trade before to go short ended in a small loss. Each trade is statistically independent and the prior trade has no bearing.

The short Eurodollar was a trade that lasted for approximately three months with 2 percent gain. Nothing to get excited about, but it offset some of the other trades that did not work. I went short March 22, 2010, and covered the short June 21, 2010. What is interesting is as always, I did not get out at the bottom. I gave back some of

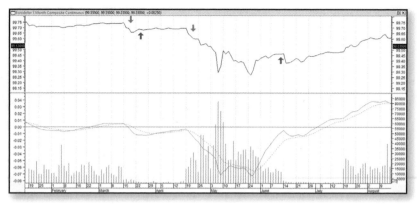

FIGURE 10.4 Eurodollar Trades

my open trade equity. My trailing stop allowed the trade to work and when the Eurodollar hit my stop, I exited. Remember, only liars get out at bottoms and at tops. Trend followers try to take a piece out of the move. We give it enough room to work but many times Murphy's law steps in and just as we exit, the trade turns around. The only solution to this is not trade. There is nothing perfect about trading. We try our best to catch trends when and if they are present. In the interim there were more small trades that I lost money on and some on which I made a small amount. Continuing, I stumbled into a nice interest rate trade in the beginning of May 2010. Trend followers do not know the future, all we try to do is follow our plan and be consistent. In the beginning of May 2010 I had a signal to purchase the 30-year bonds. That was on May 5, 2010. That trade lasted until September 10, 2010. What I want to point out on this trade was the proverbial let your winners run. You need to have patience when trend following. You cannot panic and hit the cash register prematurely. If you cannot have the patience to be in the trade for such a long period for whatever reason—greed, boredom, or fear—you need to change your thought processes. If you do not have the patience to let your winners run, you will not be in this field that long. You really need the winning trades to make up for all the inherent losses when trading.

The trade shown in Figure 10.5 returned 4.2 percent or $11,925. One day after this trade there was a signal for the 10 years. I took that trade because I did not supersede more than a 5 percent correlation in my interest rate sector. This was the last trade for the interest rate sector. I filled my quota. This is an important issue not to miss. No matter how good a trade looks, follow the plan. Make sure the plan includes the proper risk management. The 10-year trade was a good trade at a return of 2.2 percent or $6,331.

That was the good news. However, after these two unique nice trades that worked, I experienced three months of nothing but typical small losses and small profits. An example is the loss I had in corn of –$2,100 or –.7 percent. The key is to keep the losses small (Figures 10.6 and 10.7).

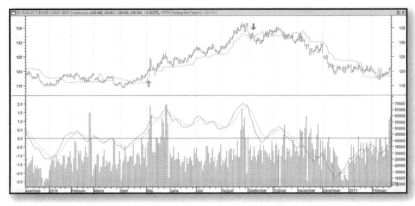

FIGURE 10.5 30 Year Bonds

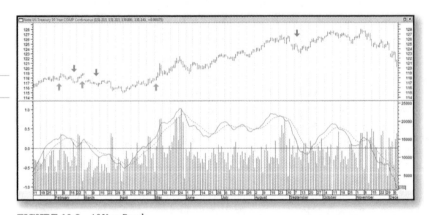

FIGURE 10.6 10 Year Bonds

There were small profits but in general I was just treading water waiting for something to trend either upward or downward.

The trade on soymeal that worked was not outstanding; rather, a 1 percent profit of $2,885. Prior to this trade there was a trade that did not work. Examples like the soymeal trade prove that one has to take every trade. We cannot pick and choose our trades. We do not know the future and we must be consistent (Figure 10.8).

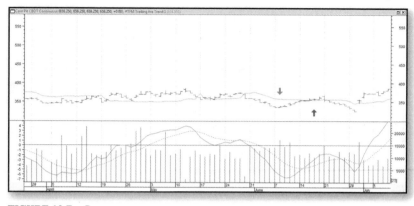

FIGURE 10.7 Corn

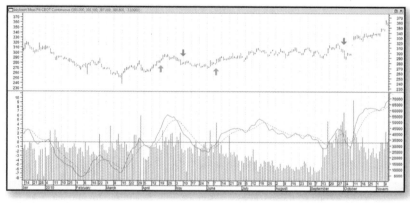

FIGURE 10.8 Soymeal

Toward the end of the three-month period in the end of July there was a beginning of a nice trend. On July 30, 2010, I entered a soybean trade. When I put this trade on I had no idea it was going to work. I ended up staying in the soybean trade until November 17, 2010. This trade highlights why you need to be patient and let the trades work (when they work). I did not get nervous or anxious to take a profit. I simply followed the tenet of good trend following—let your profits run. This trade returned $10,488 or 3.8 percent. Again, what is very important to emphasize is that the prior trade for soybeans did not work (Figure 10.9).

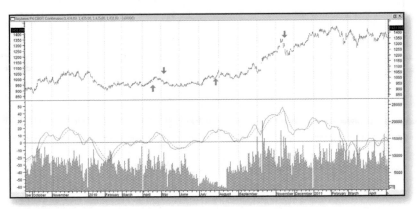

FIGURE 10.9 Soybean
MetaStock®. Copyright© 2012 Thomson Reuters. All rights reserved.

What is interesting with the period of July 2010 was that I was on vacation with my family in Greece. I remember vividly maintaining my stringent routine of waking at 5 a.m. in order that my trades could be entered the night before in Chicago. On average throughout the year there is an eight-hour time difference. There are no vacations when we are trend followers. I do my work regardless wherever I am in the world. I was in Bangkok on holiday and due to the time difference I was able to sleep in slightly. Actually, if I had not taken the soybean trade or the upcoming cotton trade, my 2010 trade returns would have been greatly impacted.

Point in fact—you must take every trade. You never know which ones will really work.

Cotton was one of those trades you step back from and say to yourself "Can you believe that? Wow." I remember watching the only TV show I might watch, *Bloomberg*, and seeing analysts stating that cotton will never go over 100. Well, they were so totally wrong (as analysts and all other gurus). Cotton knocked on the door of almost 200. I got in cotton on August 2, 2010, and patiently stayed with it till November 22, 2010. It was a huge profit, 7.5 percent or $21,730. In every trade you can learn. What can be learned from this trade is that yes, it was a unique rare trade; however, you never get out at the top or the bottom. Mr. Murphy stepped on this trade. Not that I am complaining or feel I left money on the table. I was taken out of this trade and almost immediately cotton continued on its trajectory into the stratosphere. Due to the volatility and risk I could not take the trade. I did not chase it or feel that I missed out. I thanked God for what I was able to take out of the trend. Cotton climbed and peaked slightly lower than 200. I want to emphasize this point. Anything can happen when we trade. You do not want to listen to the news or any so-called experts. No one knows any more than you. You must follow your exact plan. You must take every trade. You must have the patience to let them work. I followed them with my trailing stop and respected the stop once it was hit (Figure 10.10).

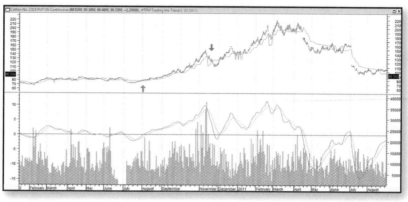

FIGURE 10.10 Cotton

During the following weeks, there were the typical small losses and small profits. Exemplifying this, I had a small loss with crude. I entered on August 16, 2010, and held on till September 13, 2010. This trade resulted in a small loss of −$663 or −.2 percent. Trades like this crude prove you should cut your losses quickly before they get out of hand. All the trades are following exactly the same plan. I am seeking a breakout, either on the upside or downside. I measure my risk, watch my correlation, watch my open trade equity, and if I can take the trade, I use my two stops as a safety precaution. Over and over again I perform the same actions (Figure 10.11).

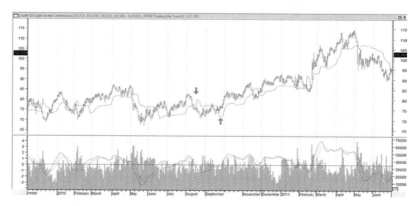

FIGURE 10.11 Crude Oil

I experienced some more small losses during the month. On August 25, 2010, I had a gold trade. I am not a gold bug and believed that as much as gold could go to $2,000 as so many were calling for, I also believed that gold could fall to $200. Either way I was willing to take the trade. The important issue as a trend follower is not to trade your opinions; rather, trade the market. Listen to what the market is telling you. I stayed with the gold till January 7, 2011. I followed the trade with my average true range trailing stop. When the stop hit, I exited. All of my trades are done without any pressure or fear. Just take the trade, let's see what happens. I know what I am trying to risk, in the case of this model .75 basis points of my core equity. I ask myself, "How much is this going to cost me to see if this trade will work?" I know statistically most of my trades do not work. There is no high win rate nonsense. Just being consistent and doing the same thing over and over again, letting the odds work over time.

The gold trade shown in Figure 10.12 returned +2.7% or $8,275. What also helped on this trade was that I was able to take advantage of position sizing. I was able to put on two contracts as opposed to one. This enhanced my profit.

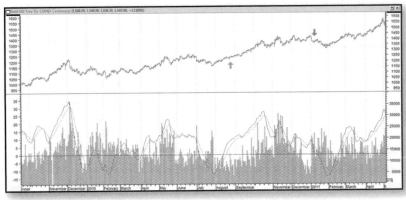

FIGURE 10.12   Gold

On August 26, 2010, I had a silver trend breakout trade. Silver was coming out of a quiet period. Actually, some of my best trades come out of times when the markets are quiet and break out. I was fortunate to have again the opportunity to put on two contracts for the same risk as a one-lot. I was in silver until January 7, 2011. This was a nice trade. This trade returned +6.1 percent or $18,420. As one could easily get frustrated, after I was taken out of this trade silver continued. I did not chase the trade. I did not feel I missed out. I appreciated what I was able to take out of the market. I received another signal a month later for silver and took another bite out of the apple (Figure 10.13).

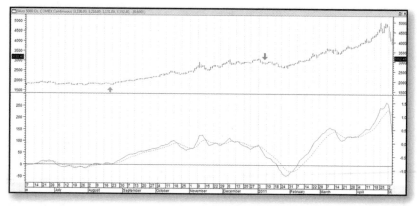

FIGURE 10.13 Silver

The month of September continued with more small losses and small profits. An example is a British pound trade where there was a breakdown short sale. I entered the short British pound on September 7, 2010, and stayed with this trade until September 15, 2010. Cut your losses quickly and let your profits run. This short sale was a small loss of –$1,725 or –.6 percent of my proprietary account. I have had and will have countless trades like this small British pound loss. I was taken out of the trade by the protective average true range trailing stop (Figure 10.14).

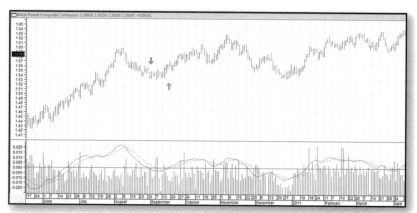

FIGURE 10.14 British Pound

On September 13, 2010, I had a trend breakout trade on the Nasdaq 100 futures contract. I stayed with this trade until I was taken out by the trailing average true range stop on March 10, 2011. I let my profits run. This trade generated $7,530 or +2.5 percent. As much as I had personal opinions regarding the stock market I took the trade shown in Figure 10.15. I learned over the years that my opinions do not make me any money.

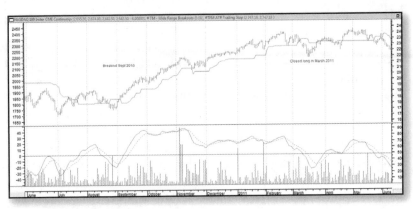

FIGURE 10.15   Nasdaq
MetaStock®. Copyright© 2012 Thomson Reuters. All rights reserved.

A couple days later on September 17, 2010, I had a trend breakout signal for the S&P 500. I held this trade until March 10, 2011. This was one of the last profitable trades I would see for months. This trade returned +2.9% or $8,688. However, this was the end of the profitable trading period. Until the end of the year all I had were small losses and some small profits. These small losses ate into the profits that were generated on a handful of the "rare" big profits (Figure 10.16).

An example of the multitude of small losses are exemplified by natural gas. I had a trend breakout to the short side on December 22, 2010, and by a short six days later I was out on December 31, 2010, with a loss of −.7 percent or −$2,700. I had trade after trade like the ones shown in Figure 10.17. I did not quit. I did not get upset. I know that as much as I get lucky at times with some big trades, the nature of trend following is to have numerous small losses.

Getting whipped around in wheat was not an exercise I like repeating; however, it is reality. I had three trades in a row that did not work. The difference between me and other traders is that if there were a fourth trade to try, I would gladly accept the risk and see what happens. I remember Paul Tudor Jones speaking about how many times

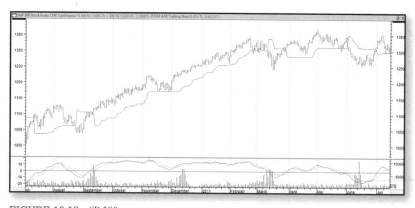

FIGURE 10.16 SP 500

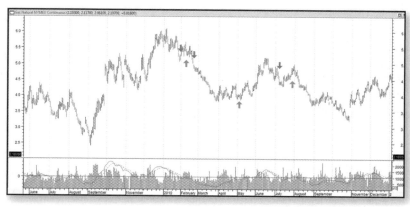

FIGURE 10.17 Natural Gas

he tried to catch a silver trade until it finally worked. This is the mindset. The last trade has no bearing on the next trade. They are statistically unique occurrences and our job as a trend follower is to let the odds work out over time. Ed Seykota's answer to whipsaw trades was very simple: "Do not trade."

The wheat trade on December 29, 2010, was a trend breakout to the upside. I exited with a small loss of –.6 percent or –$2,125 on January 11, 2011. The trailing average rate of change got me out of this. It is extremely important to honor your stops. There is no "the market will come back." At times it can get brutally worse. Wheat fell from the $1,050s to the $800s, which could have been a HUGE loss. What to glean from this is that I can have numerous trades in a row that do not work in a particular market. Due to these losses I do not arbitrarily decide to stop trading that particular market. Any market can completely surprise us, and we need to make ourselves available to all opportunities. This is in complete contradiction to many that look at the past results of a market and cherry pick which markets they decide to trade. Past results are not indicative of future results (Figure 10.18).

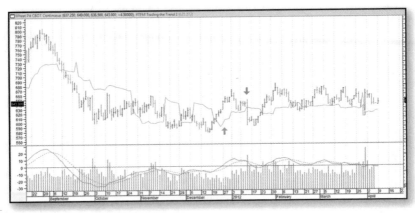

FIGURE 10.18 Wheat
MetaStock®. Copyright© 2012 Thomson Reuters. All rights reserved.

I finished the year 2010 with all the small losses, small profits, and a handful of nice trades up net +11.20 percent.

I have not seen my equity peak of November 2010 until today (March 23, 2012). Some would think 2010 was a fluke; however, as I discussed in the prior chapters, there are only four options that could have occurred.

> **Big Losses**—Did not have any of those as I had immediately placed my stops in the market. I was fortunate that there were not any big gaps or limit moves against me. These are out of my control and will happen.
>
> **Small Losses**—The majority of my trades ended up as a small loss.
>
> **Small Profits**—I had many small profits of less than .2 to 1.2 percent.
>
> **Rare Big Profits**—I was fortunate to have had position sizing enhance some of the trends that I caught and extended for months at a time.

I followed the basic tenets of trend following that so many cannot. I let my profits run and I cut my losses short.

This is trend following.

The year 2011 was not one of my better years as well as not one of the better years for many trend followers. I will detail what transpired in 2011.

Really nothing happened in January 2011 other than the typical small losses until mid-February. There were seven trades and no trends. On February 10, 2011, I had a breakout signal on silver. The trade shown in Figure 10.19 stayed until May 5, 2011. Silver hit almost $50 and imploded. I gave back a nice chunk of my profits. The velocity of the fall was shocking. Within several short days silver crashed. The profit on this trade was $8,971 or 2.4 percent (Figure 10.19).

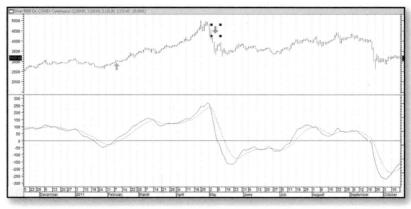

FIGURE 10.19   Silver

Throughout the month of February and all of March nothing but small losing and small winning trades. Seventeen trades transpired until the Swiss franc trade started working (see Figure 10.20). I entered the Swiss franc on April 20, 2011. I stayed with this trade until August 26, 2011, when it started to implode. I got in at 1.1272 and the Swiss franc ran up all the way to 1.4233. In one day the Swiss franc fell approximately 800 points. I exited with my trailing stop of 1.2554. This trade was profitable but the giveback was ugly. However, this is the reality of trend following. We never get out at the top. However, this trade fell apart very quickly. I profited $15,950 or 4.2 percent. I cannot stress how important it is to honor your stop. There are many who are of the "It will come back syndrome." I have seen too many people destroyed by this syndrome such as by the Nasdaq or Enron trades as glaring examples.

Months passed and nothing but the typical losses and some small profits. I had many small losses below the −1 percent range and some profits of the .2 to 1 percent range. Not until July 17, 2011, did I have a trade that made up for all of the

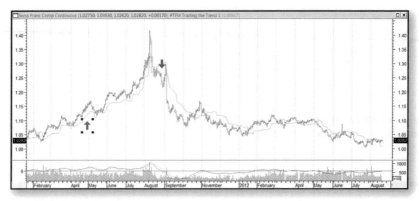

FIGURE 10.20 Franc

small losses. I had a gold trade in which I entered a trend breakout to the upside (see Figure 10.21). I entered at 1,563 and due to the tight stop was able to trade two contracts due to position size. This enhanced my result. I stayed in this trade until September 22, 2011. Gold got up to almost $2,000 and I exited via my average trend following trailing stop at 1,765.5. Gold was all over the news and the rantings of breaking $2,000 were headlines. Headlines are the dread of trend followers. Once the *Wall Street Journal* starts speaking about a particular market, the writing is on the wall of the end of the trade. However, it is never prudent to follow the news. I trust my methodology and trust it to keep me in the trade while it is working and get me out quickly when it is not.

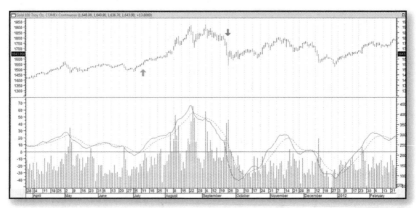

FIGURE 10.21 Gold

One of the reasons that 2011 was a lacking year was the lack of trends. The only way to make money is if one of these markets moves either up or down. Nothing happened until November 2011. Natural gas broke down on November 7, 2011. At 4.025 I had a signal to go short. This was a big trade; however, the year was lacking some trades that trended. I ended up the year 2011 with a long S&P 500 trade on December 30, 2011. I am still in this trade at the time of this writing. I entered on the breakout signal at a price of 1,251.00 (Figure 10.22).

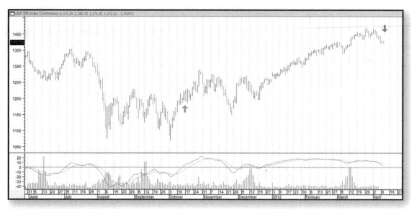

FIGURE 10.22 SP 500

In the year 2011 I had approximately 90-some trades. However, the vast majority did not work and what were lacking were those rare big trades that make the year. The year 2011 ended with a small loss of −2.1 percent.

In my model in which I trade a unit size of $150,000, which I called Global Diversified, I am willing to take on slightly more risk for more potential upside.

My beginning trades in 2009 were the typical small losses and small profit scenarios. They are almost too many to start listing. One trade that did work to some degree was a gold trade. It was your typical breakout trade, which I purchased on November 3, 2009, at $1,091. What is interesting is the trade right before did not work. If I had used the prior trade as a basis for the next trade I would have lost potential profit. The prior trade has absolutely nothing to do with the next trade. One must take every trade via one's plan. I exited this trade on December 11, 2009, as I was taken out by my trailing ATR stop. No rocket science, just repeating the same action over and over again and letting the market give me endless opportunities. Some of these present opportunities while most do not. I profited approximately 1.1 percent on this trade. There was no additional position sizing; it was a one lot for the unit size (Figure 10.23).

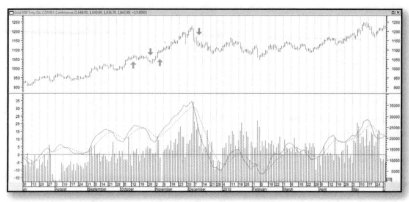

FIGURE 10.23 Gold

On the same day, November 3, 2009, I had a soymeal trade. This was a nice quick loss. I lost approximately $1,835 or −1.2 percent and exited by November 6. A month later I had a trade to go long on soymeal on December 14, 2009. This trade also did not work. I exited within a week on December 21, 2009, with a loss of −$1,575 or −1.1 percent. I did not stop trading soymeal because of these back-to-back losses. One must take each trade as it comes. There is no second guessing or picking or choosing which trades one wants. If you do this you are guaranteed to be part of the 90 percent club of losing traders. If I did not take my small loss, the situation would have been grave as soymeal fell strongly. There's nothing wrong with taking small losses. They are unavoidable! (See Figure 10.24).

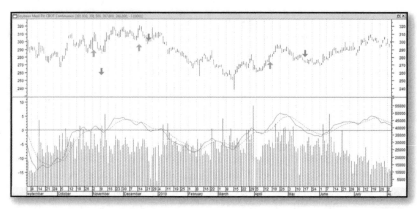

FIGURE 10.24 Soymeal

Sugar was a nice trade. Not that I did anything other than follow my plan. I entered with a breakout trade to the upside on December 11, 2009, at 15.66 with one lot per unit. This trade trended and on February 5, 2010, I was taken out by my trailing stop at 18.97. The trade resulted in a profit of 2.5 percent or $3,632. This offset some of my losing trades. This is exactly what transpires. Small losses and small profits … over and over again (Figure 10.25).

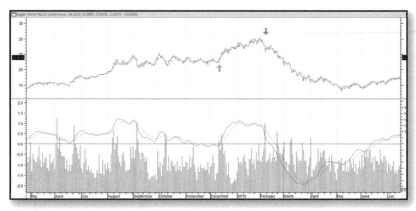

I experienced six trades in a row that did not work. One right after the next, nice. In soymeal I lost −1.1 percent, wheat lost −.9 percent, soybean oil lost −.8 percent, lean hogs lost −.8 percent, silver lost −.7 percent, and last but definitely not least, soybean oil (AGAIN) lost −.1 percent. What is important to note is that all of these losses were small. None of them were either financially or emotionally devastating. Just have to keep on putting the trades on and see what happens. Another way to think about it, which I do, is how much is this going to cost me to see if this trade will work. I like thinking in this fashion as it demonstrates I have no expectations, as well as the fact that I realize that the trade does not have to work. After my nice series of losses I was fortunate to have a series of some trades that worked. I had three trades in a row that worked. The problem is that they did not work enough. I had a wheat trade that I got in on January 12, 2010, and exited on February 16, 2010. This wheat trade resulted in a .5 percent profit or $763 per unit. There was a Eurodollar trade I entered on January 13, 2010, for a .4 percent profit or $600 per unit. This Eurodollar trade lasted until April 5, 2010. As well, during this period I had a corn trade when the grain complexes seemed to start moving in unison. I entered on January 13, 2010, and was eventually taken out of this trade on February 22, 2010, by my average true range trailing stop. The corn trade resulted in a .5 percent profit or $650 per unit. What is noted is that I filled up my correlation risk by having both the corn trade and wheat at the same time. I do not want to have more than 5 percent of my portfolio in any one sector. If I allocated heavier in a sector my correlations to risk would increase dramatically. My goal is to generate reasonable returns over time, being cognizant of the risks I am taking on at every point.

As Murphy's Law would have it, my next three trades did not work. One after the next did not work. I had a long yen trade in which I entered on January 27, 2010. This trade did not last long, as I exited being taken out by my trailing average true range stop on February 18, 2010. This trade resulted in a loss of −$1,144 or −1 percent per unit. The next trade that did not work was lean hogs (again). You have to just keep on trying to catch the breakout. You cannot pick and choose which trades you do not want to take. I went short the lean hogs on January 27, 2010. It is not common to have more than one trade in a day. I do not trade that often, and a good trading day is a day in which I do not trade. This would mean the trades that I have already entered might be working or there is too much volatility in the market so it is time to try to avoid the noise. The lean hog trade did not work and resulted in another small loss. I exited on February 23, 2010, via my trailing average true range stop. The lean hog trade resulted in a loss of −$955 per unit or .7 percent per unit, livable loss but not fun. The grind continued with a small loss in natural gas. This trade was entered on January 29, 2010, as a short trade. It was a quick trip. I exited via the trailing average range stop on February 8, 2010, with a loss of −$1,313 per unit or −.9 percent of the account. My luck started to improve with two trades in a row that worked. They worked to some extent but not a home run. On February 12, 2010, I had a breakout signal to go long cotton at 30.75. This trade lasted until April 8, 2010. I was taken out of the trade by the average true range trailing stop. What is to be noted here is the patience to let trades unfold. There are no emotions such as fear, greed, or ego. Just let the trade unfold and follow it. Your biggest profits are made by simply doing nothing. This was not the case with this trade but it was an okay trade. The trade made +1.45 percent per unit or $1,965 per unit. On February 18, 2010, I went short natural gas. This would be the first short trade in the implosion of natural gas. This trade exemplifies that trend followers do not catch tops nor exit at the bottom. We take pieces out of the trades. I had a breakdown signal to sell natural gas at 7.04. This trade continued until May 15, 2010, till a price of 6.145 was taken out by the average true range trailing stop. The short natural gas trade returned from the short side +1.6 percent per unit or $2,163 per unit. What is notable about this trade was the prior loss encountered on January 29, 2010. This loss had nothing to do with trying to go short once again. You have to have losses in order to have profits. The goal, however, is to try to keep them small (Figure 10.26).

As one starts to understand at this point from viewing all these trades I am simply accumulating small losses and small profits. The next two trades were losses but were kept to a manageable level. I had a signal to go long the Japanese yen on February 25, 2010. The entry long price was 1.1364. This trade did not work and I exited with a loss on March 10, 2010, at a price of 1.1141. The trade, like all other trades, was exited via the trailing average true range stop. The trade resulted in a loss of -$1,469 per

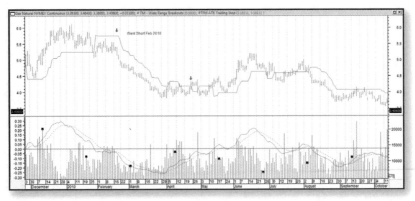

FIGURE 10.26 Natural Gas

unit or −1 percent per unit. Also, on February 25, 2010, I had a long trade on 10-year bonds. I had a breakout signal at a price of 110.20 and was taken out on March 24, 2010, for a −.8 percent loss per unit or −$1,222 per unit. This trade really never did anything after I had the buy breakout. There are times, however, when the trades start working and then turn around. You have to give them enough room to retrace; however, at times this causes not breakeven trades but losses. You cannot be afraid to take a loss. You must accept the risks when putting on a trade. No trade has to work. Finally, it was nice to stumble into a trade that worked to some degree. The S&P 500 generated a buy breakout on March 1, 2010, at a price of 1,060. I rode this trend until I was taken out on May 4, 2010, at a price of 1,129.5 via my trailing average true range stop. This trade resulted in a +2.4 percent profit per unit or $3,388 per unit. This S&P 500 offset some of those nagging small losses; however, I was still on my quest for some nice big home run trades that occur infrequently (Figure 10.27).

The rest of the month I had my numerous small losses and very small profits. None of them overly interesting to point out. Just the typical noise while trading. However, on March 22, 2010, I stumbled into a nice short Eurodollar trade. This was a breakdown trade, which I stayed with until June 21, 2010. What is interesting with this trade was the amount of open trade profit I had to give back. I entered my short at a price of 1.3435 and exited via my trailing average true range stop at 1.2406; however, the lows of this trade went down to the 1.18 range. As I have stated and restated, you never get out at the bottom. You have to be flexible in your expectations. You cannot control a trade. You have to follow the plan exactly and let the chips fall where they will. You will always have times when a trade really works that you will give back. You do not have to think you left chips on the table. You followed the plan, you made a little money, pat yourself on the back and move on. Do not think for one second that you or anyone else will know where the bottom of any trade will be. The short Eurodollar

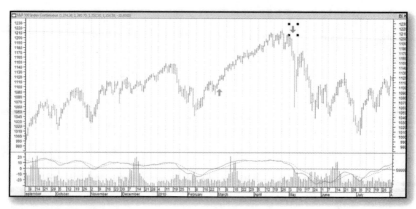

FIGURE 10.27 SP 500

trade netted out +4.5 percent per contract per unit or $6,356 per unit. This made up for a lot of losing trades. However, I was not really profitable for the year at this point. Just a lot of work for nothing. This is why patience, discipline, and controlling ego are so important. There was no one to whom I would brag about this trade. It does not matter. It is just one trade in a long series of trades. One makes money over long periods of time. Any one trade or any month really do not mean anything. This is why I compare trend following and trading to a marathon. Yes, it is grueling, but over time, when you have compounded money, you can appreciate all the hard work that went into it. There is no get rich quick. There is putting on the trades over and over again and having the patience to let the concept work over time (Figure 10.28).

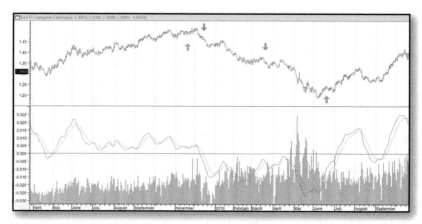

FIGURE 10.28 Euro Dollar

Nothing much happened in the month of April except, as I told you it would happen, I got somewhat impacted with a gap against me. I had a breakout signal again for cotton. I went long on April 21, 2010, at a price of 39.54. The trade lasted until May 5, 2010, in which I was taken out by the trailing average true range stop. I have attempted to risk only 1.25 percent of my account on any trade. However, due to a gap that went against me I had a larger loss. These will always happen and worse will be limit moves in which you cannot exit. This is the reality when trading. I lost 1.5 percent on this trade. This was not devastating but much more than I anticipated or wanted to lose to see if the trade would work. On the cotton trade I lost $2,105 per unit or 1.5 percent when I exited at 35.48. The only way to prevent issues like this is not to trade.

Patience is a virtue when trend following. It is as if we are fishing for trends. On April 28, 2010, I caught a nice fish. It was a 10-year bond version. I entered the long breakout at 110.57 and had the patience to ride it up till September 9, 2010. There would be those who would be unhappy with this trade. I had some open trade profit and the trade reversed and was taken out by my protective average range trailing stop, locking in $7,519 per unit per contract. Great, this was a +5.3 percent profit on the trade. However, what is so typical and what makes trend following so hard, I was taken out and the trade reversed and continued its trajectory upward. I exited at 118.17 and after being taken out the trade reversed and ran up to approximately the 122 range. That is a lot of money. However, I stuck with my plan. I did not look out the back window and complain (no one would care, anyway). More importantly, in order to educate I did not try to chase this trade. I did not have a signal. I did not feel bad. Just have to stay in the Nike moment and just keep on putting them on without any emotion. No greed. No fear. Just grind them out and let's see what happens (Figure 10.29).

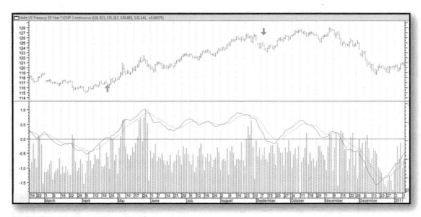

FIGURE 10.29 10 Year Bonds

Nothing much happened other than small losses and small profits all of the rest of May until mid-June. I had two trades, though, that returned in the mid-2 percent range. On June 6, 2010, I had a signal to go long soymeal again. I entered the breakout trade at 278.5. I rode this trade until October 10, 2010. I exited at a price of 310.4 on a one-lot for a profit of 2.1 percent per unit or $3,115 per unit. On June 17, 2010, I had a signal to enter the Eurodollar interest rate contract. Due to position sizing I was able to enter four contracts for the same risk as one contract. When the trade worked this benefited me. I entered the Eurodollar at 98.615 long. The trade carried on till September 8, 2010, and resulted in a 2.3 percent return per unit or $3,250.

Afterwards I had a small loss on silver of approximately −.7 percent or a loss of −$1,050 per contract. No big shakes. I hit a nice single on the Japanese yen on June 24, 2010. I entered long at 113.09 and followed the trade via the average true range trailing stop on September 16, 2010. This trade resulted in a profit of 1.8 percent per contract per unit or $2,600. In this inning of baseball trend following I had some singles, which offset all the various strikeouts and losses. These small singles make up for the aggravation of all the losses. I also had some other nice percentage winners, which started to help me. This is in complete contradiction to the upcoming year, 2011, in which I did not have that many trades work, rather a lot of small losses and whipsaws so my results were negatively impacted. You can compare the two years to understand. It really all boils down to what the markets give us, and they can be very stingy some years.

July was full of one loss after the next. Actually, five losses in a row. The reason I wanted to include this trade diary is so that you will see in reality that trades do not have to work and that you will have multiple times when trade after trade does not work.

Time to quit, nope. The next trade was like a fisherman catching Moby Dick. Before that thought my emotions were fully tested. I had a small loss on feeder cattle, −.4 percent, and soybean oil was a loss of −1 percent. Natural gas resulted in a loss of −.7 percent, and a lovely one after the next loss in lean hogs, each −.8 percent. So for all of this fun I lost 3.7 percent. One step backward and a lot of steps forward.

I was on vacation with my family, got up at my usual 5 a.m., and downloaded my data. I entered my orders and went back to vacation. I had put in an order to buy cotton. I did not know anything special nor am I an expert in cotton. I did not check the weather forecast for wherever cotton is grown. Just took the breakout long like all the other trades I take, saying to myself, "How much is this going to cost me to see if it works?" I entered on August 2, 2010, and rode this trend via my trailing average range stop until November 22, 2010. I was in the same trade as my Diversified proprietary account. Thank God. Many times the two are in different trades due to the way they are built. The cotton trade worked past my wildest expectations (actually, I did not have any). The cotton trade resulted in a 14.5 percent return per contract per unit or $21,370 per contract per unit. That was the fantastic news; however, as usual Mr. Murphy (Murphy's Law) was around. I got taken out on a retracement. Ironically, the cotton trade took me out via my trailing stop and continued on its upward path. I did not feel betrayed. I followed my plan to the absolute degree. I did not feel upset that I was taken out by my trailing stop. My trailing stop has protected me when trades have not worked, and when trades do work the trailing stop gives them enough room to run. On a back-adjusted chart the highs were approximately 112 and I was exited two bars before the pivot low of approximately 71 before the trend retraced and ran up to about 173. This is trading. You will never get out at the top. The greater the move, either long or short, there will be greater volatility as others start to jump in on these trends. One does not want to jump in on markets that are volatile. Some of the best trades I have ever had over the years started in quiet markets. You just never know what trades will work and which ones will not.

August had the typical small losing trades; however, I stumbled onto a gold trade on August 13, 2010. I entered a long breakout at 1,232.90 and was in the trade until the trailing stop took me out on November 16, 2010. This trade ended up profiting 2.7 percent per contract per unit or $4,038 per contract per unit. This helped to offset those nagging small losses.

I had a small loss on feeder cattle, which resulted in a small loss of −.8 percent.

Moby Dick had a brother. It was called silver. I cannot say it enough times. You need to make yourself available for trades to occur. You never know when or in what market you will make money (as well as lose money). Silver just so happened to be that market. I entered on August 25, 2010, and what enhanced my return was that for the same risk I was able to put on two contracts. This underscores the power of position sizing. Position sizing is such an important tool with which to compound money. It is so aptly demonstrated in this trade with silver. I entered the two lots at a price (back adjusted) of 1,885. I was patient and let the trade run its course. On January 7, 2011, I had a signal to exit via the trailing average true range stop at 285,410. This trade resulted in a 12.4 percent return for the unit or $19,232. If I had only taken one trade as in the concept of fixed size I would have left a lot of money on the table. This underscores the reality and necessity to trade via percentages. When you trade via percentages it also helps to get out of the money thought process. One should trade for percentage returns, not money. It seems a lot worse or better when you look at a loss via dollar terms. To me, trend following is a game and we need to think of it as a game in which we try to compound money (Figure 10.30).

The trends were on a roll (however, as usual they would be short lived and the ugly drawdowns would soon start). On September 13, 2010, I had a breakout signal that the S&P 500 was one of the strongest on a nominal basis of the markets I was looking at. I went long at 1,081.5 and was in this trade until March 10, 2011, when I was taken out via my trailing stop. This trade resulted in a 5.9 percent profit per contract per unit or $9,125 per contract per unit. On September 24, 2010, I had a breakout long sugar trade. Sugar was one of the strongest markets I was looking at. I want to buy the strongest if I can put on a low-risk bet and sell the weakest if I can put on a low-risk bet.

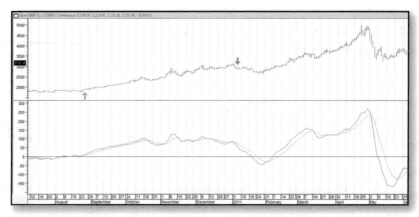

FIGURE 10.30 Silver

The low-risk bet is comparing the initial risk on the trade from the X-day breakout to the Y-day low. I look at my core equity (the amount of money I have in my account, not including open trade equity) and risk 1.25 percent of my account size. It is not as if any trade is low risk. Every day has risk and there are times my anticipated risk level is exceeded. I entered sugar at 17.22 and stayed in the trade via the trailing stop until November 12, 2010, at 21.09 (back adjusted). This trade exemplifies the tenet of good trend following: Let your profits run. There are countless trades in which I also followed the good tenet of trend following: Cut your losses short. It is almost funny to a perverted degree. I followed my rules and lost money. This is what makes trend following so hard for most people to do. The sugar trade netted me 2.6 percent per contract per unit or $4,259 per contract per unit.

For the rest of the months of 2010 I had many small losses and small profits. However, what is shocking (except I know this happens much more than we like) is that I had nine trades in a row that did not work. My equity peak of 2010 would not be seen for a long time. Currently I am still waiting to recover back to these levels. The importance of trying to risk small percentages of one's account is exemplified in the December 2010 and January 2011 periods. If I had taken bigger risks I could have easily been down in excess of 20 percent in one month. I try not to look at the upside or how much I can make. I look at how much I might lose. I attempt to mitigate the losses, but as in trading the only guarantee is uncertainty.

Chronicling these trades that did not work gives us a good idea of what to expect in your own personal trading. Seeing nine trades in a row is reality. Trend following is not "easy."

On December 17, 2010, the Canadian dollar was one of the strongest markets on a nominal basis compared to the basket of markets I trade. I entered a long trade at 9,841(back adjusted), and within a few short days on December 21, 2010, my trailing average true range stop rescued me from a bigger loss. I exited at 9,670 for a loss of −.9 percent per contract per unit or −$1,785 per contract per unit. This was loss one. There were eight more to go. On December 27, 2010, I had a signal that natural gas was one of the weakest markets and a signal to sell one contract per unit. I sold short natural gas at 4.97 and again in a few short days I was saved by my trailing stop. I exited on December 31, 2010, at 5.30 for a loss of −.9 percent loss per unit or −$1,800. I just kept on swinging on the upcoming trades. I had a signal to try to buy crude oil. At times it might seem this is not the strongest market but in nominal terms it is. It might be the best in general but not highly trending at times for a long or the worst in general for times for a short. I entered the long crude breakout trade at 100.75 on January 30, 2010, and by January 6, 2011, the fun was over and I had a loss of −.8 percent per contract or −$1,638. The Eurodollar was weakening and was the weakest on a nominal basis comparing all the markets I trade. I went short at 130.63 on January 6, 2011. This trade did not last a long time whatsoever. I exited via my trailing average true range stop on January 14, 2011. This loss was another −.9 percent or −$1,831 per contract. The losses were adding up; however, my frustration level was not affected. I have been in this story: No one ever promised me any trade had to work. I was thinking, however, that it was about time for a trade to work. However, that was not the case. I still had another five more losses to go through. On January 11, 2011, I had another bite of the apple. I had a signal to buy the Canadian dollar at 99.60. I was in this trade until January 31, 2011. This was a loss of −.6 percent or −$1,205. At this point most would start questioning their trading system or start tinkering. This would be the worst thing one could do. What was transpiring was no six sigma event. It has happened in the past and will happen in the future regardless of the meaning we put on it.

Being consistent or a glutton for punishment I had another try at crude. I had a buy signal on January 12, 2011, at 101.35. Again, another loss. I exited quickly in order to keep my losses small and was out via my trailing average true range stop on January 20, 2011. This loss was −.9 percent or $1,888 per contract per unit. Three more losses to come, but who is counting? On January 18, 2011, I had a purchase of soymeal at 400.20. This trade also did not work. I was in this trade a little more time, however. I exited the loss on February 15, 2011, at 385.50 for a loss of −.7 percent per contract per unit or −$1,515. On February 1, 2011, I took the long breakout signal for soybean oil. Again this trade did not work. The loss on this trade was −.7 percent or −$1,425 per contract per unit. One last trade and I was starting year 2011 off pretty much the way it ended for the year, ugh. This is reality and did not curb my passion or my enthusiasm for trading. I know this is expected and there was no surprise. The problem is for people who have unrealistic expectations. They are hurt by periods like this and cut themselves off from the good periods. The reason I am highlighting nine losses in a row is to accentuate the fact that it will happen in the future and might even be worse. This way you are prepared for this. It is not a shock. This way hopefully you will stay in the marathon of trading.

My last lovely loss in my series of nine trades that did not work was wheat. I went long wheat on February 2,2011, as it was one of the strongest markets and it was a breakout. I entered at 1,025.25 and exited via my trailing average true range stop. I exited on February 18, 2011, for a loss of −.9 percent or −$1,775 per unit. By the beginning of February I had a slight respite from consistent losses. I had a small natural gas trade that worked for +.8 percent. I survived the deluge and finally stumbled into a nice trade. I was down approximately 7–8 percent from the beginning of the year in a relatively short period of time. This was slightly reversed by a nice silver trade. I entered the silver trade with a trend breakout on February 9, 2011, at a price of 30.50. I was in this trade until it imploded on May 4, 2011. Silver had gotten to approximately 50.00 and then completely fell out of bed. Within a short couple of days I was out at 39.40. That was a lot to give back, but that is reality. The silver trade netted 4.3 percent or $8,826 per contract per unit (see Figure 10.30). This was a far cry from the open trade equity I had with it, but so is trading. There is no one to gripe to. This is why I write.

The small losses continued in February 2011. I had a loss of −.5 percent on a Canadian dollar trade. There was a feeder cattle loss of −.5 percent, lean hog −.6 percent, and Australian dollar with a loss of −.9 percent. Four trades in a loss until I stumbled onto a gold trade. Gold was purchased on February 23, 2011, at 1,417.20. Due to position sizing I was able to put on two contracts for the same risk as if it were a one-lot. This magnified my profit for the same small percentage anticipated risk of 1.25 percent. Gold continued in the trend until June 24, 2011. I exited when it hit my trailing average true range stop at 1,522.11. This trade resulted in a 3.4 percent profit per contract per unit or $6,836 per contract per unit. Just to clarify, per unit is referring to the model size of $150,000 per unit.

March was full of more small losses. Seven trades in a row did not work. One of the worst was−1.7 percent. This loss exceeded my anticipated losses. This will happen while you trade. The Eurodollar started out as if it would work. It had three nice up days in a row and then completely fell out of bed. I entered on March 11, 2011, and due to this fast retracement I was exited by March 28, 2011. This trade resulted in a loss of −$3,438 of my account (see Figure 10.31).

I had one trade that worked after these batch of relatively small losses. The Australian dollar trade of April 1, 2011, lasted until May 23, 2011. It was not a big profit at all. It was a welcome break after a string of trades that did not work. The Australian trade resulted in a 1.1 percent profit or $2,175 per contract per unit. No big shakes. In April and May I can easily say nothing happened. I had several more small losses and several small profits. They pretty much cancelled out each other. Almost half a year went by and pretty much nothing positive to say about my returns.

Sugar offered some relief. On June 3,2011, I entered a long trend breakout at 21.02. This long trade carried on until August 3, 2011. The trade resulted in +2.8 percent or $5,839 per unit. The rest of June was more of nothing happening. July

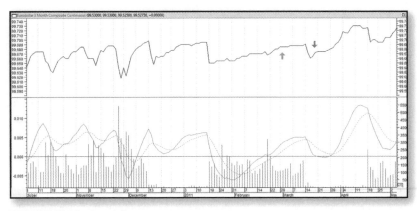

FIGURE 10.31 Eurodollar

looked like things might start turning around for the year. Trading is like football. All that really counts is what happens in the fourth quarter. The team can struggle for the whole game and in the fourth quarter win the game. There have been years like that in trading. On July 11, 2011, I entered a long gold trade at 1,561.2 with a trend breakout. I was in this trade until September 22, 2011. This trade resulted in a 3.2 percent profit per contract per unit or $6,780 (see Figure 10.32).

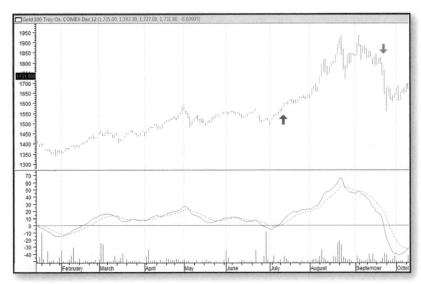

FIGURE 10.32 Gold

On the same day of entry of gold I had an entry on the Japanese yen. The yen had a long breakout trade at 125.72. This trade lasted until September 6, 2011. This yen trade resulted in a 2.1 percent profit per contract per unit or $4,313. The next day, July 12, 2011, I had a 10-year bond trade. The 10-year bond broke out to the upside and continued until I was stopped out on October 7, 2011. This trade resulted in a profit of 2.5 percent or $5,206 per contract per unit. Finally I thought I was back in the saddle and things were turning around. I could not have been more wrong. I had 18 trades not work after this point. Wow, 18 trades did not work. I had somewhat of a respite as I had 10 trades in a row that did not work and one small trade that did work. Then the fun continued; eight more trades did not work. Thank God I managed the risk. This is all that one can do. The losses were kept small, ranging from −.1 to −1.6 percent. However, losses like this are tough to take. I cannot remember when so many trades did not work. This is the reality and exemplifies why trading can be so hard. At the puke level at which most people would have wanted to quit there was the natural gas trade, which saved some of the year from being a total disaster. I am chuckling when saying a total disaster when the MF Global debacle was closing in. I entered the natural gas short trade on September 16, 2011, and was riding it along. I was able to put on a great size due to position sizing. However, this is the good news. There is bad news. I was in this trade in the thick and the thicker of MF Global and was able to transfer out all my positions the week prior to their collapse. I had updated my data version and I did not realize there was a difference between the natural gas mini contract and the full size. I was trading numerous lots of the mini size natural gas contracts for flexibility as part of my position sizing. I was able to put on more contracts due to position sizing. Again that is good news, but again I have bad news.

I stayed in this trade and as per my system, I had an exit in the beginning of December 2011 as it hit the trailing average true range stop, or so it seemed to me. However, it did not by a tick or so. I exited the position and went on my happy way with finally a nice trade that had worked after a year of countless small losses. However, I realized a couple days later when my system showed me I was still short after realizing I had a data issue. The price of natural gas had fallen sharply and I did not think it was prudent to chase the trade. However, maybe introspectively my thought of prudence was fear of losing money. I had a good trade and locked in some nice profit. However, I just got a signal and the price was rather far away from where I exited. I thought to err on the side of prudence. Natural gas went from a good trade to a great trade. I pondered if I had broken my golden rule of not letting big profits get away. Regardless of pondering, the trade did get away and I missed out on a great deal of money that would have changed somewhat my negative return in 2011 on my Diversified $150,000 proprietary account. There was no point in beating myself up or looking out the back window. The question is what to learn from this. The answer is always to get in sync with the model. I might have had some fear of losing more than 1.25 percent. Maybe I did not accept the risk that was thrust upon me. The reality is that trading is always full of lessons. The biggest issue is not following your plan or having small losses morph into large losses. The year 2011 was a year of learning. After 18 years in the markets I thought I had made every mistake and had seen every mistake. But 2011 proved me wrong.

Not that I am a glutton for punishment. October 2011 was full of some more pain for all trend followers. Ed Seykota has so aptly remarked that if you do not want to encounter whipsaw trades, do not trade. Most trend followers were in the Japanese yen trades in October 2011 and Ed Seykota's words resonated. I do not know any commodity trading advisors who quit due to these yen trades, but these were trades that we all will remember for several reasons. On October 12, 2011, I had a long breakout trade on the Japanese yen at 131.59. I held this trade for only two days. It almost immediately plunged and hit my stop. This is why stops are used. We do not know the future and need to try to keep our losses small. This trade of the Japanese yen resulted in a loss of –1.2 percent per unit of the portfolio or –$2,425 per unit. A week later my system signaled me to try the trade again. The good news I thought at the time was that due to position sizing, I could put on two contracts for the same risk. Wow, how lucky was I. Lucky was not the word. On October 31, that same lovely day that MF Global declared bankruptcy and $1.6 billion of client segregated funds supposedly "vaporized" the night before, the Japanese Central Bank decided to weaken the yen. The Japanese yen plummeted from 133.05 to 126.32. Yes, I was very lucky to have two contracts. At least they were mini contracts. This added to the pain of the MF Global collapse. It was like the icing on the cake. This trade cost me –1.2 percent or –$2,413.

When I tell you trading is tough, this exemplifies it. I use the word *marathon* quite often. I also think of the Marines, the few, the proud, the brave. I scoff at all of those that try to make trading so easy. You can watch YouTube videos in which you can use a trading robot to get rich. Thousands of people flock to learn how to day trade. At this point it should be very clear what is really entailed with trading. It is hard work emotionally. Those that can do it benefit for the rest of their lives. They have financial freedom and are independent. Traders have a choice; they can fly the plane themselves. In this book I have really taught you everything in my opinion in how to trade successfully on your own. The other choice traders or investors have is to invest in traders who will manage their accounts and sit back on the plane. Do not be deluded—there will be turbulence. Trend following and trading is not retirement in a box!

The MF Global debacle was an outright nightmare. I had wired out money on two programs that I was trading, which were substantial amounts of money. I opened up two other brokerage accounts before MF Global collapsed. I opened up with FCStone and have found them to be absolutely wonderful and feel the trading desk for CTAs is exceptional. I feel they have my back and are part of my team. I also have accounts at R.J. O'Brien with a commodity trading advisor who has traded these accounts for years. I started transferring my positions early in the week before the collapse of MF Global. I knew people at MF Global and was reassured that everything was in order and all was OK. Well, they probably were as surprised as I was on that Black Monday when they announced bankruptcy. The good news was that all my positions transferred to FCStone. The bad news was that not all my positions transferred to R.J. O'Brien. I had several Japanese yen trades, which ended up somewhere between MF Global and R.J. O'Brien. I was lucky as they were offset at R.J. I know traders that had opened positions and they were stuck. Money frozen and positions in which they could not exit. I was all in cash, and my cash was supposed to have been wired on the Friday before the collapse. This did not happen and my cash at MF Global was frozen.

Considering 2011 and what transpired, I feel very fortunate. Many traders are out of business. Lives have been destroyed. My 2011 returns for my Diversified proprietary trading were down approximately 11 percent. This was one of the worst years I can recall. As much as it was a bad year, there are years that are beyond expectations. This is really what trend following encompasses. I have been able to get through all the pain over the years, and it is still a learning process.

What this journal has done is confirm the points that I have made throughout the book. What is clear is that there are numerous small losses and small profits. There are times I stumble into some big profits, but as you can see, they are rare. The diary of my trades dispels the notion that trading is easy by a long shot. The diary shows how missing one trade can be devastating. There has not been any sugarcoating. To the contrary, there has been a lot of reality coating.

CONCLUSION

My goal in presenting *The Trend Following Bible* is to give you the ability to gain financial freedom. I have not sugarcoated anything and have given you a look at what trend following really is, no surprises. To me trend following is a lifetime strategy. It has its drawdowns and even extended periods in which profits are elusive. There will be drawdowns, there will be long periods when you do not make money, and there will be periods when you step back and say "Can you believe that?" because you stumbled onto some very large profitable trends (as rare as these are).

I have taught you exactly how I trade. It is simple in nature but hard to do in practice. The reason it is so hard is that we all have greed and fears that we need to deal with. We as traders are the weak link. This is why a key message of the book was focusing on how to think like a successful trend follower. This is no different from what William Eckhardt and Richard Dennis taught their Turtle students. The actual trading is based on Richard Donchian's breakout strategy as well as the trend retracement ideas of Alexander Elder with a strong dose of my personal risk management so often not presented. It is simple yet effective. Most of the program was spent on how to think and how to handle the emotions of fear and greed. This is also where I have tried to lay the emphasis.

Unfortunately, traders seek the holy grail. They seek the reasons why moves occur. They seek elusive trading indicators or trading systems. All one really needs is a robust methodology, strong risk management, as well as the need for patience and discipline for the plan to work over time.

The patience and discipline I cannot give you. You have to do your work. You will need to believe in the methodology and follow the plan EXACTLY. My personal thought is if trend following and the trend breakout method worked for Richard Donchian for all of those decades, why would it stop working now? I know that I will have drawdowns. I know that most of my trades will not work, but I know over time I will succeed. Trend following is a marathon.

I am here to help you in your quest to develop into a successful trader. Have patience with yourself. It is a process. You will make mistakes. You will miss trades. You will have losses. Keep in mind some of the traders mentioned in the earlier chapters of this book.

They do not know any more than you or I. They have succeeded over time due to the fact that they have a robust trading strategy, they managed the inherent risks in trading, and most importantly, they were patient and disciplined in their trading. Sound familiar?

I have stressed the ingredients needed for successful trading. Think of your trading education as money well spent. I am very grateful that you purchased this book. You have taken a positive step in your growth as a successful trend follower. I hope you internalize the methods described in the book. I would suggest you test these ideas in order to have absolute confidence in them. I have absolute confidence in them. You might want to apply these concepts to your own personality. I strongly suggest you do so.

I want to thank you once again for letting me assist you in your journey of trend following.

DISCLOSURE

Past performance is not necessarily indicative of future performance. The risk of loss in trading futures contracts, commodity options, or forex can be substantial, and therefore investors should understand the risks involved in taking leveraged positions and must assume responsibility for the risks associated with such investments and for their results. You should carefully consider whether such trading is suitable for you in light of your circumstances and financial resources.

Hypothetical performance results have many inherent limitations, some of which are described below. No representation is being made that any account will or is likely to achieve profits or losses similar to those shown. In fact, there are frequently sharp differences between hypothetical performance results and the actual results subsequently achieved by any particular trading program. One of the limitations of hypothetical performance results is that they are generally prepared with the benefit of hindsight. In addition, hypothetical trading does not involve financial risk, and no hypothetical trading record can completely account for the impact of financial risk in actual trading. For example, the ability to withstand losses or to adhere to a particular trading program in spite of trading losses are material points which can also adversely affect actual trading results. There are numerous other factors related to the markets in general or to the implementation of any specific trading program which cannot be fully accounted for in the preparation of hypothetical performance results and all of which can adversely affect actual trading results.

**The material displayed in this book is intended for education purposes only.

INDEX

10-year bond, trade journal, 183

A

Abraham Trading Company, 50–51, 77
Abraham, Salem, 50–51
Alan, 6
Alphametrix, 6
American Century Investments, 31
ArthroCare Corporation, hypothetical trade, 108
ATR. *See* average true range
attitude, 33, 157
Austin, Jeff, 70–71
average true range
   calculating, 104
   trailing stop, 102–104

B

Baidu
   buying, 128–129
   hypothetical trade, 109
Baker, Jim, 143
Barnes, Julius, 44
Baruch, Bernard, 44
Blackwater Capital Management, 70–71
Block, Paul, 44
British pound trade, trade journal, 171
broker, need for, 12
Buffett, Warren, 74
buy and hold, 41
buys

executing, 128–130
protection, 134

C

Canadian dollar, hypothetical trade, 111
CANSLIM, 92–93
capital, need for, 13–15
Chadwick Investing Group, 72–73
charting software, 20–21
Chase, Stuart, 43
Chavel, Elizabeth, 52–53
Chesapeake Capital, 62–63
Clarke Capital Management Worldwide, 64–65
Clarke, Michael, 64–65
CMG, buying, 129
Combined Fund DCF, 16
commitment, 32–33
commodity futures, trading, 100–101
commodity trading, risk measures, 89–90
commodity, hypothetical trade, 118
Complete Turtle Trader, The, 72
compound interest, 30
compounding, 7–8, 25, 28–32
computer system, 20–21
considerations, 20
consistency, 85, 154–155
control, 156–157
cool, keeping, 34
Coolidge, Calvin, 42
correlation coefficient, 87–88

Corzine, Jon, 76
cotton, 151–152
  hypothetical trade, 116
  trade journal, 168–169
Covel, Michael, 62, 72
crude oil, 123–124, 152
  selling, 131–132
CTA Expos, 6
curve fitting, 47

D

decisions, 20
Dennis, Richard, 52, 54, 54, 58, 62, 96–97,
  138–139, 193
dentist, 7–8, 142
Dighton, 4
discipline, 18–20
diversified unit, trade journal, 162–177
dollar risk per contract, 89–90
  commodity futures and, 100–101
Donchian, Richard, 45–46, 96–98, 193
Douglas, Mark, 139
drawdown, 29, 46–47
  trade journal, 163
Drury Capital, 68–69
Drury, Bernard, 68–69
Druz, David, 8, 48, 60–61, 160
Dunn Capital Management, 16, 66
Dunn, Bill, 16, 159–160

E

Eckhardt Trading Company, 56–57, 77
Eckhardt, William, 52, 54, 56–57, 58, 96–97,
  138–139, 193
The Education of a Speculator, 78
education, importance of, 13
Einhorn, David, 81
Elder, Alexander, 122
EMC Capital Management, 52–53
equity curve, stock market, 39–40
Eurodollar short, trade journal, 165–167
Eurodollar
  hypothetical trade, 117
  selling, 131–132
executing the trade, 128–133

exiting, 23
expectations, 33, 149–152

F

fear, 155–156
  losing because of, 139–140, 153
feeder cattle
  hypothetical trade, 112
  trade journal, 185–186
Fisher, Irving, 42, 44
fixed-dollar amount risk, 85–86
follower, trend, 1
Forbes, Myron E., 42
forex trading, risk measures, 89–90
full-service broker, 12
Fulton, Todd, 6
fundamental analysis, trend following vs.,
  36–38
funding, need for, 13–15
Futures, 64

G

geniuses, 74
Global diversified unit, trade journal, 177–192
GNI Fund Management, 66
gold trade, trade journal, 170, 177–178, 189
gold, buying, 130
Goodbody and Company, 43
Google, 98
Great Depression, 42–45
  bear markets since, 41
greed, 139–140
Green Light Hedge Fund, 81
gurus, 74

H

hard stops, 134
Harry, 6
Harvard Economic Society, 43–45
Hawksbill Capital Management, 54–55, 77
Heebner, Ken, 74
Hite, Larry, 81
Hoover, Herbert, 44–45
HSBC, 99
Hull Trading, 54

Hull, Blair, 54
hypothetical trades, 108–119

I

International Flavors and Fragrances,
    hypothetical trade, 113
introspection, 33–34

J

Japanese equity market, 40, 150–151
Jones, Paul Tudor, 6, 172–173
journey, trend following as, 11–13
just take the trade, 154–159

K

Keynes, John Maynard, 42
Kovner, Bruce, 70

L

Lange, Harry, 74
LCTM. *See* Long-Term Capital Management
legends, 74
lesson, 3–7
Leucadia, 99
lifetime strategy, 12
liquidity, 27, 38
The Little Book of Trading, 72
Loasby, Arthur W., 43
long buy potential, 127
Long-Term Capital Management, 74–75
    trend following and, 75–79
long-term perspective, 138
losing, due to fear, 153
losses, 28, 174
    avoiding, 158–159
    hypothetical trade, 111, 115
    recovering from, 30
low-risk trades, 28
Lowenstein, Roger, 74–75

M

MACD. *See* moving average convergence-
    divergence
margin to equity, 89

Marhedge, 54
Market Wizards, 1, 46–48, 70
markets, choosing to reduce risk, 90–91
McNeel, R.W., 43
mechanical trading systems, 36–38
    trading, 47
Mellon, Andrew W., 44
Meriwether, John, 74–75
Metastock, 20–21
MF Global, 5, 76
MFA conferences, 6
Miller, Bill, 74
mistake, by traders, 77–79
money, to start trading, 13–15
moving average convergence-divergence,
    98–100, 122–123
Mulvaney Capital Management, 66–67
Mulvaney, Paul, 66–67
Murphy, Eddie, 97

N

NASDAQ, 150
NASDAQ 100 futures contract, trade
    journal, 172
natural gas, trade journal, 177, 180–181
necessity, of broker, 12
Netflix, 100
    buying, 130
    selling, 131
New Market Wizards, 56
Niederhoffer, Victor, 4–5, 78

O

Olympic athlete, 38, 157–158
open trade equity, 89
optimization, 47
overconfidence, 85

P

pain, 155–156
Parker, Jerry, 62–63
Paulson, John, 5
Pearce, E.A., 43
percentage risk, changing, 86–87
perception, 154

perseverance, 32–33
perspective, long-term, 138
Pioneer Futures, 6
Pit Bull, 144
pitfalls, trading, 18–20
plan, 7
    following, 17
    risk and, 149
portfolio risk, 88–89, 101
position sizing, 85–86
probabilities, 147–153
profession, trading as, 10–11
profit, 27, 174
profit potential, 27, 39
protection, 134–135
pullback, identify, 127–128

R

retracement, identify, 127–128
Reynolds, Arthur, 42
rich, wealth vs., 17–18
risk management, elements of, 84–90
risk of ruin, 82–83
    formula for, 83
risk
    choosing markets to reduce, 90–91
    commodity trading, 89–90
    forex trading, 89–90
    plan and, 149
    portfolio, 88–89, 101
    sector, 87–88, 101
    trade, 84–87
    of trend following, 9–10
Robertson, Julian, 3–4
Roosevelt, F.D., 45
Royal Bank of Canada, 125–126
    hypothetical trade, 114
    selling, 132–133
ruin, risk of, 82–83
rule of 72, 4, 29

S

S&P 500, trade journal, 172–173, 181
Saxon, 58–59
Schwager, Jack, 1, 56, 70
Schwartz, Marty, 46, 144

sector, risk per, 87–88, 101
Seidler, Howard, 58–59
sells, executing, 131–133
series of trades, 25
Seykota, Ed, 8, 46–48, 60, 139
Shanks, Tom, 54–55
short sell potential, 127
short trade, hypothetical trade, 113, 116
shorts, protection, 134–135
Silowitz, Andy, 70–71
silver
    trade journal, 170–171, 175
    hypothetical trade, 119
Simmons, E.H.H., 42
simplicity, 31–32, 145–147
Soros, George, 78
soybean trade, trade journal, 167–168, 178
Steinitz, Don, 122
Sternberg, Menachem, 70
stock market, equity curve, 39–40
Stocks & Commodities (italics), 26
stops, 102
sugar, 126–127
    buying, 129
    hypothetical trade, 118
    trade journal, 179
Swiss franc, trade journal, 176

T

Tactical investment Management, 48,
    60–61
technical analysis, trend following vs., 36–38
Tharp, Van, 139
time frames, 21–23
TJX Companies, hypothetical trade, 115
TR. *See* true range
trade journal, 47, 163–192
trade
    analysis, 47
    executing, 128–133
    exiting, 23
    if it works, 102–104
    just take the, 154–159
    low-risk, 28
    number of, 100
    risk per, 84–87

series of, 25
steps before, 101–102
trading goals, establishing, 15–18
trading pitfalls, 18–20
Trading Places, 97
trading plan, 26, 140–141
trading
  money to start, 13–15
  as profession, 10–11
  successful, 138
Tradingblox, 21
transparency, 27, 39
Transtrend, 6–7
trend breakout, 96–102
  looking for, 96–98
trend follower, 1
  successful, 143–145
trend following, 2, 38–39
  fundamental analysis vs., 36–38
  as journey, 11–13
  Long-Term Capital Management and, 75–79
  requirements for, 32–34
  risks of, 9–10
  technical analysis vs., 36–38
  tenets of, 27–29
  time frames for, 21–23
Trend Following, 72

trend following wizard, 56
trend retracement rules, 105, 121–122
trend retracement, examples of, 123–127
trend, identify on time frame, 122–127
Trout, Monroe, 3–4
true range, 103
Turtle Trader, 52, 54, 56, 58, 62, 96–97, 193

U

U.S. government bond, hypothetical trade, 110
uncertainty, 91–92, 148
unexpected, planning for, 150–153

V

Vandergrift, Justin, 72–73

W

wealth, rich vs., 17–18
wheat trade, trade journal, 173–174
When Genius Failed, 74–75
Wilder, Welles, 103
Winton, 6–7

Y

yen, 123–125